Secularism, Race, and the Politics of Islamophobia

Secularism, Race, and the Politics of Islamophobia

edited by SHARMIN SADEQUEE

UNIVERSITY *of* **ALBERTA** PRESS

Published by
University of Alberta Press
1-16 Rutherford Library South
11204 89 Avenue NW
Edmonton, Alberta, Canada T6G 2J4
amiskwaciwâskahikan | Treaty 6 |
Métis Territory
ualbertapress.ca | uapress@ualberta.ca

Copyright © 2025
University of Alberta Press

Library and Archives Canada
Cataloguing in Publication

Title: Secularism, race, and the politics
    of Islamophobia / edited by Sharmin
    Sadequee.
Names: Sadequee, Sharmin, editor.
Description: Includes bibliographical
    references and index.
Identifiers: Canadiana (print)
    20240481925 | Canadiana (ebook)
    20240480821 | ISBN 9781772127928
    (softcover) | ISBN 9781772128048
    (EPUB) | ISBN 9781772128055 (PDF)
Subjects: LCSH: Islamophobia—
    Political aspects. | LCSH: Secularism. |
    LCSH: Race. | LCSH: Muslims—
    Non-Islamic countries.
Classification: LCC BP52 .S43 2025 |
    DDC 305.6/97—dc23

First edition, first printing, 2025.
First printed and bound in Canada by
Houghton Boston Printers, Saskatoon,
Saskatchewan.
Copyediting and proofreading by
Jenn Harris.

GPSR: Easy Access System Europe |
Mustamäe tee 50, 10621 Tallinn, Estonia |
gpsr.requests@easproject.com

University of Alberta Press gratefully
acknowledges the support received
for its publishing program from
the Government of Canada, the
Canada Council for the Arts, and the
Government of Alberta through the
Alberta Media Fund.

Contents

vii   *Foreword: Islamophobia's Secular and Racial Inscriptions*
        JASMIN ZINE

xvii   *Acknowledgements*

xix   *Introduction*
        SHARMIN SADEQUEE

1   **I Post-Secularity, Ethnosphere, and Neoliberalism**

3   **1 | Freeing Religion**
        ELIZABETH SHAKMAN HURD

21   **2 | The Limits of the Translation Proviso**
        The Inherent Alien within the Willed-community
        DUSTIN J. BYRD

43   3 | **New French Islamophobia in a Post-secular France**
          ALAIN GABON

67   4 | **The Best Muslims Are the Ones Who Leave**
          Neoliberalism and the Limits of Accommodation
          JINAN BASTAKI

93   **II Law, Gender, and Secular Translations**

95   5 | **Religiosity as a Threat**
          Muslims in Japan and Denmark
          SAUL J. TAKAHASHI

117   6 | **Muslim Women, Trials, and Terror under the
          UAPA in India**
          AREESHA KHAN

139   7 | **Quebec and Law 21, a Conceptual Ecosystem of Otherness**
          Between Omnipresence and Absence(s)
          ZEINAB DIAB

167   8 | **Good Islam, Bad Islam?**
          Secularism, Separatism, and Islamophobia in France
          ROSHAN ARAH JAHANGEER

193   **III Combatting Compounded Islamophobia**

195   9 | **Compounded Islamophobia**
          The Impact of Anti-Black Racism and Gender-based
          Discrimination on Muslim Mental Health in Canada
          FATIMAH JACKSON-BEST

217   10 | **Combatting Islamophobia in Canada**
          Interventions and Gaps
          KHALED AL-QAZZAZ AND NAKITA VALERIO

243   Contributors

Foreword

Islamophobia's Secular and Racial Inscriptions

JASMIN ZINE

Examining the complex and variegated formations of Islamophobia has been central to my scholarly work for almost twenty-five years. Islamophobia studies is now an emergent and growing field marked by the development of the International Islamophobia Studies Research Association (IISRA) in 2021, of which I am co-founder and vice-president. The need to attend to the global study of Islamophobia is more vital now than ever. As I write this foreword, Israel's brutal genocidal campaign in Gaza continues and is underpinned by Islamophobic propaganda and anti-Palestinian racism (Aziz and Plitnick 2023; Zine 2023). The Rohingya Muslims in Myanmar continue to suffer from mass displacement and genocide at the hands of the state and Buddhist extremists (Bakali 2021; Frydenlund 2023). Uyghur Muslims in China face unprecedented state persecution, surveillance, and forced internment (Roberts 2018) in what many nations and human rights organizations have warned constitutes genocide and crimes against humanity. India's Hindutva's government has instituted wide-ranging political and social crackdowns on Muslim citizens, who face repression, religious persecution, and violence (Thompson, Itaoui, and Bazian 2019; Kattiparambil 2023). Islamophobic ethnonationalism and the human rights abuses that are carried out against Muslims in these national contexts has become widespread and deadly. Muslims in Western nations are also subject to Islamophobic laws, policies, and practices as by-products of the "War on Terror." These global conditions warrant constant interrogation of Islamophobia as a planetary crisis.

Contributing to this call for critical engagement with Islamophobia studies, this timely edited collection grapples with the politics of Islamophobia through the critical junctures of secularism and race as colonial legacies that persist and represent both historical genealogies and contemporary challenges. On the epistemic horizon, it is common to see "post" as a prefix to terms like "colonial," "racial," or "secular," but when taking stock of global conditions, this phrasing can sound like a funeral that has taken place without a corpse. However, far from prematurely signalling the demise of colonialism, racism, or secularism, the "post" attached to these terms instead marks the continuity and persistence of these practices and, at the same time, demarcates the critical possibilities for challenging these sites of oppression as an aspirational goal. This discursive turn reminds us that the intertwined politics of colonialism, racism, and secularism have been reconfigured in new ways, but still amounts to pouring "new wine into old skins."

As this edited collection instructs, Islamophobia is the ideal phenomenon to examine the juncture of colonial, secular, and racial formations since they underpin the historical continuity, political persistence, and cultural resonance of this phenomenon.

Colonial and Contemporary Confluences
of Secularism, Race, and Islamophobia

Colonialism is an important axis in this equation and in this book, since the production of racial categories and racist logics (Goldberg 1993) along with religious chauvinism (Maldonado-Torres 2008) were intrinsic to its imperial project. Colonial expansion came hand in hand with the expansion of globalized Christian hegemony. Uplifting "savage heathens" with a Bible in one hand and a gun in the other was central to colonialism's "civilizing mission." Secular modernity emerged coterminously with European colonial expansion and sought to erase non-Christian religions, especially Islam, which had been viewed as an existential and political threat to Europe since the Crusades. Muslims have long troubled the Western secular imaginary as rivals promoting Islam's saliency in the personal and political realm instead of capitulating to secularism and its myth of neutrality (Calhoun 2012). The medieval spectre of Islam's Golden Age eclipsing Europe during its Dark Ages was a source of racial and political angst in the modern period, as the indelible imprint left by the Muslim presence in Europe required the Reconquista and Inquisition to restore historical order and white Christian rule (Mikhail 2020).

Racial politics also played a role in these historical dynamics. According to Grosfoguel and Mielants (2006), the expulsion of Arabs and Jews from Christian Spain in the name of maintaining a "purity of blood" was a proto-racist process that paved the way for colonial racial typologies to develop along with related eugenicist practices. These historical relations and global cartographies of power have shaped the way Muslims, and the West, came to be historically, politically, discursively, and racially constituted (Said 1979; Kahf 1999; Grosfoguel and Mielants 2006).

The global War on Terror also consolidated these Islamophobic racial, religious, and secular formations. In the aftermath of the 9/11 attacks, Muslims in the West became cast as threats to national security, secular democracy, and white nations. Orientalist stereotypes were weaponized and became popularized through media, popular culture, and political discourse that constructed Muslims as the new "folk devil" (Cohen 1972) around which moral panics about an imperilled Western civilization could be fomented, as Huntington (1996) famously warned.

These historical and political factors make it clear that secularism has been fundamentally a racial project. The looming threat that "religiously radical" Muslim minorities are seen to pose to secular democracy has been the hallmark of modern racial governmentality. For example, Benhadjoudja (2022) examines the formation of "racial secularism" in Quebec as the by-product of colonial nation building in Canada along with the racial capitalist project that has underpinned Western modernity. Therefore, in Canada, the Muslim presence disrupts and imperils secular hegemony and the foundations of colonial sovereignty upon which it was built. Yet white Christian privilege (Joshi 2021), on the other hand, persists. For example, the Christian cross on the wall of Quebec's legislature (only removed in 2019) has loomed in the background while cases were debated and passed prohibiting Islamic attire such as hijabs and niqab (face veils) in the public sphere on the grounds of *laïcité*. The double standards at play here were racially constituted under the guise of secular neutrality.

As this book's contributors outline, the racial formation of secularism has been institutionalized in ways that limit the freedom and human rights of Muslim minorities transnationally. This book is instructive in helping to unpack the complexities of state secularism and the ways that Islam and Muslims reside within its cultural and political confines, as well as how they navigate its inhospitable social and cultural terrain. The authors of this volume help us decode and contextualize these racial and religious inscriptions within the framework of the nation and consider how the boundaries of belonging and unbelonging are enacted.

Racialization of Religion

This collection also prompts us to take stock of the axis of religion and racialization. The racialization of religion contributes to how Islamophobia has been constituted. This occurs when racial characteristics become ascribed to religious categories and racial phenotypes are coded as religious markers (Joshi 2006). Meer (2014, 5), for example, notes that "the category of race was co-constituted with religion, and our resurrection of this genealogy implicates the formation of race in the racialization of religious subjects." The historical alignment of racial and religious inscriptions converges within Islamophobia.

In many nations, Islam and its markers, referents, and followers comprise a predominant focus of social and political disapproval, legal regulation, and cultural concern. This collection invites us to consider the historical and epistemic specificity of Islamophobia as a form of oppression and how both religion and race are invoked in its formation.

By highlighting how race, religion, and culture have shaped public policy and practices, contributors to this volume assist us in better comprehending the social-political landscape of Islamophobia.

Unpacking the Dimensions of Islamophobia

This collection continues an important legacy of scholarship that helps build nuanced understandings of Islamophobia as a social, cultural, and political phenomenon. This is necessary work for academic scholarship to undertake since Islamophobia is a term that is often misunderstood, which has led to it being contested, challenged, and strategically denied. Limiting our understanding of Islamophobia to a fear or hatred of Islam and Muslims—as the "phobia" part of the term suggests—reduces this broad-ranging transnational political, social, and cultural phenomenon to interpersonal manifestations of "intolerance." Instead, it is important to recognize the multidimensional nature of Islamophobia as a system of oppression that supports the logic and rationale of specific power relations (Zine 2006, 2022a).

In my work I have argued that Islamophobia operates through three interrelated and interdependent dimensions where this fear, hatred and racial angst is translated into actions, beliefs and practices (Zine 2022a, 2022b). This broad definition outlines the sociology of Islamophobia as a dynamic and pervasive form of oppression and power.

The most visible dimension involves individual actions ranging from microaggressions to vandalism of mosques, Islamic schools, and Muslim businesses, along with other hate crimes, including deadly terror attacks. Canada, for example, leads the G7 nations in Islamophobia- motivated terror attacks against Muslims. These attacks include the 2017 mass shooting at a Quebec City mosque that killed six Muslim men and the 2021 terror attack in London, Ontario, killing four members of a Pakistani Canadian Muslim family intentionally murdered by a truck. Both attacks occurred at the hands of white nationalists who considered Muslims a threat to Canada.

Underpinning these actions is the ideological dimension of Islamophobia, where orientalist racist discourses (Said 1979), Islamophobic conspiracy theories, and Muslim scare stories (e.g., Muslims are terrorists, a Trojan horse, and fifth column infiltrating the West to install sharia law; Muslim organizations and charities are covert fronts for Hamas and the Muslim Brotherhood) circulate with impunity and provide a justification for anti-Muslim fear, hate, violence, and activism. My 2022 study on Canada's Islamophobia Industry (Zine 2022b) outlines the ways that Islamophobic propaganda is trafficked through various anti-Muslim groups, organizations, and actors and is organized, orchestrated, networked, and monetized, thereby extending its reach and influence.

The third interrelated dimension is the institutionalization of Islamophobia, where racist ideas and discourses find expression in laws and policies. Systemic forms of Islamophobia include legislation against religious attire (Bahkt 2020; Easat-Daas 2020), racial profiling, and the securitization of Muslims as suspected radicals and jihadists, foreign threats, and illiberal minorities or "anti-citizens" (Zine 2012; Nagra 2017) as well as discrimination in private- and public-sector employment. Furthermore, over the past two decades, post-9/11 backlash and the global War on Terror has served to rationalize and fortify Islamophobic governmentality around the world.

Despite these clear articulations of Islamophobia's dimensions, some argue the term "Islamophobia" is confusing and limiting. This has led some critics to suggest "anti-Muslim racism" as an alternative. However, this volume emphasizes that it is important to keep "Islam" in the naming of this oppression. In my work I have distinguished anti-Muslim racism as a manifestation of Islamophobia that is evident through the discrimination enacted against Muslims. But since these acts rely upon the demonization of Islam to sustain and reproduce their racial logic, one does not exist without the other (Zine 2022a).

This book also highlights the intersectionality of Islamophobia. There are different social and political registers through which Islamophobia manifests and is experienced. This includes "gendered Islamophobia," which relies on vilifying orientalist tropes about Muslim oppressed women and violent Muslim men (Zine 2006; Razack 2008; Easat-Daas and Zempi 2024). Islamophobia's diverse racial registers include anti-Arab racism, anti-Palestinian racism, anti-Brown racism, and anti-Black racism. These intersectional and multidimensional dimensions of Islamophobia highlight its complexity as a system of oppression.

Contributors to this collection help us to examine the landscape of Islamophobia as a transnational, multidimensional, and intersectional phenomenon. For example, the authors present us with a global purview from Canada to France, Denmark, India, and Japan. They also critically unpack various interpersonal, ideological, and systemic dimensions of Islamophobia so that we can better appreciate the multiple yet consistent ways Islamophobia is socially, culturally, and politically configured.

Readers of this volume will find the authors have offered important insights about the nature and formation of Islamophobia in diverse contexts that they may not have otherwise considered. This book is an invitation to view Islamophobia through a wider horizon and perspective, and it comes at a critical time when dire global circumstances demand this attention.

REFERENCES

Aziz, Sahar, and Michael Plitnick. 2023. *Presumptively Antisemitic: Islamophobic Tropes in Palestine-Israel Discourse.* Rutgers University Law School, Center for Security, Race and Rights.

Bahkt, Natasha. 2020. *In Your Face: Law, Justice and Niqab Wearing Women in Canada.* Delve Books.

Bakali, Naved. 2021. "Islamophobia in Myanmar: The Rohingya Genocide and the 'War on Terror.'" *Race & Class* 62, no. 4: 53–71. https://doi.org/10.1177/0306396820977753.

Benhadjoudja, Leila. 2022. "Racial Secularism as Settler Colonial Sovereignty in Quebec." *Islamophobia Studies Journal* 7, no. 2:182–199. DOI: 10.13169/islastudj.7.2.0182.

Calhoun, Craig. 2012. "Time, World and Secularism." In *The Post-Secular in Question: Religion in Contemporary Society*, edited by Philip Gorski, David Kyuman Kim, John Torpey, and Jonathan VanAntwerpen. NYU Press.

Cohen, Stanley.1972. *Folk Devils and Moral Panics: The Creation of the Mods and Rockers.* Routledge.

Easat-Daas, Amina. 2020. "State Religion and Muslims: Between Discrimination and Protection at the Legislative, Executive and Judicial Levels-A Case Study of France." In *State Religion and Muslims*, edited by Melek Saral and Sherif Onur Bahcecik. Brill Publishing.

Easat-Daas, Amina and Zempi, Irene, eds. 2024. *The Palgrave Handbook of Gendered Islamophobia.* Palgrave Macmillan

Frydenlund, Iselin. 2023. "Theorizing Buddhist Anti-Muslim Nationalism as Global Islamophobia." *Ethnic and Racial Studies* 47, no. 5: 1034–1056. https://doi.org/10.1080/01419870.2023.2268209

Goldberg, David T. 1993. *Racist Culture*. Blackwell Publishing.

Grosfoguel, Ramon, and Eric Mielants. 2006. "The Long-Durée Entanglement between Islamophobia and Racism in the Modern /Colonial Capitalist/ Patriarchal World-System: An Introduction." *Human Architecture: Journal of the Sociology of Self Knowledge* 1, no. 1:1–12.

Huntington, Samuel. 1996. *The Clash of Civilizations and the Remaking of the World Order*. Simon and Schuster.

Joshi, Khyati Y. 2006. *New Roots in America's Sacred Ground*. Rutgers University Press.

Joshi, Khyati Y. 2021. *White Christian Privilege: The Illusion of Religious Equality in America*. NYU Press.

Kahf, Mohja.1999. *Western Representations of the Muslim Woman*. University of Texas Press.

Kattiparambil, Sheheen. 2023. "Conceptualizing Islamophobia in India." *Islamophobia Studies Journal* 8, no. 1: 123–140.

Maldonado-Torres, Nelson. 2008. "Secularism and Religion in the Modern/ Colonial World-System: From Secular Postcoloniality to Postsecular Transmodernity." In *Coloniality at Large: Latin America and the Postcolonial Debate*, edited by Mabel Moraña, Enrique Dussel, and Carlos A. Jáuregui. Duke University Press.

Meer, Nasar, ed. 2014. *Racialization and Religion: Race, Culture and Difference in the Study of Antisemitism and Islamophobia*. Routledge.

Mikhail, Alan. 2020. *God's Shadow*. Liveright Publishing.

Nagra, Baljit. 2017. *Securitized Citizens*. University of Toronto Press.

Razack, Sherene. 2008. *Casting Out: The Eviction of Muslims from Western Law and Politics*. University of Toronto Press.

Roberts. Sean R. 2018. "The Biopolitics of China's 'War on Terror' and the Exclusion of the Uyghurs." *Critical Asian Studies* 50, no. 2: 232–258.

Said, Edward W. 1979. *Orientalism*. Vintage Books.

Thompson, Paula, Rhonda Itaoui, and Hatem Bazian. 2019. *Islamophobia in India: Stoking Bigotry*. Islamophobia Research and Documentation Project, University of California Berkeley.

Zine, Jasmin. 2006. "Unveiled Sentiments: Gendered Islamophobia and Experiences of Veiling among Muslim Girls in a Canadian Islamic School." *Equity and Excellence in Education. Special Issue: Ethno-Religious Oppression in Schools* 39, no. 3: 239–252.

Zine, Jasmine, ed. 2012. *Islam in the Hinterlands: Muslim Cultural Politics in Canada*. UBC Press.

Zine, Jasmin. 2022a. *Under Siege: Islamophobia and the 9/11 Generation*. McGill-Queen's University Press.

Zine, Jasmin. 2022b. *The Canadian Islamophobia Industry: Mapping Islamophobia's Ecosystem in the Great White North*. The Islamophobia Studies Center & Islamophobia Research and Development Project, University of California, Berkeley.

Zine, Jasmin. 2023. "How Islamophobia and Anti-Palestinian Racism are Manufactured through Disinformation." *The Conversation*, October 23. https://theconversation.com/how-islamophobia-and-anti-palestinian-racism-are-manufactured-through-disinformation-216119.

Acknowledgements

The seed for this book grew out of an international conference, "Islamophobia and/in the Post-Secular States," held November 12–14, 2021, at the University of Alberta Augustana Campus, Canada, which I organized and chaired as part of my postdoctoral fellowship program at the Chester Ronning Centre for the Study of Religion and Public Life. The conference brought together scholars and practitioners who study how Islamophobia manifests in and through various social processes to develop a more comprehensive understanding and theorization of the pervasiveness of global Islamophobia. Conference contributors explored the multidimensionality of Islamophobia to measure its effects and develop recommendations to address it.

The conference was supported by the scholarly community at the Augustana Campus, including the then dean, Dr. Demetres

Tryphonopoulos, and Dr. Ian Wilson, then director of the Chester Ronning Centre for the Study of Religion and Public Life. I am very thankful for the support of Kim Wiebe, then-program coordinator of the Chester Ronning Centre, with the conference logistics. I am very grateful for the grant from the Chester Ronning Centre that supported the book's publication.

I am truly grateful for the two anonymous reviewers' insightful feedback, which was instrumental in revising the manuscript. I also want to extend my heartfelt appreciation to the contributing scholars for their professionalism, hard work, and dedication to the subject matter. Additionally, several contributors submitted original pieces that offer new, thought-provoking perspectives and theoretical analyses on Islamophobia.

I am grateful to the University of Alberta Press for the opportunity to publish this book. In particular, Mat Buntin has been enthusiastic about this volume and incredibly patient and understanding through the process.

This book is dedicated to all those who have faced discrimination, exclusion, and hatred and who courageously confront both state and structural violence in their ongoing struggle for a more just world.

Introduction

SHARMIN SADEQUEE

Several incidents made international news while I was working on this collection.[1] In late 2022, Erika López Prater, an art history professor at Hamline University in the United States, was fired for showing historical Muslim artwork depicting the Prophet Muhammad during a class lecture. The Black Muslim student complainant, Hamline University, and the local chapter of the Council on American Islamic Relations (CAIR) condemned showing this Muslim artwork as an act of Islamophobic racism.[2] However, the national CAIR office and some in the academic community disagreed with this accusation and defended the professor's academic freedom. The university later rescinded its charge of Islamophobia. López Prater's lawsuit against the university states that the complainant imposed a particular religious view on López Prater's instruction, which other students, including Muslims, did not find offensive. The lawsuit portrays the student complainant as incapable of respecting the multicultural class-room and matters of freedom of choice. Other commentators identified how race is involved in this Islamophobia controversy.

In another case, Rasmus Paludan, a right-wing politician in Sweden, publicly burned a copy of the Quran in 2023.[3] Paludan had previously stated that Muslims who do not value freedom of expression—that is, one's right to critique Islam—should leave the country. The Swedish prime minister defended Paludan's right to freedom of expression while simultaneously denouncing the burning of the Quran. Various members of the international community condemned the act as Islamophobic racism and held the secular, liberal Swedish government responsible for allowing it to occur.

Animus toward Muslims in Muslim-minority democratic nation-states has worsened since the start of the 2023 conflict between the settler-colonial state of Israel and stateless Palestinians.[4] The assault on Gaza has impacted the globe, with an exponential rise in Islamophobia and anti-Semitism across Canada, and Islamophobia alone has increased by 600 percent in the United Kingdom. In Germany, every second person supports restricting Islamic religious practice. India and Sweden have seen increases in anti-Muslim hate speech and the destruction of mosques.

The ongoing violence against Palestinians has resulted in campus uprisings of university students across North America and northern/western Europe, where they have been subjected to militarized police raids for showing solidarity with Gazans and protesting the settler-colonial state of Israel's genocide, which has included the destruction of infrastructure as well as historical Islamic cultural architecture and social institutions in occupied Palestine.[5] The Center for Security, Race, and Rights (CSRR) at Rutgers University in the US revealed that Muslims (and other pro-Palestinian activists) are being denied the liberal values of freedom of speech and assembly and are often accused of anti-Semitism.[6] These activists are being vilified and excluded from public debates in the liberal, democratic public spheres of college campuses, leading the US Department of Education to investigate rising cases of both anti-Semitism and Islamophobia in secular educational institutions.[7] The CSRR report suggests that accusing Arabs of anti-Semitism is a form of Islamophobia and that right-wing Zionism and Islamophobia are co-constituted.[8]

These incidences point not only to the persistence of antagonisms toward Muslims in traditionally secular societies like Sweden or the United States but also that right-wing ethnonationalist and ethnoreligious sentiments have become intertwined with the secular state and draw on normative liberal values and philosophies (e.g., freedom of choice and expression) to advance a far-right politics and anti-Muslim animus and actions. These controversies also reveal the problems of defining Islamophobia: is it a form of racism or religious discrimination? *Secularism, Race, and the Politics of Islamophobia* intervenes in studies of Islamophobia, shedding light on this debate and offering a conceptual clarity and theoretical framework with which to examine and analyze the manifestations of contemporary anti-Muslim racism by focusing on how the normative ideology and structure of secularism operates in the social phenomenon of Islamophobia.

Scholarship from Europe and North America generally connects Islamophobia to racism instead of critically examining the concept of religion.[9] Such work explains the rise of Islamophobia by theorizing how Muslims are treated like a "racial" group and Islamophobia as anti-Muslim racism. However, other scholars question whether Islamophobia is completely explained as racism and racial discrimination or whether it is also a form of religious discrimination (Dagli 2020a, 2020b; Sealy 2021; Kitching and Gholami 2023; Johnson and Unsworth 2023). Islamophobia *can* be a form of racism. However, it is important to examine "religion" in "Islam-o-phobia"— that is, how the discrimination Muslims encounter can also be religious. Critics of "Islamophobia as racism" foreground the importance of religion because many Muslims, whether born into the faith or having converted, identify with Islam and religious associations (Sealy 2021).

Secularism, Race, and the Politics of Islamophobia critically examines the dominant "Islamophobia as racism" thesis to scrutinize how race and religion are mixed in the process of the "racialization of Muslims" in nominally secular and/or post-secular states and societies. In this regard, this book shifts attention from representations of Islam and the things that Muslims do that cause their racialization to the foundational logic and structural frameworks of the societies, populations, and systems that do the racializing. The collection shows how secularism shapes sociocultural spheres, epistemologies, ideologies, and the disciplinary institutions of the state (i.e., law, politics, political groups, government entities, public institutions, civil society, bureaucracies, and the public sphere) to subordinate Muslims and Islam and normalize anti-Muslim racism and discrimination in both Western and non-Western nation-states.

In this introduction, I advocate for re-analyzing Islamophobia by examining how the entwinement of secularism and race operate in and construct the phenomenon—that is, the relationship of *secularism to race-making*. What role does secularism play in (re)constructing a subordinated racial and religious group and manufacturing the "outsider" and/or "foreign" Other of Islam and racialization of Muslims? Muslims are treated as a racial group partly because their external religious or cultural markers are "racialized." We must ask *how* this fusion—in the racialization of Muslims and the invention of Muslims as a "racial" category—happens in individual/personal and institutional/structural Islamophobia.

A re-examination of the "racialization of religion" thesis considers how secularism delineates Islam and creates Muslim alterity as an inferior group across secular (and/or post-secular) and postcolonial nation-states. Islamophobia, as discrimination, exclusionary, and structural practice, is foundationally grounded in the socially constructed distinction between the religion-politics of secularism.

This binary legitimizes the targeting of Muslims and Islam at the interpersonal micro level and structural macro level (e.g., the law, media, bureaucracies, educational institutions, and civil society). The politics of secularism enables the management, subordination, and/ or exclusion of Muslims and Islam through apportioning majority and elite power and hegemony across geographical, social, and political settings (settler, postcolonial, former colonial, ethnoreligious, ethnonationalist regimes). Muslims subjected to this technology of secularism through various mechanisms may explicitly or implicitly change their self-understandings, conceptual frameworks, identities, belongings, and behavioural regulations.

The Racialization of Muslims and Islam

Muslims around the world confront anti-Muslim violence. This is particularly true in nominally "post-racial" and secular (or "post-secular") societies, such as the United States, Canada, Britain, France, Japan, Denmark, and India—nation-states detailed in this collection. Post-racial[10] and post-secular societies have supposedly moved beyond racial and religious categorization; they have allegedly achieved equality and treat diversity and inclusivity with respect. Many of these societies have long histories with Islam. However, the twentieth-century migration of Muslims (including politically displaced populations) has challenged many states' ability to integrate minority groups and promote ethics of equality, inclusivity, tolerance, and neutrality. Pluralities of Muslim cultures and ethnicities have complicated these states' homogeneous self-understandings and challenged the values, philosophies, and practices of democratic pluralism.[11]

Many former colonial, settler-colonial, and postcolonial states have adopted strategies that discriminate against, exclude, and rule Muslims. This includes increasing militarization and surveillance or suspending human rights through states of emergency to ensure public safety and national security during the now decades-long global War on Terror. Other states—emboldened by the US-led War on Terror and national security politics—have executed or otherwise persecuted Muslims (e.g., China, Burma, and India) (Bakali and Hafez 2022; Alexio 2023; Beydoun 2023; Selod et al. 2024). These state-sponsored measures, combined with the global rise of right-wing ethnonationalist politics and populism, have further spread anti-Muslim and anti-Islam agendas. Muslims resist these challenges to build a more secure life; however, such structural discrimination impacts their individual and collective well-being and sense of community and belonging.

Many scholars identify the current onslaught as Islamophobia. It impacts Muslim communities, particularly in Muslim-minority geographies in North America and northern/western Europe, but also in Asia and Africa (Bakali and Hafez 2022; Ejiofor 2023; Alexio 2023) and even Muslim-majority states (Bayrakli and Hafez 2019). Notable academic, legal, and public analyses over the last two decades have increasingly framed Islamophobia within the national, regional, and global politics of empire (Kumar 2012; Kazi 2018; Abdel-Fattah 2018), ideology (Sheehi 2011; Zine 2022a), biopolitical racism (Tyrer 2013), racism, xenophobia, oppression (Esposito and Kalin 2011; Sayyid and Vakil 2011; Modood 2018, 2019; Special UN Human Rights Council Rapporteur 2021; Zine 2022a; Aziz 2022; Selod et al. 2024), epistemic racism (Grosfoguel 2012), genocide and new crusade (Alexio 2023; Beydoun 2023), tribalism (Ejiofor 2023), and coloniality (Bayrakli and Hafez 2019; Bakali and Hafez 2022). Much of this work—historical, cultural, political, ideological, and legal—sees Islamophobia as a manifestation of "anti-Muslim racism," a form of racism that exists without the *standard racialized markers* or *phenotypical similarities*. However, scholars often distance Islamophobia from critical discussions of "religion."

Race is socially constructed, with no biological basis. Critical race studies now focuses on *racialization*: the social and political processes by which certain reductive and monolithic beliefs, ideas, institutions, qualities, and practices manufacture populations as inferior for differential treatment to maintain a power structure. In North America and northern Europe, race was traditionally constructed using a phenotypical Black-white binary. However, twenty-first-century migration has challenged this dualism and expanded Blackness to include other non-white populations. The idea of race affects modes of thinking, behaving, experiencing, and being-in-the-world shaped by a dichotomous racial project and its associated legal, political, economic, and social systems. The racial binary between whiteness and Blackness is part of the racial political structure that imputes other non-white populations.[12]

Historically, religion was used to demarcate social differences and hierarchies. From antiquity through the medieval and early modern periods, Christian theologies defined and categorized non-Christian groups as "idolators," having either "false religion" or "no religion," and subjecting them to exclusion, violence, and enslavement (Maldonado-Torres 2014; Wynter 1991, 1995).[13] Religion (along with phenotypical and cultural differences) was an important component in marking differences and early race thinking, which—from the fifteenth and sixteenth centuries to the nineteenth and twentieth centuries of European colonial/modern explorations—helped develop notions of race and racial categories.[14] Religion and race were both used to legitimize European power and modern colonization; however, religion-based differences were often camouflaged as *nonreligious* categories. Those who were classified as having "false religion" and/ or "no religion" from the perspectives of Christian theology were inferiorized and racialized. The categories of "false religion" and "no religion" were *substituted* and *translated* to secular ethnoracial categories such as "Indians/Indios" "Mongloid," or "Negroid." In the nineteenth and early twentieth centuries of the modern Enlightenment movement and Darwinian evolutionary revolution, the idea of race became more "scientific" and secular (i.e., phenotypic and biological) and was decoupled from its close religious associations.[15] This *secularly* defined biological/physical determinism based on discernible signifiers displaced the role of religion as the primary marker of difference. This shift from and *substitution* of nonsecular/religious to secular "scientific" categories at this time helped shape ideas of modernity and progressivity and the modern/colonial ideologies and practices of racial formations and racism.

This secular European Enlightenment-influenced conceptualization of race (devoid of religious affiliation) dominates critical studies on race, racial theorization, and racism studies. Muslims are treated as a racial group; their diverse cultural and religious markers have become fused with various phenotypes, ethnicities, and nationalities to signify their non-whiteness and the creation of a new racial category (Rana 2011), a racial Muslim (Aziz 2022), as well as a global racial enemy (Selod et al. 2024). Sahar Selod and colleagues (2024), as well as Sahar Aziz (2022), further explain how race and religion operate in the process of contemporary racialization:

> ...a religious *identity acquires* racial meaning without relying only on phenotypical or biological factors, like skin tone, which allows for its use in countries that do not acknowledge racial classifications. (Selod et al. 2024, 13, emphasis added)

> The co-constitutive nature of religion and race means *neither identity* exists in isolation but rather interacts to produce a racial-religious hierarchy. *Religious identity* in certain contexts *functions as a racial marker*. (Aziz 2022, 5–6, emphasis added)

In this scholarly theorization, religion/the nonsecular fits into racial and racialization schemes as "identity." It takes religious practices as a "sign" to mean a self-referential category, representing group membership, which functions as demographic information. Markers that are (mis)identified as belonging to the "religion" of Islam are "racialized"—that is, religious beliefs and cultural traits are *substituted* for biological ones. Such external identity signifiers displayed by/on Muslim bodies include the hijab, beard, thobe, public congregational prayers, and workplace and spatial accommodations. States and their publics racialize Muslims, focusing on these materialities of religion and the "negative dimensions of Islamic theology and Muslim lifestyles, rendering these as incompatible with nation-states' visions and values" (Selod et al. 2024, 10). State apparatuses and ordinary citizenries read these external behaviours and lifestyles as signs of "fundamentalism," "terrorism," "extremism," "patriarchy," and "docility" (i.e., for Muslim women). These approaches focus on *what Muslims do* that *causes* their racialization by outsider entities. The "racialization of Muslim" thesis does not question *how* these religious *practices* are read as "signs" and registered as "negative dimensions" and problematic by the secular and/or post-secular state and its public.

However, defining visible expressions of religious practices as a function of just "identity" and a form of "racial" identity, where neither identity functions separately but can be *substituted for* or *translated into* Other, relegates one's self-understanding and piety, and ethical practices (connected to certain cosmologies) to an external identity category that facilitates targeting for discriminatory, exclusionary, and/or multicultural politics.[16] This process of demarcating groups into identities *reduces* their complexities into this or that identity category. This way of defining populations is common in so-called secular and post-secular neoliberal capitalist democracies like North America and northern/western Europe, where identity politics shape and assign individuals and categorize groups within a hierarchical social structure; members are unequally positioned and ranked within the Black-white racial spectrum.

The racialization process of Islamophobia has dialectical micro-personal/individual and macro-institutional/structural elements (Kundnani 2014; Beydoun and Choudhury 2020; Kumar 2021;

Bakali and Hafez 2022). The micro version of Islamophobia entails individual perpetrators' sentiments as driven by fear or hatred of cultural and religious differences. Structurally, Islamophobia is a social, cultural, and political phenomenon connected to, produced through, and enacted by state institutions (legal and other government bureaucracies and public institutions). The social process of Othering relies on orientalism (Said 1979) and operates in and through the law, politics, and the media, which manufacture and perpetuate anti-Muslim racism.[17] Islamophobia, as a form of anti-Muslim racism more broadly, is an interlocking system of exclusionary social and political practices that enables cultural and structural racism to serve particular political, imperial, and global power interests (Rana 2011; Kundnani 2014; Modood 2019; Kumar 2021; Zine 2022a; Aziz 2022; Bakali and Hafez 2022; Beydoun 2023; Selod et al. 2024). In this way, the social process of Islamophobia has turned Islam into a "race" and Muslims into a racialized people (Vakil 2011, 276; Bayoumi 2006, 270).

The "Islamophobia is racism/anti-Muslim racism" thesis is an important analysis of a very complex and interwoven system of ideological, social, political, and historical factors. Identifying Islamophobia as a phenomenon of racism based on identity helps produce demographic statistics to address the material, political, and juridical inequality of discrimination and/or hate violence. Recognizing injustice against and oppression of Muslims as a racial experience helps bring about greater justice and social change in multicultural, liberal-secular and/or post-secular societies through affirmative action and hate-crime laws. However, this approach implies that race and racial identity are more "real" than religious affiliation. Little work considers how the project of nation-states and their citizenries deploy the colonial category of "religion" to racialize Muslims (Sadequee 2018). In the United States, law scholar Asma T. Uddin has questioned the "racialization of Muslims" scholarship, which undermines the religious component of Muslim experiences with negative consequences for their free exercise of religious piety.[18] Aziz tries to address this gap by taking a US-centric historical perspective to conclude that the "racialization of immigrant Muslims [in the US] is grounded in a racial-religious hierarchy, [not only] a racial hierarchy" (2022, 5).

Muslims are treated as a racial group by government institutions, the general public, and Islamophobia-focused scholarly works alike and this makes it difficult to consider the targeting of Muslims as infringing on their religious sensibilities, lives, and practices. As a result, Islamophobia has become entrenched in *race politics* (Tyrer 2013; Aziz 2022). The racialization of Muslims has also become a global phenomenon that "transcends geographical boundaries, highlighting that this racial project can no longer be described as the 'West vs. the Rest'" (Selod et al. 2024, 28). For Reza Gholami (2021)[19] and others, however, this approach does not adequately explain *why* and *how* Muslims experience Othering and marginalization *globally*.

The Concept of "Religion" in Islamophobia

The current racialization thesis seems to avoid analyzing the concept of religion and "religion qua religion" in the Islamophobic experiences of many Muslims, for whom religious tradition operates as the primary affiliation (Sealy 2021). Others have raised the issue of how we understand manifestations of Islamophobia in places like India, Nigeria, and China, where the population appears phenotypically somewhat alike (Ejiofor 2023; Selod et al. 2024). How does one explain situations in Muslim-majority states where certain Muslims, devoid of criminal conduct, are targeted by citizens and the state for discrimination, exclusion, and execution under the policies and practices of "countering violent extremism" in the global War on Terror? Selod et al. (2024) suggest the concept of the "global racialization of Muslims" to understand the shared construction of Islamophobia between western Europe, North America, and non-Western contexts of China and India, where

Muslims are racialized using the same orientalist tropes. However, an examination of the modern category of religion and its critical study—like the contemporary category of race and critical race studies—should be used to conceptualize and theorize anti-Muslim racism and the racialization process of Islamophobia.

The scholarship on the racialization of Muslims eschews religion in analyzing Islamophobia. For Deepa Kumar (2012, 2021), Islamophobia is at all not about religion. For David Tyrer (2013), a focus on religion and religious identity hinders an understanding of the racial politics of Islamophobia. Aziz (2022) *substitutes* and frames public religious attributes as racial formations in constructing racial-religious hierarchies. Tariq Modood (2019) deals with the question of religion by proposing the integration of Muslims through multicultural policies, accommodation, and collective religious group recognition. Atiya Husain (2019, 594) claims that "religion" is a factor where "Muslimness" is seen as a "foreign influence," and she positions "Muslimness" (i.e., external religious markers) within and in relation to the Black-white binary racial logic. Approaches like these, however, do not consider *how* the modern/colonial category of "religion" is conceptualized and formulated in the phenomenon of Islamophobia in the first place (at the interpersonal and systemic-structural level) and why external religious signifiers are imputed in a particular way and targeted for racialization. Canar Dagli (2020a) further outlines how Islam (religion qua religion) is conceptualized in the racialization thesis:

> The way Islam is brought into the framework of
> intersectionality does not add another parameter
> of discrimination (that of religious bigotry) to the
> existing matrix of oppression but instead inserts
> religion into the already existing hierarchy by using
> the concept of racialization. In this view, only races,
> genders, classes, and sexual orientations constitute
> real groups. Religious bigotry *sits on the lap of racism*

instead of having its own seat at the table of intersecting hierarchies. (Emphasis added)

Shifting focus away from neoliberal, atomized identity politics, which ignore religion, to structures and systems that perpetuate domination (Cho, Crenshaw, and McCall 2013), intersectionality continues to *substitute* and *translate* religion/the nonsecular as "race" to be considered for oppression. The circumvention and elision of religion imply that critical and intersectional racial, social, and legal analyses of Islamophobia do not consider religion a "real" or *material reality* enough to warrant further examination. When "religion" and "religious affiliation" are understood as an "internal matter" or "personal choice," it becomes easy to ignore, substitute, or discard the nonsecular/religion from having its own place at the intersections of oppression. After all, *secular* epistemology and systems of knowledge focus on the material and the visible, making intersectional analysis of religion as a discriminatory parameter difficult. This approach reveals the embeddedness of the theories of intersectionality and their connected resistance and liberatory activism in secular epistemes that understand injustice and/or justice only in the material form. When Islam is considered for examination, it is accepted as a "religion" based on "ascriptive definitions of what constitutes Islam and Muslim identity" (Aziz 2022, 18–19). Certainly, some scholars suggest expanding intersectionality theories and analysis to include "religion" as an axis of structural discrimination (Gholami 2021). However, Islam is not just an external/visible/material signifier; it is an evolving tradition with lived and embodied experience that structures adherents' personal and social lives (Asad 2003; Mahmood 2005; Deeb 2006). Explorations of the concept of "religion" in Islamophobia must theorize discrimination (i.e., resulting from the outside, based on ascribed identity) and emphasize how to address it based on what Muslims consider important (Sealy 2021; Gholami 2021).

Crucially, Islamophobic discrimination can occur in the *absence* of visible expressions of religion. This is the case where populations are phenotypically similar when people convert to Islam. Such individuals are often worried about "coming out" as Muslim and facing Islamophobia (Jones et al. 2018; Sealy 2021). National elites and co-religionists in Muslim-majority postcolonial nation-states may also target particular Muslims who adhere to certain Islamic hermeneutics (Bayrakli and Hafez 2019; Ejiofor 2023). In societies where science and liberal interpretations of scripture are understood as markers of modernity and social progress, negative views of Islam—as "anti-science," with "scripturally deterministic" beliefs—are used to demarcate differences between religious and racial groups (Jones et al. 2018, 175).

The current approach to examining "religion qua religion" in Islamophobia demonstrates how variously situated outsiders ascribe and perpetuate discrimination against Muslims to produce racialization or "religification" (Gholami 2021). However, scholarship on "religion qua religion" in Islamophobia studies does not explain *how* the contemporary designation and relationship of religion to post-secular states (some are settler-colonial states) helps demarcate Islam to produce Othering, exclusionary practices, and global racialization. In other words, how do the so-called secular and/or post-secular states and their publics and civil societies understand "religion" and perpetrate Islamophobia on Muslims? Islamophobia studies often avoid addressing whether and to what extent the "Islamophobia as racism" and "Islamophobia as religious discrimination" theses depend on a particular *structural* understanding of "religion" in secular and/or post-secular states.

This collection argues that Muslim experiences of Islamophobia, whether as "racism" or "religious discrimination," are co-constituted and are both connected to and produced by secularism. How have *secularism* and *race* become entwined to produce the subordination and racialization of Muslims and Islam? Specifically, how are modern/colonial orientalist perceptions of Islam and Muslims that manufacture Islamophobia as structural/systemic

Otherization or racialization rooted in secularism? How does secularism work with neoliberal capitalism and the global economic system to perpetuate structural Islamophobia? What *mechanisms* of secularism produce and reproduce racial categories out of religious markers? Furthermore, how do the general public, state institutions, and even scholarly theorizations of Islamophobia rely on secularism (thereby continuing the racialization, Othering, exclusion, and structural domination of Muslims)?

Orientalism is Secularism, Secularism is Racialism

Orientalism is the foundation of the scripts and ideologies that construct the ongoing racialization of Muslims in the phenomenon of Islamophobia, based on the imagined European perceptions about Muslims and Islam that have solidified twenty-first century Euro-American neocolonial expansion amid the global War on Terror. Orientalist perspectives continue to define Islam as an "aggressive political ideology" hostile to Christianity (Aziz 2022, 12). They "divide... the world into two clashing civilizations, 'Islam and the West,' eternally locked in a crusade that constructs the most vulnerable Muslims into villains and scorches the earth in the name of empire" (Beydoun 2023, 39). Orientalism and "neo-orientalism [focus] more on the negative dimensions of Islamic theology and Muslim lifestyles, rendering these as incompatible with nation-states' visions and values" (Selod et al. 2024, 10) and producing "the building blocks" for Islamophobia: Muslims become a racial category and Islam a "monolithic" religion "separate from and inferior to the West" (Green 2015, 98–99). As Kumar (2021, 51–52) states, orientalism is "built on Enlightenment theories of race and the notion that Muslims are a distinct race...locked within their sacred customs and a set of moral and religious codes that kept them static....cast[ing] [Muslims] as premodern, backward, primitive, despotic, static, undemocratic, and rigid." Indeed, "Orientalist ideologies shape Islamophobic imaginaries and provide the rationale for systemic practices through which Islamophobia becomes institutionally embedded and reproduced" (Zine 2022b, 36). As Bakali and Hafez further note:

> The securitisation of Muslims is made possible
> through the WOT [War on Terror] discourse, which
> is based on Orientalist views...This process of
> securitization facilitated the state apparatus that
> institutionalised Islamophobia in its laws and policies.
> (2022: 23–24)

In other words, orientalist (mis)representations of Islam (re)produce the current form of (global) racism and violence against Muslims.

However, the "Islamophobia as racism" thesis uncritically employs orientalism to explain the phenomenon of Islamophobia and rests on the same modern/colonial knowledge structures that gave rise to orientalism and persist in scholarly and public spaces.[20] Like Said's *Orientalism*, the approach of the "Islamophobia as racism" thesis to "religion" is rooted in the modern/colonial European Enlightenment concept of "religion." This approach does not go beyond the secular, *modern* concept of "religion" that forms the *bedrock* of orientalism and the orientalist approach to Islam and Muslims. The "orientalism as racism" and "Islamophobia as racism" theses show how orientalism misrepresents Islam/Muslims and drives anti-Islam and anti-Muslim agendas. These scholarly theorizations demonstrate various ways that (neo)orientalism depicts Islam (as violent, dogma, backward, etc.)— that is, as the opposite of enlightened European Christianity—but *do not question* this formulation.[21] However, as Said writes,

> *Modern* Orientalism *derives* from *secularizing* elements
> in eighteenth-century European culture...But if these

interconnected elements represent a *secularizing tendency*, this is not to say that the old religious patterns of human history and destiny and "the existential paradigms" were simply removed. Far from it: they were *reconstituted, redeployed, redistributed in the secular frameworks*...For anyone who studied the Orient, a *secular vocabulary* [translations] *in keeping with these frameworks was required*. (1979, 120–121, emphasis added)

In other words, premodern European Christianity reconfigured itself within a secularizing framework for the modern period at a time when Europe was also expanding the colonization of non-European geographies in the nineteenth century. Gil Anidjar argues that "[s]ecularism is Orientalism, Orientalism is Christianity" (2006, 66). What this means is that western European Christianity demarcated its ethnic heritage and identity as white and secular, positioning itself above its particular metaphysics and allegedly became modern and secularized by making distinctions between secular and religious, rational and irrational, civilized and uncivilized, and progression and regression (Anidjar 2006; Ahmad 2017). Orientalism, then, relies on the hierarchical and dichotomous schemes of secularism. Essentially, secularism is the name Christianity gave itself to act as "the transcendent mediation" (Asad 2003, 5) and now claims to be undogmatic, unbiased, and neutral, so as to produce and universalize its Eurocentric culture and ethnosphere by designating and reproducing other traditions and cultures as not universal but particular, localized "religions." This understanding of secularism, as an expression of Eurocentric and white racial superiority, played a significant role in the nineteenth-century modern/colonial economic and political expeditions that dismantled the "polycentric and noncapitalist" globe and established "monocentric" capitalism, authorizing the control and management of "economy, subjectivity, [and] gender and sexual norms" (Mignolo 2011, 3–7). Secularism—that is, European Christianity's (mythical) dissociation between "religious" and "secular"—is connected to the rise of the modern capitalist system of nation-state power and control. Based on Europe's self-definition as secular and modern, the modern/colonial enterprise that violently extracted resources and exerted power and control over non-Europeans managed both non-Christian *religions* and non-white *populations* (Asad 2003; Masuzawa 2005; Mignolo 2011; Kahn and Lloyd 2016; Hallaq 2018; Maldonado-Torres 2014; Menon 2024; Yountae 2024). The European modern/colonial conceptualization of "religion" has continued into contemporary religious hierarchies, positioning "religion" as an adversary to secular rationalism, scientific progress, and modernity. The co-emergence and operation of secularism, coloniality, capitalism, modern categories of race and religion, and their relationship to (neo) orientalist formulations of Islam, then, is critical for theorizing the *racial politics* of Islamophobia and the *global* racialization of Muslims that perpetuates the continued global War on Terror.

The "racialization of Muslims/Islam," which is said to have been driven by orientalist constructions, is articulated in and through the grammar of secularism. When orientalism is secularism, then secularism (re)produces Islam as Other and Muslims as a distinct racialized population. Orientalist racism is the foundation of Islamophobia, and secularism underpins orientalism; therefore, secularism fuels current-day Islamophobia and the racialization and Othering of Muslims and Islam globally. Secularism racializes Muslims (and Islam) and enables anti-Muslim racism, manufacturing racial categories out of religious markers. Vincent Lloyd elaborates on the entwinement of secularism and racism:

> Secularism evokes a religious domain that is managed by power and is circumscribed by nonreligious forces. The analogy for race: racial-minority communities are managed by power and circumscribed by nonminority, that is, white, forces…Put more starkly, whiteness is

secular, and the secular is white. The unmarked racial category and the unmarked religious category jointly mark their others. Or, put another way, the desire to stand outside religion and the desire to stand outside race are complementary delusions, for the seemingly outside is in fact the hegemonic. (2016, 4–5)

Perhaps secularism and race-making make more sense in places with binary Black-white racial structures (e.g., North America or northern/ western Europe). However, as Bayrakli and Hafez (2019) show, the powerful elite in some postcolonial Muslim-majority nation-states adopt colonial epistemic frameworks, resulting in anti-Muslim discrimination and racism. Islamophobia in both Muslim-majority and -minority societies "stem[s] from similar ideological and epistemological backgrounds...between Westernized secular Muslim elites and conservative Muslim masses...that aims to undermine a distinct Muslim identity [which is viewed as 'bad' Muslim]" (2019: 1–2). Hatem Bazian defines Islamophobia in Muslim-majority nation-states as:

A political, social, economic, military, cultural, and religious process emerging out and shaped by the Colonial-Eurocentric hegemonic discourses dating to the late eighteenth century, constituted and internalized through an imitative project by postcolonial elites that posited itself or was designated by Western powers as the custodian for the modern, secular, nationalist and progressive Muslim nation-state projects. (2019, 22)

In the postcolonial Muslim-majority states, secularism and classism operate together to produce Islamophobia that is rooted in the experiences of European colonial modernity, where Islam is conceptualized through the grammar of secularism. In these societies, the elites and institutions in power have internalized secularism and undermine the materiality of certain Islamic hermeneutics as "bad," targeting and discriminating against certain Muslims. In Western contexts, secularism underwrites the reading and demarcating of Muslim religiosity in Muslim-minority places like Australia (Abdel-Fattah 2018) and the United States, where a Muslim who "drinks alcohol, engages in premarital sex, or associates exclusively with non-Muslims… is perceived as secularized and modern" (Aziz 2022, 10)—a "good" Muslim in service of Eurocentric whiteness. A combined examination of secularism *and* racialization and how secularism constructs Islam and Muslims in postcolonial and settler colonial nation-states and in the global international system (Hurd 2009, 2015; see also Chapter 1 by Hurd) can productively advance understandings of Islamophobia and the global racialization of Muslims and Islam.

Post-secularity, Religion, and Structural Islamophobia

Eurocentric cultural and historical perspectives suggest that religion has declined or will decline with the spread of scientific rationalism and technological progress. The separation of religion and politics would then propel secularization processes and generate secular, modern, rational individuals.[22] This particular Eurocentric self-understanding introduced certain "behaviors, knowledge, and sensibilities" that have formed contemporary citizens and societies and their relationship to and concepts about "the religious" and "the secular" (Asad 2003, 25). Transmitted over generations, these learned behaviours and sensibilities have encultured individuals and shaped certain emotional and intellectual dispositions about and relations to religious/nonsecular traditions. In this social reality, religion is (or should be) absent and/or private, which has helped form a new way of knowing (i.e., a secular episteme) and being-in-the-world (ontology) that informs and demarcates the temporalities, spaces, and laws of nation-states (Asad 2003). In this white Eurocentric, socially constructed, modern/colonial worldview, progression is evaluated through hierarchical and antagonistic binaries in perpetual conflict: reason *above* religious dogma, (secular) politics *versus* religion, science *against* religion, internal spirituality *over* external religiosity. Secularization (the supposed declining role of religion in society) and secularism (confining religion to the private realm) are the key characteristics of typically secular nation-states.[23] Anxieties about religion generally position it as a personal matter with no place in the public sphere or public debates. Formally or nominally secular states promote a "neutrality" that obstructs public displays of religious traditions that have been repressed and are supposedly re-emerging.

Jürgen Habermas (2010) and Charles Taylor (2007) have identified increasingly secularizing environments in northern/western Europe and North America that have seen the growing presence of diverse faith communities (particularly non-white migrants/immigrants). Post-secularity aims to produce a more inclusive and multicultural democratic society that incorporates religious citizens into political debates and public spheres. Habermas asserts that unlike traditional secularism, which strictly divided the private and public, the religious and secular must learn from each other. Religion cannot be subordinated to the domestic realm by secular publics and states. However, religion must also be rendered in secular, rational terms—comprehensible and acceptable to the majority public—to be considered for inclusion in post-secular societies and public spheres. Religion needs to be *translated* (by neutralizing its religious components) and *formatted* to fit Christian secular sensibilities if it is to contribute to post-secular, multicultural, pluralistic societies (Habermas 2010). Taylor (2007) agrees that this particular secular configuration of religion is an appropriate method for managing religious diversity; he likewise affirms that religious concepts, language, identity, and culture should be neutralized and made legible to modern secular systems and citizens.

The formulation of religious concepts into secular or "neutral" categories is not, however, just a verbal or cognitive exercise but a social and political process by which concepts, customs, traditions, and cultural categories that have emerged from a particular spatiotemporal location (i.e., language, culture, structure, history) are *substituted* for and *configured* to fit others. It is the process by which an "embedded local practice [tradition, behaviour, worldview, etc.] is decontextualised (and secularised) in a manner that enables it to be translated, or rendered intelligible entirely—and only—in cosmopolitan [secular] terms" (Menon 2024, 17). As language and culture intertwine and shape each other and our worldviews, the process of this translation to and substitution of the nonsecular/religious with the secular alters and displaces values, modes of reasoning, meanings, and sensibilities as it moves from one religio-socio-spatiotemporal sphere to another.[24]

The adaptation of the religious into Eurocentric secular logic is nothing new. This process of translation was identified and discussed in Said's *Orientalism* and has long been a feature of the modern/colonial Enlightenment-influenced white ethnic project that converted and transplanted its medieval Christian religious categories and experiences into secular and modern, but claims to be neutral. This Eurocentric process of *translation* and *reformulation* of religious into secular has become *structurally* embedded in the foundation of contemporary nation-states, laws, and civil society, as well as instituted in postcolonial state structures, as chapters in this collection illustrate. However, this *morphing* of religion and *reformatting* of religious concepts into a secular, "neutral" framework presumes the normativity of liberal secularism, which defines and separates private and public spheres of life (Asad 2003, 2018; Mahmood 2005, 2015).

The normativity of liberalism that underlies nation-state societies also gives rise to the rationality of economic neoliberalism of late capitalism and underpins global governance structures and frameworks (During 2009, 2010; Mueller 2011; Crocket 2021). Neoliberalism is a cultural and political project "premised [on] a shift toward governmentalities that merge market and state imperatives [such as secularism in order to] produce self-regulating 'good subjects' who embody ideals of individual responsibility" (Bernstein and Jakobson 2013). Rationality, neutrality, and material reality are central to the normativity of (neo)liberalism, generating mass consumerist and surveillance cultures, which are also internalized and reproduced by peoples and societies residing in the nation-state structures (During 2010; Mueller 2011; Barnet and Stein 2012; Bernstein and Jakobson 2013).

The mechanism of normative secularism—the private-public categorization of spheres and spaces—affects knowledge systems, ways of understanding the world, cosmologies, and one's interactions with religion. The normative project of secularism is not just about the separation of church and state. It involves concealing outward religious markers, becoming nonreligious self-governing citizens, choosing religion autonomously, and promoting freedom of (secularly defined) religion and multiculturalism. It is a *cultural* and *political* project that interpellates and reformats the religious into a secular conceptual and cultural framework, brings religions and religious groups within/ under its purview, manages "practices and bodies...[and] lives of ordinary people" (Lloyd 2016, 6), administers human behaviour within and between societies, and regulates how individuals and groups relate to each other. How secularism articulates and functions in various nation-states—such as the United States (Sullivan 2020) and France (Fernando 2014)—is nonetheless different from how it operates in Egypt (Agrama 2012; Mahmood 2015), Malaysia (Moustafa 2018), India and Pakistan (Stephens 2018; Menon 2024), or China and Russia (Marsh 2011).

As discussed in the forthcoming chapters, secularism is part of the nation-state's biopolitical power and mechanism of governing, which uses laws and policies that define and control religion and regulate the lives of populations. As seen in the transnational targeting of Muslims in the global War on Terror, whether in North America, Europe, or Asia, secularism creates the condition where (minority) religion-based communities are seen as an existential and biological threat to the nation-state, which needs militarized security measures for control and domination. This "management of the religious [is also] connected with...technologies of governmentality, such as the management of race" (Lloyd 2016, 6). Secularism activates the biopolitical legal and political measures of the nation-state to exclude populations from the boundaries of national, political, and cultural belonging. It also empowers the state and its public to manage and control gendered experiences and interactions and normalizes the secular policing of Muslim women's bodies (discussed in Chapters 7, 8, and 9 of this book by Diab, Jahangeer, and Jackson-Best, respectively). It operates with neoliberalism to demarcate economically desirable and undesirable racial and religious populations and maintain socioeconomic inequality and the sovereignty of the state (as discussed in Chapter 3 by Bastaki). It also works with neoliberalism to demarcate acceptable and unacceptable "religious" subjects, as was seen in a 2007 New York Police Department report's theorization of "radicalization," which explained that departing from a consumerist lifestyle and the secular world are "signs" of "religious extremism" (Sadequee 2018).[25] Secularism, co-constituted with neoliberalism, is the *structural* framework of the contemporary nation-state and global governance system that shapes peoples and societies and governs human behaviours and relationships.

In demarcating which racial, ethnic, gender, and religious groups (or religious interpretations) are included and excluded in its national polities and boundaries, secularism also helps maintain the cohesiveness of the nation-state (liberal or authoritarian) and its power structure as well as the dominance of the ethnoreligious and/or racial majority (or the postcolonial state elite). Right-wing and populist movements also legitimize their power to restrict Islam and Muslims in and through secularism (as discussed in Chapters 3, 6, and 8 by Gabon, Khan, and Jahangeer, respectively). The normative arrangements and ideological underpinning of secularism give rise to the politicization of right-wing nationalism and religious politics (Bose 2009; Hurd 2009; De Roover 2015), as seen in the growing rise of populism and right-wing political power in the institutional structures of typically secular nation-states such as India, the United Kingdom, the United States, or Norway. From the beginning, George W. Bush framed the US-led War on Terror within liberal and secular values of tolerance, freedom, and the colonial civilizing mission: "This is not, however, just America's fight. And what is at stake is not just America's freedom. This is the world's fight. This is civilization's fight. This is the fight of all who believe *in progress and pluralism, tolerance and freedom*" (Bush 2001, emphasis added). Narendra Modi also claimed when he came into power, "We are secular not because the word was added in our Constitution. Secularism is in our blood. We believe in Sarva Pantha Sambhava."[26] Secularism helps produce populism and right-wing ethnonationalism as the dominant ideological category for political parties to use for specific political purposes (Nandi 2003; Bose 2009).

Secularism thus creates unequal racial and religious hierarchies that regulate and dominate both religion and race. It organizes and forces people to live, experience the world, and relate to others in particular *unequal* and *hostile* ways based on its Eurocentric antagonistic binaries of progression and regression. Through its mechanisms and ideological processes—the normative divide between private-public and its reformatting to fit the religious into the secular—secularism interprets and misrepresents religion and religious practice as an identity/sign/signifier, reads such traits as "backwardness" and "extremism," and facilitates the processes of racialization. The entanglement of the state's governing of religion, biopolitical management of race, and regulating gendered and social behaviour in and through secularism results in ongoing exclusionary policies, securitization, and structural violence. This is evident in the practices of the last twenty years that drive the geopolitics of the continued global War on Terror on Muslims.

Secularism is the underlying *governing logic* and *structural foundation* of contemporary nation-states; it is likewise the subtext of national security and counterterrorism regimes and the regulatory forces of the state that continue to target, surveil, police, and imprison Muslims. It is the foundational mechanism of the international and foreign policy order that defines religion and manufactures hierarchical racial categories out of religious markers of populations, engineering the War on Terror and bolstering Islamophobia. I now turn to normative secularism and its role in individual/personal Islamophobic racism.

Secularism and Individual/ Personal Islamophobic Racism

Canada and America have a *separation of church and state* which makes *religion a personal matter* while Islam has a much closer *integration of state and religion* and religion is not a personal matter, hence with the growing Muslim population in these countries comes the issue of more *Muslim involvement in politics which scares the public of religious extremism.* (Christian clergy, Camrose, Alberta, emphasis added)[27]

I would call myself a devout person with faith, I have very strong convictions about who God is, what's God's nature you know, so um but, *I'm not the sort of person who wears it outwards.* I don't think most Australians are religious in the same way, you know, *it's an internal thing, not something you wear,* so I can work with people and they'd never know. (Danielle, a Euro-Australian mother and member of an anti-Islam group in Australia, emphasis added; quoted in Abdel-Fattah 2018, 41)[28]

I say I'm a Christian but I never go to church. But I still have Christian values, and you know, I would marry in a church and I would hold a funeral in a church, and baptize my children in a church. But I think one of the things with Muslims is this, you know, need, what is it—four or five times a day, to pray. And you know, *everywhere we go we're getting prayer rooms, we're getting prayer rooms in stations*. (Don, a Euro-Australian, construction industry employee in Australia, emphasis added; quoted in Abdel-Fattah 2018, 41)

I look at the Islamic world at the moment...well, Christianity was under reformation in Europe, and there were very dark times in Europe with the Catholic Church being a massive overlord, we had the Inquisition, just complete control, and people were kept in the dark. And I find that in Islam. I think that *Islam needs a reformation*, but their religious laws, *I just can't see how...Islam can separate from Sharia*. I think that if Islam could separate, then things would be much better. (Adrian, a Euro-Australian IT specialist and member of an anti-Muslim group in Australia, emphasis added; quoted in Abdel-Fattah 2018, 46)

[Islam is] the enemy of everything. It's the enemy. And we're just blindly wandering into it. We're not hanging on to the *insights of Enlightenment*, which to me is the *primacy of reason over dogma*. We're turning our backs on that, and it's absolutely terrifying. I'm not sure what's going to happen. (White British nonreligious member of the public, emphasis added; quoted in Jones et al. 2018, 169)

Islam is a totalitarian ideology and movement *contrary to the Constitution* of Norway, legislations, and Norwegian society…Islam is *incompatible with democratic and humane values worldwide through the legislative system of sharia.* Stop The Islamization of Norway. (Anti-Islam group Stop the Islamization of Norway, emphasis added; quoted in Kinsella 2022)

Muslim values, to the extent they are embraced, are deeply *antithetical to American values, i.e., gender equality, religious pluralism,* extolling dissent and the ability to *freely criticize* anyone and anything. (Former conservative blogger and Trump supporter in the United States, emphasis added; quoted in Hawley 2019)

Islam has never found reform from moderates, so *the only hope is assimilation,* and there is no push for that in America or the West at this time under multiculturalism. (Trump supporter, emphasis added; quoted in Hawley 2019)

I would even submit to you that *Islam is not even a religion.* It's a *social political system that uses a deity* to advance its agenda of global conquest. (Former US state representative John Bennett, emphasis added; quoted in Branch 2014)

Humanists should *assess Islam using the same standards* applied to all belief systems. This means, in practice, that humanists support the concept of *a democratic secular state, with complete separation of religion and government…*Basing the law of the land on literal interpretation of ancient texts not only stands in stark opposition to the whole concept of *separation of church and state*, it also violates basic *human rights*. *Humanist* tolerance for a nation's preference for a given religion does not extend to using such a preference to shield *mass violations of such primary freedoms. Governing modern societies by literal application of Shari'a law is a backward reversion* and should be recognized as such. (American Humanist Association 2014, emphasis added)

Remarks like these from individuals or members of civil society (who may target Muslims) usually get identified as Islamophobia, the result of misconceptions and/or prejudice. These comments may be driven by individual ignorance, fear, hatred, and bias and are deemed racist. However, a closer examination reveals the ethnosphere and the conceptual ethnocultural and ethnoracial framework that underpins the evaluations of Muslims and Islam. These sentiments distinguish between external-internal religiosity, reason-dogma, and religion-politics to define and demarcate subordinated categories of Islam and Othered Muslims. Muslim religiosity and commentators' views of Islam do not seem to align with religiosity in the Christian tradition. These statements draw on European Christianity's *medieval* dispositions as well as Christianity's experiences with modernity and secularity in appraising Islam and Muslims. They translate their European experiences of "religion" onto Islam and Muslims in and through the binary grammar of secularism. The chapters in this book by Gabon (Chapter 3) and Jahangeer (Chapter 8) illustrate how secular nation-states and their citizenries are incapable of using "neutral" conceptual frameworks but instead rely on premodern Christianity to judge contemporary Islam and Muslims. Deploying the hostile binary categories of secularism, the general public *substitutes* and *translates* a particular Eurocentric religio-ethnic historical experience of/with "religion" onto Islam and Muslims.

These commentaries and views also reveal how "whiteness enrolls a range of specific affective registers, and shapes certain emotional discourses and responses to Muslim bodies, behavior, things, and spaces" (Abdel-Fattah 2018, 4). The normative mechanism of secularism produces the racialization of Muslims in relationship to whiteness as micro-level individual/personal Islamophobia. This process is also observable in Muslim-majority nation-states, as discussed earlier, where colonized elites in power internalize and mirror Western (white Christian) secular epistemologies in differentiating between "good" and "bad" Muslims.

Perpetrators of individual/personal Islamophobia target, exclude, and racialize Muslims based on Muslims' visible external comportment as assessed in and through secularism. These secular binaries—religion-reason, private-public, science-religion, and religion-politics—shape ideological self-understandings, attitudes, and practices at both the micro and macro versions of Islamophobia. These dichotomous distinctions help create an imagined ethnoreligious and ethnoracial majority identity (or elite identity in Muslim-majority places) of contemporary (liberal and authoritarian) nation-states, perpetuating the racialization of Muslims and provoking conflicts.

According to the "Islamophobia as racism" thesis, race and religion merge to racialize Islam and Muslims. However, religious groups are racialized by the normative distinction of secularism between religion and politics as registered in and through the divide of private-public as well as through the processes of substitution, translation, and reformatting to fit the nonsecular/religious into the secular. This technology of secularism undergirds sociocultural systems, nation-states, and the international order that defines and governs "religion" and racializes groups as "friends" or "enemies" based on the politics of the time. Secularism, then, is the political tool that international and nation-state powers instrumentalize to devise policies in the maintenance of neocolonial imperial, neoliberal, and capitalist power structures and authority. It also informs both right-wing and liberal Islamophobia, as well as the intersectional, scholarly critical race discourses that have tended to erase examinations of the contemporary concept of religion and its connection to race politics and racial formation.

Organization and Structure
of the Collection

This volume makes a new contribution to the "Islamophobia is racism" thesis by analyzing how secularism organizes and constructs the racialization of Muslims and perpetuates anti-Muslim racism. It examines the rise of Islamophobia in societies around the globe that are considered nominally secular or post-secular and includes scholarly investigations of and policy recommendations for the current moment. The authors have diverse approaches to secularism and/or post-secularism—as political and social discourse and/or practice—which offer various considerations for our overall understanding and theorization of Islamophobia. Empirical case studies add nuance to the collection's argument that secularism is the foundational ideological and normative organizing principle of nation-states, civil society, and the epistemologies of their citizenries that has flourished in local histories and cultural contexts in varying ways, construing and racializing Muslims. Chapters show that secularism, instead of promoting its values of freedom, equality, inclusivity, tolerance, neutrality, and pluralism, emboldens states to use these values as weapons to produce intolerance, racism, inequality, and violence.

The collection is divided into four interrelated parts, each demonstrating that the "racialization of Muslims and Islam" in the phenomenon of and scholarship on Islamophobia cannot be understood without considering how the notion and mechanisms of normative secularism operate to conceptualize, interpret, and regulate religion and race. As such, each part illuminates how secularism distinguishes and subordinates Islam and maintains the racialization of Muslims in various social and national contexts where Muslims have been well integrated in secular societies but continue to face racism in the post-secular age.

Part I, "Post-Secularity, Ethnosphere, and Neoliberalism," addresses the intricacies of the way religion interacts with politics, race and ethnicity, coloniality, and the neoliberal economic order in governing and as a civilizing discourse and practice of racial exclusion and inclusion, furthering macro-level Islamophobia. In Chapter 1, Elizabeth Shakman Hurd brings attention to how the category of religion is understood and politicized in and by the foreign policy establishment of secular and/or post-secular nation-states. The chapter demonstrates the complexities around the politics of religion and how the international system moulds *global* religio-political culture in particular ways that both shape and diverge from the lived experiences of ordinary people. Hurd argues that the powerful global construct of good religion/bad religion differentiates who is and is not included within the international community. This classification impacts various faith communities, including Islam and Muslims. Disaggregating the category of religion into "expert religion," "lived religion," and "governed religion," Hurd illustrates how programs to "counter violent extremism" and promote "religious freedom" authorize and politicize particular religions and religious interpretations. This macro-structural formulation of secularism based on the distinction between religion and politics names and empowers "moderates" (i.e., appropriate religious national subjects) and disempowers religious "extremists" (inappropriate [inter]national religious subjects). Those who are inappropriate subjects (or misrecognized) are racialized as "bad Muslims" or "terrorists" via the collective racialization of Muslims and the manifestation of anti-Muslim racism or Islamophobia. Recognizing the structural framework of the international order and the foundational formation of the nation-state in defining and regulating "religion" is necessary for understanding how Islam and Muslims are racialized in local contexts.

While diverse bodies constitute the global international order, particular majority ethnospheres operate in the foundation of each nation-state structure. Focusing on Western societies, Dustin Byrd (Chapter 2) discusses how religion and ethnicity/whiteness become structurally co-constituted in European and North American ethnospheres, impacting Islam and Muslims. Since the Enlightenment, many northern/western European and North American countries have moved from ethnic-based identities to intentional democratic willed-communities, in which historical foundations based on shared ethnicity, language, religion, history, etc. (supposedly) no longer define the *modern* citizenry. An intentional or willed-community is based on "ascribed citizenship," founded on the general acceptance of constitutional ideals, values, and principles of a democratic society—which Muslims can achieve by translating religious concepts into a secular logic. Although Muslims can ascribe to these democratic political ideals and are legal citizens of many traditionally secular and/or post-secular societies, Byrd suggests that they are viewed as ethnically—and religiously—alien to the white "ethnosphere" of the West. Byrd points out that there is a limit to this translation in post-secular societies. Even when Islam is reformulated into secular grammar, which allows Muslims' political and legal participation, they are not accepted as part of the shared cultural ethnoreligious sphere and heritage by nationalist and populist ethnos or ethnic groups (of white European ancestry). Not only the politics of religion and secularism (the mechanics of the private-public dichotomy) but also the shared cultural heritage/ethnicity of the majority are considered to be *structurally* embedded in the imagined identity and formation of the state and society (Anderson 1983; see also Chapter 6 on Hindutva in India, and Chapters 3 and 8 on France in this volume).

For many on the far right in countries like Canada and France, for example, Muslims have been seen as an external biological and physical threat to Western societal Christendom (also to Hindutva in India; see Chapter 6 by Khan). However, under post-secularism, Muslims are viewed as all-encompassing metaphysical threats from within. In the view of far-right adherents, ethnic "nations" could accommodate similar ethnicities but not wholly different ethnicities, races, religions, or cultures. Byrd argues that this segment of the European/white population continues to reject the possibility of "Others" as part of the national culture within their own closed ethnosphere, perpetuating white Christian supremacism and making it difficult for so-called modern secular societies to integrate Muslims. Byrd writes, "It is not 'the Muslim' who threatens modern Western identity—or a Western way-of-being-in-the-world—but rather the Westerners who cannot grasp the modern Enlightenment concept of the willed-community." The presence of Muslims and diverse non-white immigrants and faith communities allows the West to attain modernity, even while the far right tries to impede this process.

Similarly, in Chapter 3, Alain Gabon discusses how the dominant Catholicism pervades the French public sphere, but it is only Muslims' public expressions of Islam—the faith tradition of a marginalized group—that are targeted for relegation to the private sphere through various exceptional legal and political measures in the global War on Terror. Gabon argues these exceptional state measures are derived from and a continuation of French coloniality. Citing France's Charter of the Principles of Islam, Gabon discusses how the secular French state *modifies* its grammar of liberal secularism when it defines and regulates Muslims' devotion to Islam, even for those who have *successfully integrated* into French society. Muslims are fully incorporated into French society but the coloniality of modern France continues to perpetuate the current form of Islamophobia that operates ideologically as well as subliminally to exclude and discriminate against Muslims. Gabon argues that French secularism, *laïcité*, was designed for the state to practise neutrality and does not apply to civil society or the general population—citizens are free to practise religion in public and collectively. However, *laïcité* has been weaponized by the state and various politicians (see Chapter 8 by Jahangeer on how right-wing politicians take advantage of French secularism) to impinge on the religious lives and autonomy of French Muslims. In other words, it is the French state and its dominant ethnosphere that appear to be *incapable* of managing diversity and upholding secular Enlightenment-influenced liberal values of freedom, tolerance, equality, and pluralism. In employing secularism, the French state racializes Muslims and Islam and denies French Muslims freedom, equality, and autonomy. Gabon argues that how the French state is handling Islam has led to France becoming a post-secular situation, where a gravely falsified version of *laïcité*, a pseudo *laïcité*, functions to control French Muslims (i.e., operating like a theologian).

Islamophobia likewise needs to be understood within the global economic order of neoliberal capitalism, which conceptualizes itself as colourblind and borderless. The way many states have encroached on Muslims' autonomy in the global War on Terror contradicts this normative global political and economic order, as neoliberal capitalism aims to limit the scope of governments to ensure individual freedom in all aspects of human life. Juxtaposing Europe's accommodation of Muslim tourists from the wealthy Gulf states with President Trump's travel ban on Muslims from impoverished Muslim-majority nation-states, Jinan Bastaki (Chapter 4) illustrates how neoliberal post-secular nation-states, which also self-identify as post-racial, regulate economically desirable and undesirable Muslim (im)migrants and perpetuate ethnonationalist white supremacy and racism. On the subject of wealthy Muslim tourists in Britain, Bastaki writes: "Within the current context of neoliberalism, Muslims are generally portrayed as unfit for neoliberal subjectivities. Muslims— whether at home or abroad—are racialized and seen as inferior due to their cultural and religious practices; thus, they need some intervention by neoliberalism." Yet, at the same time, Bastaki argues that when economically desirable people look like the undesirable members but do not make a demand on public institutions, "neoliberalism welcomes Muslims [with markers of religiosity] when large amounts of capital are involved." In other words, neoliberalism commodifies the markers of devotion to Islam (the materialities of religion displayed by/on bodies of Muslims), which are usually understood by secular nation-states as unacceptable, and engenders a spiritual marketplace in which the state seems to favour adherents who behave as self-governing consumers and benefit from the borderless movement of capital. In Britain, where secularism operates differently than in France, religion is seen as a public good, especially when it benefits the state in accumulating capitalist wealth. This treatment of Muslims is not about favouring Islam and Muslims, Bastaki argues; it is a paradoxical move by post-secular, neoliberal states that contradicts their so-called neutrality and self-defined secularism. Neoliberalism and ideas of multiculturalism operate together to create a sense of colourblindness and an Islam-friendly veneer for the so-called secular state, when in actuality they function together to racialize Muslims and maintain structural racism and ethnonationalist white supremacy. This intersection of the processes of neoliberalism and secularism and their deployment of a multicultural politics also constitutes a foundational trait of structural Islamophobia by perpetuating the distinction between desirable and undesirable religious and economic subjects. A desirable religious subject disassociates from politics (i.e., no demand on the state) but invests in consumerism. Religious subjects who make political demands get racialized and excluded as undesirable and unacceptable (national and global) subjects needing neoliberal and secular intervention for reform.

Part II on "Law, Gender, and Secular Translations" illustrates how the mechanism of the private-public category of secularism impacts women and how the secular translation of the law and the public sphere empowers the biopolitical authority of the state (or its institutions) in racializing, targeting, excluding, and reforming

Muslims. Saul J. Takahashi in Chapter 5 employs international human rights law to examine the securitization of Islam and anti-Muslim discrimination by the so-called secular states of Japan and Denmark. From the outset, Takahashi highlights the mechanism of secular translations: "Though current practices would theoretically appear to constitute religious, as opposed to racial, profiling, [the UN Human Rights Council Special Rapporteur] noted that 'in practice, most terrorist profiles [of Muslims] use ethnic appearance and national origin as proxies for religion, as religious affiliation is normally not readily identifiable.'" Directing attention to the courts and religious freedom in Japan, which has seen increased religious minorities in the public sphere, the public expression of religiosity is targeted for "Othering" and understood as both a security problem and threat to the Japanese Shinto-based majority ethnosphere. Takahashi argues that "It is the devotion of Muslims and the manifestation of those beliefs that, in the minds of policymakers and society at large, marks them as different and threatening in (and to) secular society." As religion is considered a private matter, excesses of religion associated with notions of piety are used by the Japanese government's surveillance program to racialize Muslims. In the lawsuit brought against the Japanese surveillance program, the court disregarded issues of religious freedom and identified the *outward* conduct of Muslims as a necessary target for surveillance, to distinguish between peaceful Muslims (religiously acceptable subjects) and violent Muslims (religiously unacceptable and thus racialized subjects who can be targeted).

Euphemistically highlighting Muslims' non-white European heritage, the Danish state substitutes "Muslim" as an identity connected to religion to the secular "non-Western" category and relegates Muslims into socioeconomically impoverished communities by legally labelling such locations as "ghettos." Takahashi contends that under the "ghetto" laws the state requires Muslim children to attend schooling to learn "Danish values." This *translation* and *reformulation* of nonsecular/ religious markers into a nonreligious "neutral" category racializes

Muslims, allowing the secular Danish state to circumvent any accusation of "religious discrimination." The Danish government enforces policies to reform and control Muslims' way of life—a process of de-Islamization. Through secularism's private-public classification, the state hegemonically exerts its version of identity and sovereignty over Muslims. It curtails Muslims' autonomy to freely and creatively choose and express their own identities.

Similarly, the much-celebrated secular Indian state has been exerting its ethnoreligious Hindutva politics using the Unlawful Activities (Prevention) Act (UAPA) to target Muslim men emboldened by the US-led War on Terror. The state targets Muslim men suspected of loyalty to Muslim-majority Pakistan instead of the state of India. The connection to co-religionists in a foreign country establishes Muslim men in India as "terrorists." Entrapping and arresting Muslim men on fabricated crimes, writes Areesha Khan (Chapter 6), the Hindutva Indian state marks biopolitical boundaries of who is included and excluded in the nation and encroaches upon the private realm of the family and women. Mirroring the West and its European colonizers, the Hindutva Indian state essentializes and racializes Muslim men and places women in vulnerable conditions. In these circumstances, the public sphere becomes important to women's collective organizing efforts in resisting the state, thereby blurring secularism's distinction of private-public.

Although women invoke religious standpoints in seeking justice for their loved ones, their beliefs and sentiments are *substituted* into the language of rights and secular, judicial justice to make them accessible and employable for resistance in the public sphere by members of civil society. Khan points out that the public sphere is also considered a male-dominated space, whereas both women and religion have been relegated to the private sphere by secularism. In other words, the conceptual framework of secularism's private-public distinction that subordinates religion also interiorizes women, establishing which gender is more acceptable and privileged in so-called modern secular regimes. Far from "rescuing" vulnerable Muslim women from the violence of the Indian state, Indian secularism and its associated patriarchy subject women to abject conditions in the global War on Terror.

Zeinab Diab, in her discussion of gender and the secularism Bill (or Law) 21 in Quebec, Canada (Chapter 7), shows how multiple forms of secularism intersect with Islamophobia/anti-Muslim racism to construct a gendered alterity of Muslims, focusing on the hijab and women's bodies. While secularism purportedly aims to liberate Muslim women from the hijab and Muslim patriarchy, secular Bill 21 fixated on the bodies of Muslim women to racialize them and regulate Islam. By denigrating the normative Canadian Charter and modifying the Quebec Charter, the secularism of Bill 21 deploys the distinction of private-public discursively on Muslim women to demarcate the boundaries of Québécois ethnoreligious Catholic nation from anglophone Canadians and Muslims, while also omitting and Othering Indigenous communities in Canada. For Diab, this omission exposes the intertwined operation of race and settler colonialism in Québécois secularism that perpetuates religious discrimination and/or violates religious freedom as well as racializes Muslims.

Muslim women are at the centre of Canadian regional identity politics, and in the erasure of various populations through Bill 21, hijabi Muslim women are deployed in constructing the alterity and racialization of Muslim and anti-Muslim racism. Far from emancipating Muslim women and recognizing their autonomy, secularism controls and infringes on their freedom in Quebec. What Diab's chapter also reveals is that the presence of hijabi Muslim women (i.e., those outwardly demonstrating their religious markers) in the Canadian public sphere is *central* to the preservation of ethnoreligious and ethnonationalist white Catholic superiority in the Québécois secular regime. Through the erasure of various forms of Otherness and the racialization of Muslim women in and through Bill 21, the Quebec province attempts to maintain its sovereignty and separation from the dominant anglophone Canadian nation.

However, the French *laïcité* that Québécois borrow for targeting Muslim women and constructing their own ethnoreligious identity
is considered illiberal by Roshan Arah Jahangeer (Chapter 8; see also
Chapter 3 by Gabon). Crossing the Atlantic, Jahangeer likewise shows
how the new "separatism law" has modified the grammar of historical
liberal secularism in the French state to target and shut down Muslim
social justice and humanitarian organizations like the Collective Against
Islamophobia in France (CCIF), with accusations of breeding "Islamist"
activity. The "new secularism" law proposed by right-wing politicians,
instead of centring the conflicts between the Catholic Church and the
state, positions Islam as its main rival. Right-wing political parties envi-
sioned the re-establishment of state authority by crafting a particularly
French ethnoracial identity and religious governance. Instead of maintaining the separation of religion and state, right-wing parties see Islam
and Muslims as endangering the sanctity of the Christian European
cultural and religious heritage of French society, which needs to be
protected by weaponizing secularism against Islam.

The separatism law has allowed the French state to expand
its authority to securitize Muslims, subject them to surveillance, and
devise reform policies for Islam. Securitization of Muslims occurs in
and through the distinction of the private-public category of secularism, through which Muslims are targeted for their "visible" displays of
"religiosity," defined as "Islamism." Jahangeer writes that the French
state defines "Islamism" not as violence, but as modes of "correct
conduct"; however, certain behaviours that are foundational to Islam
are interpreted as "political" or "radical," thereby revealing how the
memory of particular premodern sociohistorical and modern experiences within and with institutional Christianity is evoked by the
French state and its citizenries in evaluating and translating the basics
of Islam and Muslim religiosity. The separatism law aims to refashion
Islam into a secularized French Christian version, reproducing neocolonial discourse and practices of biopolitical inclusion and exclusion to
maintain the power of the French state and its ethnoreligious majority.

In this way, the French state reproduces racial differences, perpetuates anti-Muslim racism, and strips Muslims of their freedom to self-define and build community outside the control of the militant secular state.

Part III, "Combatting Compounded Islamophobia," includes an exploration of the impact of multilayered Islamophobia on the mental health of Muslims and examples of grassroots initiatives and policy recommendations on how to address Islamophobia in the Canadian context. Fatimah Jackson-Best (Chapter 9) explores how Islamophobia is a threat to the physical and mental well-being of Muslims and examines how Muslims seeking mental healthcare and their therapeutic relationship with providers can be impacted by Islamophobia. Muslims who experience anti-Muslim harassment and violence can suffer mental health impacts and their experiences can likewise be intensified by mental health service providers' inadequate or secularly biased understandings of religious identity markers. Focusing on the gendered and anti-Black experiences of Islamophobia that Black Muslim women encounter, Jackson-Best writes that secular understandings of religion, race, gender, and mental health rest on a concept of humanity that has historically excluded Black people and can exacerbate particularly Black Muslim women's access to healthcare and health professionals' approach to them. Black Muslim experiences of anti-Black Islamophobia cannot be separated from the histories of settler colonialism and enslavement that have exerted racialized violence on people of African descent. This historical racism continues to shape their experiences in Canadian society, and mental health providers need to be aware of this specific history and these experiences when providing services to Black Muslims.

Jackson-Best shows that although mental health institutions have shifted to a community-based approach, they continue to apply a universal model built upon whiteness, patriarchy, and secularism that understands the mind (private) and body (public) as separate realms. This one-size-fits-all model focuses on managing symptoms and ignores patients' worldviews, identities, and religions, which constitute our sense of self and shape personal and social experiences in a society. Jackson-Best suggests that mental health institutions in Canada disregard the multiple experiences of patients and promote a Western secular biomedical approach to illness instead of incorporating a holistic wellness and diversity approach. Black Muslims, who experience multilayered marginalization, may face additional practitioner-related biases because of their discriminatory beliefs about race and religion. Jackson-Best makes several recommendations to improve mental health institutions for Muslim seekers of mental health assistance in an age of rising Islamophobia in Canada.

The collection ends with Chapter 10 by Khaled Al-Qazzaz and Nakita Valerio, offering policy suggestions by focusing on their grassroots anti-Islamophobia efforts in Canada. They suggest that anti-Islamophobia advocacy and policy solutions need to be based on multi-level and multifaceted approaches. They offer insights into how local approaches might build upon existing strategies, with a focus on safety and overall wellness for Muslims.

Conclusion

Secularism, Race, and the Politics of Islamophobia intervenes in the Islamophobia scholarship to offer a theoretical and conceptual framework to understand better the phenomenon of Islamophobia. It shows how racial thinking and exclusionary practices emerge in the institutional structures of secular and/or post-secular settler-colonial and postcolonial nation-states and societies with growing ethnoreligious and ethnonationalist politics. It brings attention to the "racialization of Muslims/Islam" thesis and illustrates how secularism co-produces religious and racial Others and facilitates the processes of race-making and racial politics. It shifts the focus of Islamophobia from the materialities of Islam—that is, outward performances of Muslims that supposedly facilitate their racialization—to the modern/colonial knowledge system, institutional structures, and epistemological mechanisms that undergird contemporary micro-individual and macro-structural processes of society that construct and perpetuate Islamophobia.

While secularism may have diverse articulations and manifestations, it nevertheless functions ideologically as a form of normative rationality and governmentality that reshapes and transforms human lives in the context of the global War on Terror. It is a political, ideological, and cultural project that governs human conduct and behaviour within societies, shaping and structuring how individuals and groups relate to each other and weaponizing nation-states and their publics to enforce policies and laws to control and discriminate against Muslims.

The chapters in this collection add to these discussions by tracing the history and machinery of secularism and race-making and their connections to law, power, and nation-state sovereignty in various geographical contexts. This nexus of secularism and race in the phenomenon of Islamophobia divides the world into "us and them" and perpetuates anti-Muslim racism, discrimination, and violence. Secularist and right-wing ethnonationalist forms of Islamophobia share similar foundations (even if right-wing Islamophobia is more overt and aggressive). This connection lies in a shared ethnoreligious heritage—even though the philosophical, political, and social framework of secularism operates differently in various contexts and times—that structurally empowers both the state and its public to discriminate and, in the process, govern race, religion, and gender. The contributors to this collection argue and illustrate that Islamophobia is a form of racism that materializes through the normativity of secularism and targets Muslims as racial subjects and Islam for reformation in the global War on Terror.

NOTES

1. The chapters in this collection (except for one) were born as presentations given at the second International Fellows Conference, "Islamophobia and/ in Post-Secular States: Law, Religion, and Science" at the University of Alberta—Augustana campus in 2021.

2. This debate revealed the existence of a contested or inadequate understanding of "Islamophobia" by major American civil rights organizations such as the Council on American Islamic Relations between its local and national chapters. CAIR-National, some activists, and the academic community defended the liberal value of academic freedom over the liberal value of autonomous individuals' sense of injury and the religious freedom of the Black Muslim student. See, for example, CAIR, "CAIR Announces Official Position on Hamline University Controversy, Islamophobia Debate," press release, January 13, 2022, https://www.cair.com/press_releases/ cair-announces-official position-hamline-university-controversy- islamophobia-debate/. This news generated public remarks from various segments of the broader American society and highlighted the issues of religious freedom, academic freedom, and the operation of anti-Black Islamophobic racism. See, for example, Amna Khalid, "Most of All I Am Offended as a Muslim," *Chronicle of Higher Education*, December 29, 2022, https://www.chronicle.com/article/most-of-all-i-am-offended-as-amus- lim. See also remarks by Kayla Wheeler and Edward Curtis on anti-Black racism: "The Role of Blackness in the Hamline Islamic Art Controversy," *Religion News Services*, January 12, 2023, https://religionnews.com/2023/01/12/ the-role-of-blackness-in-the-hamline-islamic-art-controversy/. The controversy led to the filing of a lawsuit against the university, and others wrote petitions in support of the instructor. See the news piece on this by Vimal Patel, "After Lecturer Sues, Hamline University Walks Back Its 'Islamophobic' Comments," *New York Times*, January 17, 2023, https://www. nytimes.com/2023/01/17/us/hamline-lawsuit prophetmuhammadreligion. html. Also, see the petition in support of the university instructor by Christian Gruber, "Petition in Support of Dr. Erika López Prater," Change. org, December 24, 2022, https://www.change.org/p/petition-in-support- of-dr-erika-l%C3%B3pez-prater-the-dismissed-hamline-instructor wrongly-accused-of-islamophobia.

3. The Swedish Constitution, along with a growing number of right-wing and nationalist entities, continues to allow and encourage the exercise of the

liberal tradition of expressing oneself by burning the Quran. See more on this by Jones Hayden, "Quran-Burning in Sweden Exacerbates Tensions with Turkey over NATO Bid," *Politico*, January 2023, https://www.politico.eu/article/quran-burning-in-sweden-exacerbates-tensions-with-turkey-over-nato-bid/; *Al Jazeera*, "Turkish Anger after Quran Burning, Kurd Protests in Sweden," January 2, 2023, https://www.aljazeera.com/news/2023/1/21/turkey-cancels-swedish-minister-visit-over-right-wing-protest.

4. The State of Israel's genocide of Palestinians has had a global impact and caused the rise of anti-Palestinian Islamophobia and targeting of Arabs, South Asians, Muslims, and any pro-Palestinian activists. See more on this by Selen Rasquinho, "European Parliament Holds a Session on Combating Islamophobia, Antisemitism," AA.com.Tr, February 8, 2024, https://www.aa.com.tr/en/europe/european-parliament-holds-session-on-combating-islamophobia-antisemitism/3131064#; Dylan Robertson discusses the case of Canada in "Anti-Islamophobia Envoy Warns of Chill on Speaking Out about Gaza, Hate Crimes," *Canadian Press*, January 27, 2024, https://www.thecanadianpressnews.ca/politics/anti-islamophobia-envoy-warns-of-chill-on-speaking-out-about-gaza-hate-crimes/article_565be62a-143a-54e3-80d2-e9b2f0a0c73f.html, as does Peter Zimonjic in "Rise in Antisemitic, Islamophobic Threats has Canadians 'Scared in Our Own Streets,' PM Says," *CBC News*, November 8, 2023, https://www.cbc.ca/news/politics/trudeau-antisemitism-gaza-islamophobia-1.7022244. Christoph Strack discusses "Muslims in Germany: Life Post-Hamas Attack 'Like after 9/11,'" *Deutsche Welle*, January 12, 2024, https://www.dw.com/en/muslims-in-germany-life-post-hamas-attack-like-after-9-11/a-67959092; see also Monica Pinna, "Can Germany Be Neutral When It Comes to the Gaza War?" *Euronews*, February 16, 2024, https://www.euronews.com/2024/02/16/has-the-israel-hamas-war-fuelled-political-polarisation-in-germany. Anti-Muslim violence in India has also seen a rise, as Kanishka Singh shows in her article, "Anti-Muslim Hate Speech Soars in India, Research Group Says," *Reuters*, February 26, 2024, https://www.reuters.com/world/india/anti-muslim-hate-speech-soars-in-india-research-group-says-2024-02-26/. Sara Monetta discusses the rise of Islamophobia in the UK in "Anti-Muslim Cases Surge in UK since Hamas Attacks, Charity Finds," *BBC News*, February 22, 2024, https://www.bbc.co.uk/news/uk-england-68374372. Michael Makawoski covers the rise of Islamophobia in Germany in "In Germany, Historic Guilt Is Fueling Islamophobia, Anti-Immigrant Policies," *The Progressive Magazine*, October 25, 2023, https://progressive.org/latest/

germany-historic-guilt-makowski-20231025/. Focusing on Sweden, Alexandra Enberg details that a "Mosque in Sweden's Capital Again Targeted by Islamophobes with Threatening Graffiti," AA.com.Tr, February 22, 2024, https://www.aa.com.tr/en/europe/mosque-in-swedens-capital-again-targeted-by-islamophobes-with-threatening-graffiti/3145288.

5.   Amy Goodman and Juan Gonzales critique universities' violation of students' right to protest in recent Gaza encampments in "300+ Arrested in Police Raids on Columbia and CCNY to Clear Gaza Encampments," Truthout.org, May 1, 2024, https://truthout.org/video/300-arrested-in-police-raids-on-columbia-and-ccny-to-clear-gaza-encampments/. Kate Wagner writes about how the destruction of cultural and historical heritage sites like mosques constitutes Islamophobia; this is a tactic of ethnic cleansing used in colonization to ensure there is no trace of any history and sense of place left to which people can return. See "What Israel's Destruction of the Great Omari Mosque Means," *The Nation*, January 24, 2024, https://www.thenation.com/article/world/great-omari-mosque-urbicide-gaza/.

6.   See "Presumptively Antisemitic: Islamophobic Tropes in Israel-Palestine Discourse," Center for Security, Race, and Rights, Rutgers University Law School, November 2023, https://csrr.rutgers.edu/issues/presumptively-antisemitic/.

7.   Kiara Alfonseca discusses the launch of the US Department of Education's investigation of racism in higher education in "DOE Launches Investigation into Harvard following Islamophobia, Anti-Arab Complaint," *ABC News*, February 6, 2024, https://abcnews.go.com/US/doe-launches-investigation-harvard-islamophobia-anti-arab-complaint/story?id=106998802.

8.   Alongside the CSSR report, Hilary Aked analyzes how the organized politics of pro-Israel groups fund the Islamophobia industry in the US to vilify Palestinians and Arab Muslims; see "The Undeniable Overlap: Right-wing Zionism and Islamophobia," *Open Democracy*, September 29, 2015, https://www.opendemocracy.net/en/undeniable-overlap-right-wing-zionism-and-islamophobia/.

9.   The concept of Islamophobia became popularized in the 1990s by the Runnymede Trust report in the United Kingdom entitled "Islamophobia: A Challenge For Us All." It defined the concept as a form of "fear, hatred, and dread" by focusing on the "religion of Islam" but not on how it manifested and impacted the lived experiences of all diverse non-white Muslim adherents in British society. Scholarship on Islamophobia, as a result, attempts

to explain on-the-ground policies and their impacts on various societies and human lives, as well as its local, transnational, and global formations. The Runnymede Trust, however, modified its definition in a 2017 report, unpacking issues such as integration, hate crime, xenophobia, gender, identity, and racism to include in the conceptualization of Islamophobia. For more on the Runnymede reports, see https://www.runnymedetrust.org/ publications/islamophobia-a-challenge-for-us-all.

10. I use the term "post-racial" to generate more inquiry into this concept for societies with Black-white racial divides but that self-define themselves by dismissing their history of racism. In the context of the United States, with the presidency of Barack Obama, Americans as well as many Europeans, using Obama's presidency, have tried to redefine their Euro-American heritage and cultural superiority by claiming to have moved "beyond racism." David Theo Goldberg and Stephanie Boulila demonstrate how the post-racial thought processes in these societies, in denying or overlooking racism, sustain structural racism, where the historical and structural relationship between Blackness-whiteness has not been dismantled but continues with claims of post-raciality. See, for example, David Theo Goldberg, *Are We All PostRacial Yet?* (Polity, 2015). For more discussion on this, see Stefanie C. Boulila, *Race in Post-racial Europe: An Intersectional Analysis* (Rowman & Littlefield, 2019).

11. Democratic pluralisms in this collection mean the normative understanding of modern constitutional nation-states and the pluralistic characteristics or nature of diversity of their polities in places such as North America, northern Europe, or India.

12. Scholars agree that a heightened awareness of Muslim presence in Muslim-minority places coupled with Muslim non-state actors' global activities have added to the current racialization of Muslims in the global War on Terror. Extensive academic literature exists on this racialization of Muslims. Louis Cainker and Sahar Selod reviewed this scholarship since the global War on Terror to examine how the racialization process has produced the racial category of Muslims in their 2018 article, "Review of Race Scholarship and the War on Terror," *Sociology of Race and Ethnicity* 4, no. 2: 165–177. Selod adds that racialization is "the process by which bodies become racial in their lived realities because of biological and/or cultural traits as a result of the intersection and cooperation between ideologies, policies, laws, and social interactions that results in the denial of equal treatment in society" (2018, 23), in Sahar Selod, *Forever Suspect: Racialized Surveillance of Muslim*

Americans in the War on Terror (Rutgers University Press, 2018). Both Eric Love's *Islamophobia and Racism in America* (NYU Press, 2017) and Sahar Aziz's *The Racial Muslim* (University of California Press, 2022) take a comparative and historical approach to this by examining various minorities in the US with the added feature of religion in Aziz. See also Steve Garner and Saher Selod's 2015 article, "The Racialization of Muslims: Empirical Studies of Islamophobia," *Critical Sociology* 41, no. 1: 9–19. In the European context, the racialization process is defined as cultural racism in Nasar Meer and Tariq Modood (2009), "Refutations of Racism in the 'Muslim Question,'" *Patterns of Prejudice* 43, no. 3–4: 335–354, and also in Nasar Meer (2013), "Racialization and Religion: Race, Culture, and Difference in the Study of Antisemitism and Islamophobia," *Ethnic and Racial Studies* 36, no. 3: 385–398.

13.   Discrimination and racism toward Muslims based on truth claims of Islamic theology have existed since antiquity. Saint John of Damascus, a theologian who also served as an official in the Islamic Umayyad Empire, wrote one of the first books, *Fount of Knowledge*, where he critiques theologies of Islam, and Muslims are labelled derogatorily as Ishmaelites, Saracens, Agarness, desert or tribal people, etc., and declared Muhammad a false prophet and Islam a false religion (https://archive.org/details/writings-thefount0037john/page/n487/mode/2up). See also Daniel Janosik, "John of Damascus on the Qur'an: Evidence for an 8th Century Canonization," http://danieljanosik.com/wp-content/uploads/2015/11/John-of-Damascus-on-the-Quran.pdf. These theologically based categorizations continued through to the European Middle Ages in Catholic western and Byzantium Orthodox eastern Europe. Stefan Stantchev explains that papal bulls were issued to demarcate the relationship between Christians and non-Roman Christians as well as their interactions with Jews and Saracens (Muslims), who were both viewed as "infidels" by Roman Catholics. See Stantchev's (2014) "'Apply to Muslims What Was Said of the Jews': Popes and Canonists between a Taxonomy of Otherness and 'Infidelitas,'" *Law and History Review* 32, no. 1: 65–96. See also *The Western Perception of Islam between the Middle Ages and the Renaissance* by Cary Nederman and Marcigliolo (Pickwick, 2017). In *Islamic Thought Through Protestant Eyes*, Mehmet Karabela explains how Protestant theologies were developed by engaging with Islamic theologies, particularly Sunni Islam, but post-Reformation Europeans also categorized all Muslims as "Turks" as well as used Islamic theologies as a foil to differentiate themselves from Catholics (Routledge, 2021). For more examples of how Islam played a crucial role in the evolution of Christianity, see John Tolan, *Faces of*

Muhammad: Western Perceptions of the Prophet of Islam from the Middle Ages to Today (Princeton University Press, 2019); Kecia Ali, *The Lives of Muhammad* (Harvard University Press, 2014). For a history of Islam in the United States see Thomas Kidd, *American Christians and Islam: Evangelical Cultures and Muslim from the Colonial Period to the Age of Global Terrorism* (Princeton University Press, 2008).

14. Modern/colonial or modernity/coloniality are concepts formulated by Walter Mignolo and Aníbal Quijano to show how early explorations and discoveries and colonization are co-constituted in creating knowledge systems and the structures of modernity. The authors highlight colonial exploration's connection to white, European power structures that gave rise to modern categories of religion and race. See Mignolo's *Local Histories, Global Designs: Coloniality, Subaltern Knowledges and Border Thinking* (Princeton University Press, 2000), as well as Quijano's "Coloniality of Power, Eurocentrism, and Latin America," trans. Michael Ennis, *Nepantla: Views from South* 1, no. 3 (2000): 533–80.

15. The replacement of religious differentiation with secular racial categories is the result of long wars within European Christianity where various Christian theocracies conducted extensive "holy war" military campaigns against one another. In the aftermath of these terrible conflicts and influenced by the spread of Renaissance humanism and the advent of science during Enlightenment in the nineteenth century, Europeans began to move toward a separation of religion from all governmental, political, and legal institutions to stop the intra-religious violence and authoritarianism, and to cultivate tolerance. See Harold Berman, *Law and Revolution II: The Impact of the Protestant Reformations on the Western Legal Tradition* (Belknap Press, 2003).

16. Scholars such as Talal Asad and Saba Mahmood have critiqued the interpretation of religious practice as a sign or signifier, representing and standing for a self-referential identity. This way of viewing and understanding religious practices denies the ontic readings of being. It is also grounded on the Kantian secular concept of the "inner self" and "outer self" that separates the mind and body and is pervasive in contemporary societies. See, for example, Immanuel Kant, *Critique of Pure Reason* (Cambridge University Press, 1998) and *Anthropology from a Pragmatic Point of View* (Cambridge University Press, 2006). In both state and academic analysis, Muslim religiosity and its markers of piety are read as symbols of "identity" that distort the understanding of Muslim-majority societies as well as those living in Muslim-minority contexts, causing them to be treated as "foreign" outsiders. See more on this in

Talal Asad, *Genealogies of Religion: Discipline and Reasons of Power in Christianity and Islam* (Baltimore: Johns Hopkins University Press, 1993) and Mahmood's *Politics of Piety*.

17. Islamophobia's dialectical aspects of individual/personal and institutional/ structural systems reinforce each other to perpetuate and maintain structural racism against Muslims. Elements of the structure here include state and legal institutions such as law enforcement and congressional agencies as well as their policies and actions. The dialectical force of structural Islamophobia, explained by Khaled Beydoun, becomes intense in moments of crisis when governmental actions authorize Islamophobia against ordinary citizens. See, for example, Khaled Beydoun, *American Islamophobia: Understanding the Roots and Rise of Fear* (University of California Press, 2018).

18. For a detailed discussion on this, see Asma T. Uddin's *When Islam Is Not a Religion: Inside America's Fight for Religious Freedom* (Berkeley: Pegasus, 2019). Uddin also shares concerns about how the "racialization of Muslim" discourse may have disadvantaged Muslim Americans' claims of religious freedom in her interview with the Institute for Social Policy and Understanding, on October 3, 2019, https://www.facebook.com/theISPU/ posts/pfbidoLdH3eJur72e9xVcT4HpJ5seg8DPvJCWhnq6iodXFZpACpDszzq-J1xr7zZKtKTeKXl. Uddin critiques the Christian evangelists and political right-wing entities that want to weaponize traditional religion, as well as the political left (secularists) who are against the mixing of religion and politics, advocating for Muslims' constitutional rights to religious freedom. As Hurd will discuss in Chapter 1, in constitutional liberal, secular democracies, religious freedom laws and discourses are themselves part of the legal and political technology that defines the boundaries of what is and is not a religion and religious freedom. For more on this, see Hurd's *Beyond Religious Freedom*, Winnifred Sullivan's *The Impossibility of Religious Freedom*, and Saba Mahmood's *Religious Difference in a Secular Age*.

19. Thank you to the anonymous reviewer for their suggestion regarding the works of Reza Gholami.

20. Wael Hallaq, in *Restating Orientalism* (Columbia University Press, 2018), critiques Said's *Orientalism* for failing to specify when colonialism began and ended and how nineteenth- and twentieth-century colonial domination and capital extraction involved not just economic and political subjugation but erasure and reformulation of Indigenous and local knowledge systems, along with replacing local systems with secular modern epistemologies and institutions. Modern European colonial empires evolved with and under

secular liberalism, with the mission of conquering the worldviews and epistemologies of local cultures, thereby committing epistemic violence. While
Said critiqued the Western production of oriental knowledge and European
authors' connections to the political time in supporting colonization, Said
himself engaged in secular knowledge production and perpetuated orientalism. A similar trend is in place in much of the Islamophobia scholarship.

21. Although Edward Said's *Orientalism* has been instrumental in addressing
the relationship between knowledge production, power, and domination
in manufacturing the oriental Other in colonial modernity, scholars have
pointed out how, in his critique of Western/the Occident's production
of knowledge about Islam, Said has reproduced the very thing that he
was critiquing—Western modernity, coloniality, secularity—because
of his inability to see and question the category/definition/secularity
through which the Western Occident understood "religious lives" in
post-Enlightenment European modernity. Religious lives in Europe were
not viewed/understood as "dogma" in premodern times but have come
about or been viewed in such a way with European modernity. A growing
number of scholars have demonstrated how Said makes the "secular" and
"secularism" an authoritative presence in his critique of the Occident and
maintains the Occidental, modern, and secular understanding of "religion
as dogma" concerning Islam. Nelson Maldonado-Torres contends that Said
"presupposes a transhistorical and transcultural view of [universal] religion"
in "Secularism and Religion in the Modern/Colonial World-System: From
Secular Postcoloniality to Postsecular Transmodernity," in *Coloniality at
Large: Latin America and the Postcolonial Debate*, edited by Mabel Morana,
Enrique Dussel, and Carlos Jauregui (Duke University Press, 2008), 376.
For more on this, see Khaled Furani (2020), "Said and the Religious Other,"
in *Comparative Studies in Society and History* 52: 604–625; Joseph Massad
(2004), "The Intellectual Life of Edward Said," *Journal of Palestine Studies* 43,
no. 3: 7–22; Amir Mufti (1998), "Auerbach in Istanbul: Edward Said, Secular
Criticism, and the Question of Minority Culture," *Critical Inquiry* 25: 95–125;
Yazid Said (2013), "Edward Said, Religion, and the Study of Islam: An
Anglican View," *Journal for the Academic Study of Religion* 26, no. 2: 129. Also see
Lucy Pick, "Orientalism and Religion," *Middle East Institute*, April 20, 2012,
https://www.mei.edu/publications/orientalism-and-religion.

22. Many nineteenth-century European scholars, like Edward Burnet Tyler
in *Primitive Culture* (1871), theorized that with technological and scientific
advancement, societies would give up religious beliefs and religions would

be brought under the domain of scientific understanding. This way of thinking continued in the twentieth century where scholars such as Peter Berger defined secularization and modernization are processes in which society and culture free themselves from the domination of religious institutions and symbols; see Berger, *The Sacred Canopy* (Doubleday, 1967). Along with technological and economic growth, modernization generates certain ways of thinking and behaving that are incorporated into the everyday life of a society that give individuals varied viewpoints and options through which they can separate thought processes for public and private life; see Peter Berger, Brigitte Berger, and Hansfried Keller, *The Homeless Mind: Modernization and Consciousness* (Vintage, 1974). See also Peter Berger, *A Rumor of Angels: Modern Society and the Rediscovery of the Supernatural* (Doubleday, 1970).

23. Others have also defined these concepts in various ways—for example, Jose Casanova explains that the term "secular" is a central modern theological-philosophical, legal-political, and cultural construct that codifies experience or reality as separate from the religious. Secularization is the social process developed first in modern Europe and which then travelled with globalization and technological transformation as a normative teleological human progression and development from the primitive "sacred" to the modern "secular." Secularism refers to either ideologies or principles of governance and statecraft, the separation of church and state, or religion and politics. See more on this in Jose Casanova, *Public Religions in the Modern World* (University of Chicago Press, 1994).

24. For discussion on the connection between language, culture, and thought and how language shapes worldviews and cultures, see Christine Jourdan and Kevin Tuite, *Language, Culture, and Society: Key Topics in Linguistic Anthropology* (Cambridge University Press, 2006); also see Svenja Völkel and Nico Nassenstein, *Approaches to Language and Culture* (De Gruyter, 2022).

25. The word "secular" appears fourteen times in the NYPD's report "Radicalization in the West: The Homegrown Threat." See https://www.brennancenter.org/sites/default/files/legacy/Justice/20090000.Radicalization.in.the.West-Statement.of.Clarification.pdf. This secular government agency clearly distinguishes and privileges "secular" worldviews and lifestyles over what it views as "religious" and thus "extremist." Those leaving or giving up materialism, consumerism, and capitalistic competitive worldly endeavours are considered "bad" people who are "dangerous" to/for the society. Any contemporary environmentalist would

disagree with this characterization of those who give up a consumeristic lifestyle as bad and dangerous for the global community; see, for example, Naomi Klein, *This Changes Everything: Capitalism vs. The Climate* (Simon & Schuster, 2015), and Gregory Claey, *Utopianism for a Dying Planet: Life After Consumerism* (Princeton University Press, 2022). The report also assumes everyone in the world must also have the same definition and distinguish, like the NYPD, between the "secular" and "religious." For an Islamic concept of the secular, see Sherman Jackson, *The Islamic Secular* (Oxford University Press, 2024).

26. Narendra Modi on X on April 29, 2014: https://x.com/narendramodi/status/460685920652390400?lang=en.

27. An undergraduate student research paper by Syed Faran, Spring 2022, entitled "Islamophobia in Camrose," on Islamophobia in the local community, for the course "Constructing Muslims and Islam" at the University of Alberta, Augustana Campus. Quote reproduced with permission from the student.

28. Like my student in Camrose and unlike the focus of most Islamophobia studies on the impacts on and categorizations of Muslim performances (for example, *The Racial Muslim* by Sahar Aziz and *American Islamophobia* by Khaled Beydoun), Abdel-Fattah investigates Anglo-Australians and their everyday attitudes of/about Muslim's religiosity. She typologizes these Anglo-Australians as "political Islamophobes"—those Euro-Australians involved in hate groups and anti-Islam organizations—and "Everyday participants"—regular everyday citizens not connected to anti-Islam hate groups.

REFERENCES

Abdel-Fattah, Randa. 2018. *Islamophobia and Everyday Multiculturalism in Australia*. Routledge.

Agrama, Hussein. 2012. *Questioning Secularism*. University of Chicago Press.

Alexio, Aiden. 2023. "Islamophobia Leads to the Persecution and the Genocide of Muslim Minorities." Justice For All (Canada). https://www.justice-forallcanada.org/uploads/4/6/8/9/46897513/globalislamophobia report-2023-03-15.pdf.

American Humanist Association. 2014. "Statement and Resolution on Islam." September 15. https://americanhumanist.org/key-issues/statements-and-resolutions/islam/.

Anidjar, Gil. 2006. "Secularism." *Critical Inquiry* 33, no. 1: 52–77.

Asad, Talal. 2018. *Secular Translations: Nation-State, Modern Self, and Calculative Reason*. Columbia University Press.

Asad, Talal. 2003. *Formations of the Secular: Christianity, Islam, Modernity*. Stanford University Press.

Aziz, Sahar. 2022. *The Racial Muslim: When Racism Quashes Religious Freedom*. University of California Press.

Bakali, Naved, and Farid Hafez. 2022. *The Rise of Global Islamophobia in the War on Terror Coloniality, Race, and Islam*. Manchester University Press.

Bayoumi, Moustafa. 2006. "Racing Religion." *New Centennial Review* 6, no. 2: 267–293.

Bayrakli, Enes, and Farid Hafez. 2019. *Islamophobia in Muslim Majority Societies*. Routledge.

Bazian, Hatem. 2019. "Religion-building and Foreign Policy." In *Islamophobia in Muslim Majority Societies*, edited by Enes Bayrakli and Farid Hafez. Routledge.

Bernstein, Elizabeth, and Janet Jakobsen. 2013. "Introduction: Gender, Justice, and Neoliberal Transformations." *The Scholar & Feminist Online*, no. 11.1–11.2. https://sfonline.barnard.edu/introduction-for-gender-justice-and-neoliberal-transformations/.

Beydoun, Khaled. 2023. *The New Crusades: Islamophobia and the Global War on Muslims*. University of California Press.

Beydoun, Khalid, and Cyra Choudhury, eds. 2020. *Islamophobia and the Law*. Cambridge University Press.

Branch, Chris. 2014. "State Rep. John Bennett Stands By Anti-Islam Comments: 'Islam Is Not Even A Religion.'" *Huffington Post*, September 22. https://www.huffpost.com/entry/oklahoma-john-bennett-islam_n_5863084.

Bush, George W. 2001. George W. Bush Address to a Joint Session of Congress and the American People, September 20. Transcript. https://lifetime-learners.org/uploads/Bush-Speeches.pdf.

Cho, Sumi, Kimberlé Crenshaw, and Leslie McCall. 2013. "Toward a Field of Intersectionality Studies: Theory, Application, and Praxis." *Signs: Journal of Women in Culture and Society* 38, no. 4: 785–810.

Crockett, Clayton. 2021. "Neoliberalism, Postsecularism, and the End of Religion." *Religions* 12: 631.

CSRR. 2023. "Presumptively Antisemitic: Islamophobic Tropes in Israel-Palestine Discourse." Center for Security, Race, and Rights. Rutgers University Law School. https://csrr.rutgers.edu/issues/presumptively-antisemitic/.

Dagli, Caner. 2020a. "Muslims Are Not a Race." *Renovatio*, February 6. https://renovatio.zaytuna.edu/article/muslims-are-not-a-race

Dagli, Caner. 2020b. "Muslims are not Racialized." CanerDagli.com, September 16. https://canerdagli.com/2020/09/16/muslims-are-not-racialized/.

Deeb, Lara. 2016. *Enchanted Modern: Gender and Public Piety in Shi'i Lebanon.* Princeton University Press.

De Roover, Jacob. 2015. *Europe, India, the Limit of Secularism.* Oxford University Press.

During, Simon. 2009. *Exit Capitalism : Literary Culture, Theory and Post-Secular Modernity.* Taylor & Francis Group.

During, Simon. 2010. "Completing Secularism: The Mundane in the Neoliberal Age." In *Varieties of Secularism in a Secular Age*, edited by M. Warner, J. VanAntwerpen and C. Calhoun. Harvard University Press.

Ejiofor, Promise Frank. 2023. "Decolonising Islamophobia." *Decolonising Islamophobia, Ethnic and Racial Studies* 46, no. 13: 2863–2892. https://doi.org/10.1080/01419870.2023.2181670.

Esposito, John, and Ibrahim Kalin. 2011. *Islamophobia: The Challenge of Pluralism in the 21st Century.* Oxford University Press.

Fernando, Mayanthi. 2014. *The Republic Unsettled: Muslim French and the Contradictions of Secularism.* Duke University Press.

Gholami, Reza. 2021. "Critical Race Theory and Islamophobia: Challenging Inequity in Higher Education." *Race Ethnicity and Education* 24, no. 3: 319–337. https://doi.org/10.1080/13613324.2021.1879770.

Green, Todd. 2015. *The Fear of Islam: An Introduction to Islamophobia in the West.* Minneapolis: Fortress.

Grosfoguel, R. 2012. "The Multiple Faces of Islamophobia." *Islamophobia Studies Journal* 1, no. 1: 9–33.

Habermas, Jürgen. 2010. *An Awareness of What is Missing: Faith and Reason in a Post-Secular Age.* Translated by Ciaran Cronin. Polity Press.

Hallaq, Wael. 2018. *Restating Orientalism: A Critique of Modern Knowledge.* Columbia University Press.

Hawley, George. 2019. "Ambivalent Nativism: Trump Supporters' Attitudes Toward Islam and Muslim Immigrant." Brookings Institute, July 24. https://www.brookings.edu/articles/ambivalent-nativism-trump-supporters-attitudes-towardislam-and-muslim-immigration/.

Hurd, Elizabeth Shakman. 2009. *The Politics of Secularism in International Relations.* Princeton University Press.

Hurd, Elizabeth Shakman. 2015. *Beyond Religious Freedom: The New Global Politics of Religion*. Princeton University Press.

Husain, Atiya. 2019. "Moving Beyond (and Back To) the Black-White Binary: A Study of Black and White Muslims' Racial Positioning in the United States." *Ethnic and Racial Studies* 42, no. 4: 589–606.

Jones, Stephen, and Amy Unsworth. 2024. "Two Islamophobias? Racism and Religion as Distinct but Mutually Supportive Dimensions of Anti-Muslim Prejudice." *British Journal of Sociology* 75, no 1: 5–22. https://onlinelibrary.wiley.com/doi/10.1111/1468-4446.13049.

Jones, Stephen H., et al. 2018. "'That's How Muslims are Required to View the World': Race, Culture and Belief in Non-Muslim's Descriptions of Islam and Science." *Sociological Review* 67: 161–177. https://doi.org/10.1177/0038026118778174.

Kahn, Jonathon, and Vincent Lloyd. 2016. *Race and Secularism in America*. Columbia University Press.

Kazi, Nazia. 2018. *Islamophobia, Race, and Global Politics*. Rowman & Littlefield.

Khalid, Amna. 2022. "Most of All I am Offended as a Muslim." *Chronicle of Higher Education*, December 29. https://www.chronicle.com/article/most-of-all-i-am-offended-as-a-muslim.

Kinsella, Victoria. 2022. "Attitudes Towards Muslims & Islamophobia in Norway." *Life in Norway*, November 4. https://www.lifeinnorway.net/attitudes-towards-muslims-islamophobia/

Kitching, Karl, and Reza Gholami. 2023. "Towards Critical Secular Studies in Education: Addressing Secular Education Formations and their Intersecting Inequalities." *Discourse: Studies in the Cultural Politics of Education* 44, no. 6: 943–958. https://doi.org/10.1080/01596306.2023.2209710.

Kumar, Deepa. 2012. *Islamophobia and the Politics of Empire*. Haymarket.

Kumar, Deepa. 2021. *Islamophobia and the Politics of Empire: Twenty Years after 9/11*. Verso.

Kundnani, Arun. 2014. *The Muslims are Coming: Islamophobia, Extremism, and the War on Terror*. Verso.

Lloyd, Vincent. 2016. "Introduction." In *Race and Secularism in America*, edited by Jonathan Kahn and Vincent Lloyd. Columbia University Press.

Mahmood, Saba. 2005. *Politics of Piety: The Islamic Revival and the Feminist Subject*. Princeton University Press.

Mahmood, Saba. 2015. *Religious Difference in a Secular Age: A Minority Report.* Princeton University Press.

Maldonado-Torres, Nelson. 2014. "Race, Religion, and the Ethics in the Modern/Colonial World." *Journal of Religious Ethics* 42, no. 4: 691–711.

Marsh, Christopher. 2011. *Religion and the State in Russia and China: Suppression, Survival, and Revival.* Continuum.

Masuzawa, Tomoko. 2005. *The Inventions of World Religions: Or, How European Universalism Was Preserved in the Language of Pluralism.* University of Chicago Press.

Menon, Nivedita. 2024. *Secularism as Misdirection: Critical Thought from the Global South.* Duke University Press.

Mignolo, Walter. 2011. *The Darker Side of Western Modernity: Global Futures, Decolonial Options.* Duke University Press.

Modood, Tariq. 2018. "Islamophobia: A Form of Cultural Racism." *Sociology, Politics and International Studies: A Submission to the All-Party Parliamentary Group on British Muslims on 'Working Definition of Islamophobia.'"* June 1.

Modood, Tariq. 2019. *Essays on Secularism and Multiculturalism.* Rowman & Littlefield.

Moustafa, Tamir. 2018. *Constituting Religion: Islam, Liberal Rights, and the Malaysian State.* Cambridge University Press.

Mueller, Julie. 2011. "The IMF, Neoliberalism and Hegemony." *Global Society* 25, no. 3: 377–402.

Rana, Junaid. 2011. *Terrifying Muslims: Race and Labor in South Asian Diaspora.* Duke University Press.

Sadequee, Sharmin. 2018. "Surveillance, Secular Law, and the Reconstruction of Islam in the United States." *Surveillance & Society* 16, no. 4: 473–487.

Said, Edward W. 1979. *Orientalism.* Vintage.

Sayyid, Salman, and AbdoolKarim Vakil. 2011. *Thinking through Islamophobia: Global Perspectives.* Columbia University Press.

Sealy, Thomas. 2021. "Islamophobia: With or Without Islam?" *Religions* 12, no. 6: 369. https://doi.org/10.3390/rel12060369.

Selod, Saher, Inaash Islam, and Steve Garner. 2024. *A Global Racial Enemy: Muslims and the 21st Century Racism.* Polity Press.

Sheehi, Stephen. 2011. *Islamophobia and the Ideological Campaign Against Muslims.* Clarity Press.

Special UN Human Rights Council Rapporteur. 2021. *Report on Countering Islamophobia/Anti-Muslim Hatred to Eliminate Discrimination and*

Intolerance Based on Religion or Belief. Special Rapporteur on Freedom
of Religion or Belief. 46th Session of Human Rights Council,
April 4–5. https://www.ohchr.org/en/documents/thematic-reports/
ahrc4630-countering-islamophobiaanti-muslim-hatred-eliminate.

Stephens, Julia. 2018. *Governing Islam: Law, Empire, and Secularism in Modern South
Asia*. Cambridge University Press.

Sullivan, Winnifred. 2020. *Church State Corporation: Construing Religion in the US
Law*. University of Chicago Press.

Taylor, Charles. 2007. *A Secular Age*. Belknap Press.

Tyrer, David. 2013. *The Politics of Islamophobia: Race, Power and Fantasy*. Pluto Press.

Uddin, Asma. 2019. *When Islam Is Not a Religion: Inside America's Fight for Religious
Freedom*. Pegasus.

Vakil, AbdoolKarim. 2011. "Is the Islam in Islamophobia the Same as the
Islam in Anti-Islam; Or, When Is It Islamophobia Time?" In *Thinking
Through Islamophobia: Global Perspectives*, edited by Salman Sayyid and
AbdoolKarim Vakil. Columbia University Press.

Wynter, Sylvia. 1991. "Columbus and the Poetics of the Propter Nos." Annals of
Scholarship 8, no. 2: 251–286.

Wynter, Sylvia. 1995. "1492: A New World View." In *Race, Discourse, and the Origin
of the Americas: A New World View*, edited by Vera Lawrence Hyatt and
Rex Nettleford. Smithsonian Institution Press.

Yountae, An. 2024. *The Coloniality of the Secular: Race, Religion, and Poetics of World-
Making*. Duke University Press.

Zine, Jasmin. 2022a. "The Canadian Islamophobia Industry: Islamophobia's
Ecosystem in the Great White North." Islamophobia Studies Center.
University of California.

Zine, Jasmin. 2022b. *Under Siege: Islamophobia and the 9/11 Generation*. McGill-
Queen's University Press.

I

Post-Secularity,
Ethnosphere,
and Neoliberalism

1

Freeing Religion

ELIZABETH SHAKMAN HURD

There are far more terrorists today than there were on 9/11. It is imperative that the United States and the international community find more effective ways to both halt violent extremism's expansion, and ultimately to eliminate the drivers and root causes of this phenomenon. While we have made significant strides against terrorism, today I would argue the biggest deficit we have is not on the countering side, but on the preventing side.

> —*Lieutenant General Michael K. Nagata,*
> *former director of Strategic Operations and*
> *Planning, National Counterterrorism Center*
> *(USAID 2020)*

One day while sitting on a plane, I got an email from a program officer in the US State Department's US Speaker Program, part of the Bureau of International Information Programs. It was a "call for experts," a phrase that attracted my attention as someone interested in the politics of expertise. The US Embassy Niamey, in Niger, was putting together a program on Countering Violent Extremism, or "CVE." The State Department's US Speaker Program was seeking "a French-speaking countering violent extremism and/or religious freedom expert" to address a closed audience for thirty minutes as part of the program. The event would be held at the embassy in Niamey and was described as follows: "The goal of this program...is to start a dialogue about CVE [Countering Violent Extremism] issues in the Sahel region. Having direct knowledge of CVE and technology situations from TechCamp participants will help us better match subject matter experts and technologists to the needs of our participants, enabling us to host a more impactful TechCamp event. The main viewing group will be gathered at the American Center in Niamey, Niger. The themes are empowering civil society groups, religious freedom and countering violent extremism." The call for experts also described the anticipated audience: "The audience of the main viewing session will be 20–30 religious leaders and young civil society leaders selected by Post and our TechCamp implementing partner, the National Youth Council of Niger. Audience members will be francophone Africans. Audience members will all come from demographics targeted by recruiters from extremist organizations."

I found the email perplexing. What is a "countering violent extremism and/or religious freedom expert"? What are the qualifications for this expertise? What does the "and/or" in that sentence mean? Is it right to assume that experts in violent extremism are also experts in religious freedom, and vice versa? What exactly is an "extremist" organization? Is it any organization that opposes US policy in the Sahel? Is it anyone who espouses political radicalism? Is it limited to those who use violence to express their opposition? What if the United

States is using violence against them? What forms of knowledge about religion, freedom, and extremism are being mobilized in this call, by whom, and to what ends?

Since 9/11 and the intensification of counterterrorism policy, US- and internationally sponsored religious interventionism has flourished, assuming new forms and mobilizing new resources. Government-led programs and projects intended to support moderate forms of religiosity and suppress violent ones have become the norm. These efforts encompass advocacy for religious freedom, interfaith dialogue, and legal protections for religious rights. Increasingly, they also include countering or preventing violent extremism (CVE/PVE).[1] Such efforts have become the bread and butter of "soft" foreign and security policy in most liberal democracies. Most initiatives, though not all, are directed at surveilling and reforming Muslims. Their goal is to ensure public health and welfare by ensuring that individuals who may be attracted to un-American or anti-American political tendencies are challenged and reformed. The aim is to nip terrorism in the bud.

These programs operate on a host of uninterrogated assumptions about the proper relations between religion, freedom, power, and security. Like the discourse of national security, of which it is a part, CVE/PVE, paradoxically, implicitly defines and then explicitly bypasses the question of religion. US domestic CVE programming posits a psychological element which is said to inhabit radicals who sympathize with foreign or fanatical forces. That element is neither captured nor protected in the notion of "religious belief," however. True religious belief is understood to form a kernel of truth that the state cannot and should not access or influence. It is set apart. But the rest, the remainder, can and must be modified, tamed, sculpted, and converted into the naturalized, unmarked pro-American subject of disestablished modern religion (Hurd 2021). At the same time, and in part for reasons having to do with the First Amendment to the US Constitution, CVE claims to stand above both politics and religion. It positions itself as social and psychological rather than theological or political. It operates from a purportedly universal and "acultural" position. CVE speaks the language of American exceptionalism: the US (or "the West") is the home of universal human rights, democracy, tolerance, and peaceful dissent. Americans enjoy limitless political and religious freedom. CVE, it is said, protects and enhances those freedoms. Promoting religious freedom (RF) overseas exports them.

Rather than representing a solution to the problem of violent forms of political and religious opposition to American and/or Western policy objectives, however, the CVE/RF agenda exacerbates tensions by empowering US and European-friendly religions and their representatives and by politicizing divisions between them and their rivals (Hurd 2015). The empowerment of US-friendly religions and leaders and marginalization of their rivals leads to a series of mini-religious and political establishments that aggravate the very tensions that such programs claim to resolve. Following a brief introduction to CVE/RF, this chapter develops this critical perspective on state-sponsored attempts to prevent religious extremism and promote religious freedom.

State-sponsored Religious Interventionism

There is an operative consensus in international policymaking circles that free religion catalyzes democratization and takes the wind out of the sails of extremists. In this view, secular and religious reformers are advised to cultivate the conditions in which secular states and their religious subjects become tolerant, believing or nonbelieving consumers of free religion, and practitioners of faith-based solutions to collective dilemmas. States are counselled to marshal resources, gather information, and train bureaucrats to achieve these aims. Experts are summoned—and many have emerged willingly to meet the demand. Analyses of religious actors and beliefs on political outcomes are ubiquitous. Professional associations have sections on religion. Foundations and think tanks fall over each other to meet demand for knowledge about religion in relation to every conceivable domain of human life. Solutions for anxious policymakers are sought and found. The security industry and rule of law consultants are anxious to "bring religion back in."

Actors and decision makers in this global "religion industrial complex" conceptualize religion as singular, separate, and prior to other lifeways and forms of sociality. In other words, there are things out there in the world called "religions" that interact with that which is "not religion." Religions are taken to be bounded entities with agency that can be studied, engaged, or reformed. In this view, religion is both an explanation for and a cause of political behaviour. It causes people to do things. Global government-sponsored interventions to fashion religion and politics in particular ways are needed to shape these responses. This is where the CVE/RF agenda comes in.

CVE programming, like advocacy for international religious freedom, is a bipartisan affair that has been gaining momentum for decades. CVE was initiated by the Obama administration. The former undersecretary of state for civilian security, democracy, and human rights in the Obama administration, Sarah Sewell, described the move to CVE as motivated by "learning" from "more than a decade since the searing experience of 9/11." Near the end of Obama's presidency, she observed that "[o]ver the last two years, the Obama administration has dramatically elevated CVE in the international agenda," developing a "preventative, civilian-led framework" (Mozirdazeh 2016). USAID and other government agencies have taken steps to incorporate CVE into their programming (USAID 2020). For the US government, CVE represents a kinder, gentler way to "get at the roots" of the perceived problem posed by violent extremism by moving beyond security-focused counterterrorism toward a broad-spectrum, preventive approach.

When Trump took office in 2017, he vowed to narrow the ambit of countering violent extremism programs to "Countering Violent or Radical Islamic Extremism." Throughout his administration, it remained unclear how those in charge of such programs were supposed to identify an "extreme" interpretation of Islam or how exactly a case could be made that the job of US government is to define and promote particular interpretations of Islam. Opponents of Trump's plan criticized the lack of surveillance of neo-Nazis and white supremacists responsible for domestic terrorism from Charleston to Charlottesville to El Paso. These concerns were lost, or intentionally misplaced, by the administration. During the Biden administration that took office in 2021, there was some movement toward including white supremacists in CVE programming. Funding for CVE continued apace.

Religious interventionism in foreign policy is not new and it takes many forms. Across the US political spectrum, it is common practice to employ American soft power, religious and secular, to cultivate good relations with allies abroad. The US had Navy chaplains giving Quran lessons to citizens in Afghanistan for decades in an effort to embolden particular pro-American understandings of Islam. Since 2009, one of the official duties of US military chaplains has been to engage proactively with local religious leaders overseas to advance US strategic objectives, gather cultural intelligence, promote religious tolerance, and patch up shaky relations with local citizens whose lives have been impacted by US or US-sponsored violence. Military chaplains effectively serve as religious counterinsurgents. A program called "Voices of Religious Tolerance" had the Marines taking Afghan elders and politicians from Helmand Province on what was described as a "collaborative influence program" tour to Amman, Jordan, to learn about "life in a religiously tolerant country." One former ambassador-at-large for religious freedom called for using US "muscle" to engage religious leaders abroad.

Most legal scholars agree that these activities would be unconstitutional, or at the very least deeply suspect, if undertaken by the US government domestically (on the disconnect between domestic and foreign religion policy in the US, see Hurd and Sullivan 2021). But Americans have never disestablished religion as a matter of foreign policy. The US Constitution does not apply, and never has applied, overseas. The politics of disestablishment shifts hues when it comes to foreign policy. For as long as it has had the ability to project power on behalf of its interests, the US has actively promoted its interests by co-opting and cooperating with religious institutions and leaders abroad.

9/11 and the rise of counterterrorism led to an explosion of new forms of US government-sponsored religious interventionism at home and abroad. In my book *Beyond Religious Freedom*, I use the term "religious interventionism" to refer to government programs and policies that support what is understood to be "moderate" or "good" religion and seek to reform or suppress what is seen as "bad" or "violent" religion. This takes different forms, including the promotion of religious freedom, interfaith dialogue, CVE/PVE, and advocacy for legal protections for religious minorities. All these efforts are enabled and emboldened by a global consensus that has concluded that the flourishing of free religion is a basic requirement to emancipate societies from a host of social, political, and economic ills, including intercommunal violence, economic deprivation, environmental degradation, and gender discrimination. In this view, the right kind of religion has emancipatory potential if recognized and supported by states and other authorities. Religion scholars, leaders, and policy experts play a leading role in advocating for and advancing this consensus. Again, this is not new; the US foreign policy establishment has a long history of collaborating with scholars and others. Understanding how these collaborations actually work and their disjuncture with and implications for lived religion was a central objective of *Beyond Religious Freedom*.

It is not only the United States that has taken up the CVE/RF agenda—it has been an international effort. In the aftermath of 9/11, the UN Security Council unanimously adopted Resolution 1373 (2001), which established the Counter-Terrorism Committee (CTC), consisting of the fifteen members of the Security Council, to monitor the implementation of Resolution 1373. The CTC is supported in its work by its executive directorate (CTED), which implements policy decisions and conducts expert assessments of member states. In the context of the global war on extremism, more partnerships are emerging among experts, religious authorities, and government officials. As suggested by the Niger programming mentioned earlier, there is robust demand for expertise on religion, counter-extremism, and religious freedom.

To understand the politics of religion in international partnerships to free religion and counter violent extremism, it is useful to break down the category of religion into three "heuristics": expert religion, lived religion, and official religion. Disassembling the overly broad construct of religion into these three categories sheds new light on these programs. Rather than simply repressing extremists and empowering moderates, it becomes clear that the CVE/RF policy agenda intervenes and shapes entire religio-political fields in particular ways. It presses religious representatives and authority and expertise into the service of Western power and interests. These programs empower Western-friendly religions and their representatives and disempower and disable their opponents, rivals, competitors, and dissidents. They authorize particular leaders to speak on behalf of US, UN, or EU-sanctioned constituencies. As these religions and those leaders are empowered, both politically and religiously, they create a series of "mini establishments."

Expert Religion, Lived Religion, Official Religion

The first category is *expert religion*. In the Niger call for experts, the US State Department was looking for something called a "CVE/religious freedom" expert. What exactly is that? It is helpful here to employ the notion of expert religion, which is religion as defined by those who generate what is considered policy-relevant knowledge. This includes scholars, policy experts, think tank and media pundits, and government officials. Today, a particular version of expert religion dominates the airwaves, congressional hearing rooms, and classrooms. This is what I call "the two faces of faith," to borrow a phrase from former British prime minister Tony Blair. When we hear experts talk about religion in international policy circles, they are either celebrating religion as a source of morality, community, and freedom (the first face of faith) or are warning against it as a danger to be contained or reformed (the second face of faith).

This way of understanding religion, or what scholars call a "discourse," underlies and motivates global religious governance. It drives the CVE and freedom agendas. It defines extremism as an unhealthy, even pathological, disorder that causes and is caused by distorted forms of religion that have illicitly made their way into politics. Religion is understood simultaneously as an aspect of social difference that is a potential problem—a cause of violence and discord—and as its own solution, if interfaith cooperation can be institutionalized, extremists marginalized, and religion's benevolent tendencies properly harnessed by the right authorities. In this perspective, if governments study and shape religion effectively, it will contribute to international peace and security, and the potential for violence will diminish. This consensus serves as the background condition for the email invitation from the State Department with which I opened this chapter. It is how policymakers talk and think about religion. Global religious freedom advocacy appears from this perspective as a mode of enforcing particular understandings of what it means to be religious and to be free. CVE appears as a securitized form of internal and transnational governance that prescribes and proscribes particular forms of religious and political expression. We can now see more clearly why the "call for experts" understands these two forms of expertise as related.

This brings us to our second heuristic: *lived religion*. Lived or "everyday" religion is religion as it is practised by ordinary people as they interact with authorities, rituals, texts, and institutions, navigate their lives, connect with others, and find their places in the world. Lived religion may be indifferent, opposed, supportive, or unassimilable to the terms of expert religion. It is helpful to think of lived religion as "small r" religion, in contrast to "Big R" religion, which I will describe in a moment. "Small r" religion, as Winnifred Fallers Sullivan (2014) explains, is a nearly ubiquitous and perhaps even necessary part of human society and culture. "Big R" religion, on the other hand, the religion that is designated and protected in constitutions, human rights law, and liberal political theory, is not. "Big R" religion is a modern invention and a tool of state and global governance. It is the religion of the law and of the state.[2] It is the religion of state-sponsored religious freedom.

The third heuristic is *governed religion*. This is religion as defined by those in positions of legal, bureaucratic, and/or religious power. Governed religion is articulated through the law, public administration, foreign policy, and other authorities such as supranational courts, the European Union, and international and nongovernmental organizations, as well as churches and other religious organizations. Viewed through this prism, religion is seen as both a governance problem as well as its own solution. Refracting the email invitation from the State Department through this lens, the objective of US Embassy Niamey's programming is to generate particular forms of governed religion that conform to US interests in the Sahel. In the US government's view, this is what it means to have achieved religious freedom. This also clarifies why religious freedom advocacy and CVE dovetail into one project. "Freedom" is construed as conformity to American economic, political, and security interests, which includes adherence to official US understandings of what it means for religion to be "moderate" and "free." Violent religion leads to extremism; free religion leads to peace. Note that in this narrative, "free" religion naturally aligns with American political objectives. To be "free" is to be pro-American. To be "religiously free" is to practise legible, Protestantized forms of religiosity that do not threaten US interests.

These three heuristics allow us to appreciate the complex intersections of religion, security, and governance. They clarify how religion is politicized in contemporary international relations. They also clarify the impossibility of religious freedom. Lived or "small r" religion is in tension with expert and governed religion, the "big R" religion defined and protected in constitutions, by governments, in international legal instruments. Foreign policy experts and decision makers often forget about "small r" religion altogether. When they look for religion, they look for religious leaders and institutions, texts, and orthodoxies. They look for leaders with impressive robes and formidable hats. These individuals matter, but they do not exhaust the field. There is always a gap between legal and governmental constructs of religion, religious freedom, and violent extremism as defined by the State Department, Global Affairs Canada, the Department of Defense, national and international courts, EU governing bodies, and religious hierarchies, on one hand, and the broad and shifting fields of practice, belonging, and belief, on the other. It is difficult to reconcile official constructs of religious governance—such as freedom, disestablishment, counter-extremism, as defined by experts and enforced by states—with the ambiguities of the diverse spiritual worlds that they purport to govern. My work suggests a need for careful attention to this disjuncture.

Despite these concerns, government advocacy for religious freedom and the empowerment of moderate religious leaders continues apace. These programs are seen by many political leaders as a legitimate means of protecting pre-existing religious individuals and communities, empowering moderates, and shunning extremists. According to this mindset, the world is divided into good religionists and bad religionists. The job of the government is to resist the latter and empower the former by supporting the "moderates in our midst." We see this language becoming salient in attempts to engage "moderate" Palestinians in efforts to rebuild Gaza after the devastation wrought by the Israeli Defense Forces in 2023 and 2024. Discourses of moderation and toleration that are embodied in the language of "strategic peace" distract from the need to transform the conditions of structural inequality that often lead to conflict in the first instance (Caicedo and Manrique 2023).

A Civilizing Discourse?

The global religious interventionism of the early twenty-first century is a combination of expert and official religion of a very particular kind. It is a civilizing discourse and part of the global War on Terror. It produces particular forms of politics and religion and empowers particular political and religious subjects. Viewed from this angle, CVE and religious freedom programs are strategies for controlling the political and religious lives of foreign subjects. This explains how the US State Department can represent these programs as a single field of expertise: by definition, shunning whatever the authorities define as "extremism" is understood to be a means of achieving "religious freedom." Freedom is perceived as the opposite of extremism. The potential for the politics of religious freedom to *itself* embody a form of extremism is unimaginable. An intensive focus on Islam as the problem and CVE/RF as the solution displaces politics, in political theorist Bonnie Honig's (1993) sense of the term. It distracts decision makers from the wide array of structural challenges that contribute to violence, including economic inequality, climate crisis, unjust governance, racism, and so on in favour of a laser-like focus on religious reformation. Patrick Eddington (2016) develops this point:

> CVE-related actions...shift the blame away from the federal government for its role in helping create and sustain ISIS—first by invading and destabilizing Iraq and Libya, and second by doubling-down on a failed security-centric approach to counterterrorism in the Arab and Muslim world. That disastrously overly-militarized approach to militant salafism, combined with federal support for de facto anti-Arab and anti-Muslim CVE programs at home, only help groups like ISIS make the case that America is, contrary to all public statements to the contrary, at war with Islam.

To adapt a phrase from Mahmood Mamdani's critique of Nicolas Kristof, religious interventionism contributes to "the reduction of a complex political context to a morality tale unfolding in a world populated by villains and victims who never trade places and so can always and easily be told apart." Like Kristof's account of the war in Darfur, CVE reduces a series of complex political contexts to a morality tale that unfolds in a world populated by ("bad," often Muslim) villains and ("good," often non-Muslim) victims who never trade places and can easily be told apart (Mamdani 2007). The complex histories that contribute to episodes of discrimination and violence are brushed aside in a wave of excitement at the prospects of religio-political reform and collective security.

Yet CVE is never neutral. It privileges whatever the authorities define as tolerant beliefs and practices that carry the promise of accommodative or quiescent forms of politics. It creates a divide between "most-favoured" religious beliefs and practices and those associated with varieties of political and religious nonconformity, dissidence, and, at times, violence. Seen in this light, CVE programming may in fact exacerbate rather than assuage social tensions by politicizing and policing the divide between the religion/politics of those in positions of power and those on the outside. Naz Modirzadeh (2016) explains how this works in her discussion of the UN's Preventing Violent Extremism Plan:

> If the Plan is implemented as the SG hopes, then *every state in the world* will have a national plan of action on CVE. States will dedicate resources and energy towards this effort. They will draft new laws. They will change where development and aid money is invested. Their officials will refer to communities that are "vulnerable" to terrorism, or ethnic or religious groups that must be "protected" from their own tendency to be drawn to "violent extremism." These communities will be scrutinized and surveilled under the banner

of CVE; states will engage in efforts to make religious people more "moderate," or to teach them that their religious texts say something other than what they believe...by CVE's own internal logic it might produce as many "violent extremists" as it prevents.

Anthropologist Darryl Li (2015) suggests that it would be a mistake to banalize violence by writing it off as the product of imperial blowback. The greater challenge, he explains, is to take "radicalism seriously as a political orientation, whether its idiom is Islamic, communist or anarchist. The challenge is how to understand the distinctiveness of jihadi groups without lapsing into an all-too-often racialized exceptionalism." As Li concludes, "the fundamental problem is not only how Islam is discussed; it is how politics is understood."

Conclusion:
Beyond the Politics of Religion

The modern category of religion is an unstable and unreliable foundation on which to base foreign policy, write laws and constitutions, make asylum decisions, protect vulnerable communities, conduct rights advocacy, or combat extremism. CVE and religious freedom advocacy target specific forms of religion and religious leaders for reform, condemnation, celebration, or eradication. In the process, these programs blind policymakers to a much more complex series of social, legal, religious, and political realities and histories.

Second, the religion that is celebrated or condemned by these programs does not and never will align with the diverse and shifting forms of belonging, belief, and practice that characterize lived religiosities on the ground. Instead, these programs privilege moderate, American-friendly, quote-unquote religion. This leaves it to policymakers to determine what counts as religion and to distinguish between tolerable and intolerable forms of it. They become state theologians.

Third, CVE/RF programs actively politicize the field of religious difference by producing "religious" groups as political actors and "faith communities." Religious engagement officers in Washington or Brussels breathe sighs of relief: "finally, we've found the partners we've been waiting for." The problem is that there is no set of religions that is waiting offstage to be empowered and ushered into a "pure" secular public life. That which falls under the heading of religion is a contested and shifting mash-up of diverse families of beliefs, institutional forms, texts, traditions, and fields of attachment, practice, and experience. State-sponsored religious interventionism attempts to distill this unwieldy field into something governable. It squeezes a vast and shifting array of practices, beliefs, and ways of life into the awkward mould of whatever those in power define as identifiable, amenable, and tolerant religions deserving of legal protection and political engagement. This enacts a divide between officially favoured Religions and the rest of the world's religions. Governments and the international community marginalize practices that don't look like "the right kind of religion." These often include traditions that are considered sacred by their practitioners but that do not meet the bar to qualify legally as religions, those that are associated with political opponents and/or religious dissidents, and those that represent the interests of historically marginalized populations such as formerly enslaved persons and Indigenous communities. Seen through this prism, CVE/RF exacerbates political and religious tensions by politicizing the divide between the "religion" of those with power and those without it. Far from representing a solution to the quandaries of how to live together, it fans the flames of partisanship and division along religious lines.

In today's halls of power, the languages of religious freedom and counter-extremism exert a gravitational pull. Governments trip over each other to be the first to encourage individuals and groups to constitute themselves as tolerant, freedom-loving participants in peaceful, pro-Western/pro-American faith communities. Laws incentivize individuals and groups to represent themselves in these terms. Development and military aid packages are contingent upon the inclusion of this programming. Many individuals and groups naturally respond by demanding their religious rights and freedoms, contributing further to the sense of empowerment of "religious" voices and perspectives. This snowball effect lends agency and authenticity to groups that are designated as (good) religions. A global faithscape takes shape (Colbert Report 2006). This avalanche of programming sharpens boundaries between religions, and between religion and nonreligion. It encourages muscular corporate forms of religious agency. This is evident in the US Supreme Court's *Hobby Lobby* decision, which reinforced corporate notions of religious freedom and elevated them above individual women's reproductive health and choice (see Sullivan 2020, Chapter 3). On this faith-based political landscape, those who cannot or choose not to speak in a religious register go unheard. This includes claimants for justice, equality, and dignity who cannot or choose not to speak as religionists. It includes Indigenous individuals and groups whose practices fail to register legally or officially as religious. It includes practitioners of Afro-descendant traditions that are treated as anachronistic, if not illegal. It includes Palestinians and their allies who refuse to conform to definitions of "moderation" that demand quiescence in the face of inhumane levels of Israeli state violence. It includes scholars, such as myself, who remain unsympathetic to the freedom agenda and its tireless demand for knowledge and expertise.

It is easy to picture TechCamp in Niger, with an American "expert" benevolently counselling "at-risk" locals on how to be tolerant, free, and not *too* anti-American. At best, such programs are distractions that divert scarce resources from efforts to address the real causes of violence and discrimination through initiatives supporting education, economic opportunity, environmental justice, and democratic governance. At worst, they intensify and politicize religious and racial difference, fomenting the very radicalization they are intended to prevent.

NOTES

1. Counter-extremism programming travels under different names ("Countering Violent Extremism," "Preventing Violent Extremism," and so on) and is rebranded frequently even as the interventions themselves remain largely unchanged. As of this writing, Department of Homeland Security programming in this domain travelled under the heading of "Targeted Violence and Terrorism Prevention" (TVTP).

2. I make no attempt to romanticize lived religion as prior to structures and relations of power, nor to identify pure or "authentic" forms of lived religion. Each of these categories has porous boundaries that are themselves the product of law and governance.

REFERENCES

Caicedo, Alhena, and Carlos Manrique. 2023. "Religiones, Espiritualidades y Construcción de Paz en Colombia." In *Después del Acuerdo ¿Como va la paz en Colombia?*, edited by Laura Betancur Restrepo and Angelika Rettberg. Ediciones UniAndes.

Colbert Report. 2006. "The De-Deification of the American Faithscape." *Comedy Central*, February 27. https://www.cc.com/video/a6q2os/the-colbert-report-the-de-deification-of-the-american-faithscape.

Eddington, Patrick. 2016. "America's Muddled Approach to Fighting ISIS." *Just Security*, January 28. https://www.justsecurity.org/29041/americas-muddled-isis-approach/.

Honing, Bonnie. 1993. *Political Theory and the Displacement of Politics.* Cornell University Press.

Hurd, Elizabeth Shakman. 2015. *Beyond Religious Freedom: The New Global Politics of Religion.* Princeton University Press.

Hurd, Elizabeth Shakman. 2021. "Border Religion." In *At Home and Abroad: The Politics of American Religion*, edited by Elizabeth Shakman Hurd and Winnifred Fallers Sullivan. Columbia University Press.

Hurd, Elizabeth Shakman, and Winnifred Fallers Sullivan, eds. 2021. *At Home and Abroad: The Politics of American Religion.* Columbia University Press.

Li, Darryl. 2015. "A Jihadism Anti-Primer." *Middle East Report* 276 (Fall). https://merip.org/2015/12/a-jihadism-anti-primer/.

Mamdani, Mahmud. 2007. "The Politics of Naming: Genocide, Civil War, Insurgency." *London Review of Books* 29, no. 5 (March 8). http://www.lrb.co.uk/v29/n05/mahmood-mamdani/the-politics-of-naming-genocide-civil-war-insurgency.

Modirzadeh, Naz. 2016. "If It's Broke, Don't Make it Worse: A Critique of the UN Secretary-General's Plan of Action to Prevent Violent Extremism." *Lawfare* (blog), January 23. https://www.lawfaremedia.org/article/if-its-broke-dont-make-it-worse-critique-un-secretary-generals-plan-action-prevent-violent-extremism.

Sullivan, Winnifred Fallers. 2014. "The Impossibility of Religious Freedom." *The Immanent Frame*, Social Science Research Council, July 8. https://tif.ssrc.org/2014/07/08/impossibility-of-religious-freedom/.

Sullivan, Winnifred Fallers. 2020. *Church State Corporation: Construing Religion in US Law.* University of Chicago Press.

US Agency for International Development (USAID). 2020. "Policy for Countering Violent Extremism Through International Development." April, Washington, DC. https://www.usaid.gov/sites/default/files/documents/USAID-publication-Policy-for-Countering-Violent-Extremism-through-Development-Assistance-April2020.pdf.

2

The Limits of the Translation Proviso

The Inherent Alien within the Willed-community

DUSTIN J. BYRD

Beginning with the Enlightenment, most western European and North American countries have moved from an ethnic-based community (*Volksgemeinschaft*) to an intentional democratic willed-community (*Willensgemeinschaft*), wherein the pre-political foundations of historical communities, such as ethnos, language, religion, and shared history no longer define the demos. Rather, "ascribed citizenship," as Jürgen Habermas calls it, is predicated on the general acceptance of constitutional ideals, values, and principles (Habermas 1996, 492–493). Acceptance of those ideals, values, and principles can earn the immigrant a place within the citizenry, a place understood by law to be on equal footing with "legacy citizens," those who are the bearers of the pre-political foundations. As such, within *Willensgemeinschaften*, anyone in the world is a potential American, Canadian, French citizen, Dutch citizen, Italian, etc. Although ascribing

21

to these democratic political ideals, Muslim communities nevertheless find themselves the victims of harassment, discrimination, and
terror attacks because they are viewed as being ethnically—and/or
religiously—alien to the white "ethnosphere" of the West. It seems
that those political ideals taken to heart among Muslims have gained
Muslim citizenship within Western countries but have not gained
them sincere inclusion into the pre-political foundational community,
which continues to define itself via that which cannot be ascribed:
ethnos. As such, the Muslim, especially the immigrant Muslim,
remains the "inherent alien" within the white ethnosphere: a tolerated or sometimes non-tolerated Other who is *homoiusius* with the
legacy ethnic community—sharing similar characteristics—but not
homousius—not "identical" with the "legacy" Westerner. While the
Westernized Muslim remains a legal citizen, they remain the cultural/
ethnic Other—an object of suspicion whose growing presence is a
source of frustration and uneasiness. Additionally, their presence is a
reminder to many on the far right that the identity of the demos is no
longer homogenous (or what is imagined as homogeneity). Especially
in modernity, the ethnosphere, which once determined who belonged
to what identity, has become blurred, as it is no longer a matter of
Geworfenheit (thrownness) (as defined in Heidegger 1962) that one
finds oneself already existentially "thrown into" a certain ethnic
community by the fact of being born into that community; rather,
one can—through an act of *will*—choose one's community based
on preference.

The fundamental tension that exists between the idea of the
Volksgemeinschaft and the *Willensgemeinschaft* is that while intellectual
elites, liberals, globalists, and others on the political left, by and large,
have accepted the willed-community as an appropriate form of democratic group identity within modernity, much of the masses within
Western nations have either (1) never fully accepted such a synthetic
formulation of national identity, or (2) simply refuse to do so and thus
continue to maintain an ethnos-based concept of nationhood. Such

an open concept of the nation was merely a philosophical construct made by Enlightenment elites and their universalist conceptions of humanity. For the masses, the abstract ideals of *liberté*, *égalité*, and *fraternité* were articulated for white Westerners by white Westerners and were not meant to open the West to non-Westerners. In places like North America, the closed ethnosphere of each particular European nationality was opened up, albeit slowly, to other particular European nationalities, thus creating the generic "white person" out of the myriad European peoples and identities (Allen 2012). This inter-ethnic openness was not understood in its initial articulations as being an invitation to those outside of western Europe's ethnicities to join what they thought was exclusively a "white society." Nevertheless, as the contemporary willed-communities of the North American states continued to struggle for ethnic expansion of their societies to those outside of the European ethnospheres, negative reactions have followed suit. Seeing traditional identities based on pre-political foundations slowly opening up to non-European "Others" led to reactionary retreats into the concept and language of the *Volksgemeinschaft*—the exclusive ethnic community. With "historic" ethnic identity threatened by multiculturalism, racial diversity, and religious pluralism, the abstract ideals of the Enlightenment, which formed the philosophical basis of the willed-community, were abandoned, especially by those who felt threatened by demographic change.

Beyond Race and Ethnicity: Geist

Although race and ethnicity are the most poignant markers of Otherness, the far right's objections to the inclusion of others is also a *metaphysical* protest against the amalgamation of nations: it is a violation of the spirit (Geist) of each people—an intangible yet animating essence that resides in the *Dasein* of each ethical community, particular only to themselves. While citizenship could be ascribed, and members of one nation can theoretically "adopt" individuals of another nation, matters of the spirit are much more complicated, as the metaphysical nature of "belonging" is not present-at-hand (*Vorhanden*, to use Martin Heidegger's term) for utilitarian purposes. Since the birth of modern nationalism, it has been understood that the Geist of a nation is something one is born into. National Geist, unlike modern political citizenship, cannot be ascribed; the individual must rather find themselves thrown into it (*Geworfenheit*) as part of their being within a particular community determined by its ethnos (Heidegger 1962, 174–175). Thus, Geist is an integral part of one's cultural and ethnic inheritance and is constitutional to the "essential sameness" (*Artgleichheit*) of the ethnos: the necessary condition for "homogeneity" (*Gleichartigkeit*) in an ethnic community (Schmitt 1933, 17, 35). To better understand the nature of the ethnos-bound Geist, we should consider Johann Gottlieb Fichte's thirteenth address to the German nation (1806), wherein he says:

> Spiritual nature was able to present the essence of humanity in extremely diverse gradations in individuals and individuality as a whole, in people. Only when each people, *left to itself*, develops and forms itself in accordance with its *own peculiar quality*, and only when in every people each individual develops himself in accordance with that common quality, as well as in accordance with his own peculiar quality—then, and then only, does the manifestation of divinity appear in its true mirror as it ought to be...Only in the invisible qualities of nations, which are hidden from their own eyes—qualities as the means whereby these nations remain in touch with the source of original life—only there is to be found the guarantee of their present and future worth, virtue, and merit. *If these qualities are*

dulled by admixture and worn away by friction, the flatness
that results will bring about a separation from spiritual
nature, and this in its turn will cause all men to be fused
together to their uniform and conjoint destruction.
(Fichte 2017, 114–115, emphasis added)

Echoing Fichte, the *Rassengeist* (race spirit) or "ethno-spirit" (*theoû génos*) for Italian fascist philosopher Julius Evola was the "determinate spirit" that "constitutes [the ethnos'] internal aspect" and its "formative cause" (Evola 2018, 1–2). As such, the spirit can be defined as the intangible essence of a people, that which the people understand to be exclusively theirs and is readily apparent to them, but may be imperceptible to others outside of their ethnosphere. The spirit is the group's normative way-of-being-in-the-world; a matrix of defining characteristics that determines the worldview and praxis of a people. Such a spirit is born out of the ethnos' collective memory, commonality of language and tradition, shared worldview, common social characteristics, and collective aspirations and projects. Such commonalities are the result of hundreds or thousands of years of shared experiences that continue to dwell within the collective identity of the group and inform their collective *Dasein*. In this sense, the spirit of the ethnos is not born out of "undifferentiated human matter" but proceeds from a closely knit biological and cultural entity, existing in a singularity (Camus 2018, 25, 191). Any mixing of the races/ethnoi is a betrayal of the races/ethnoi, as it forecloses on the "formative cause"—the historic task—of the *Rassengeist* (Allen 2012).

The resurrection of Fichte's notion of a given ethnos' "spiritual nature" poses a direct challenge to the possibility of post-secular inclusion in democratic states. Brought into the present, what Fichte's logic suggests is that even if Muslims become an integrated part of the Western *demos*, they will remain a *perpetual and inherent alien* by virtue of not organically belonging to the "spiritual nature" of the historic *ethnos*, for the ethnos' spiritual nature is biologically closed off to them.

They will remain, even if alienated from their national community of origin, a part of their native ethnos' spirit. In this sense, Fichte's logic creates a spiritual iron cage, wherein no matter how integrated or assimilated an immigrant is, they are locked outside of the spiritual nature of the ethnic "nation" they reside within.[1] Thus, they become citizens of a state but are, by virtue of their foreign ethnos of origin, permanent aliens within their adopted demos.[2]

For the far right, multiculturalism—wherein numerous cultures are confirmed and promoted within an enclosed geographical space once defined by a single ethnos—is the wholesale destruction of the ethnic community's "essence," its "Geist," in favour of a "flattened" reality, "dulled by admixture" (to use Fichte's words). From this perspective, the immigrant, especially the Muslim—who has served as the menacing shadow of Europe since the beginning of Islam—is a threat to the very metaphysical identity of the West. Their modern claim to Westernality, by virtue of being a citizen of a Western state, creates compounded confusion as to what a Westerner is: Are Westerners merely citizens of a Western country, or is there a metaphysical basis for Westernality? Does one have to be a bearer of an inherited Western Geist, or is to be Western merely a political act of ascription? The Enlightenment's argument for the universality of humanity, against the particularity of ethnicity, race, and civilization, suggests that Western ethnoi (ethnos, plural) are expendable, nonessential, or even simply replaceable. On the other hand, far-right critics of this universalism find Western ethnoi to be essential for identity, as ethnoi are the initiators, bearers, and maintainers of particular spirits. Clearly, the retreat into this pre-Enlightenment thought, as expressed by many far-right critics of multiculturalism, serves as a defence against what they view as the "flatness" or ambiguity of identity that results from the cultural and ethnoi "admixture."[3]

While liberals, leftists, and even certain religious voices— including Pope Francis, who is open to modern multiculturalism—see the possibilities of birthing a new and modern spirit from the construction and nurturing of religiously, culturally, and ethnically mixed *Willensgemeinschaften*, they too must conclude that such a new and open spirit is incompatible with the old ethnic spirit as articulated by Fichte. The old exclusivist spirit must die for the new, inclusive one to be born. Consequently, there is no greater symbol for the death of the old spirit than the integration of Muslims in the Western world via the constitutional state. It is understood by many on the far right that Muslims were historically the menacing *physical threat* from *outside* of Christendom, but now, within the conditions of post-secularity, they are the all-encompassing *metaphysical threat* from *within* the remnants of Christendom. In other words, the *Dār al-Islam* once threatened Christians with physical subjugation (especially by the Ottomans) from outside of Christendom; now, within the liberal conditions of post-secularity—with its openness, multiculturalism, and multi-confessionalism—the Muslim immigrant, refugee, and citizen threaten the West's entire identity *from within*. Never in the history of Christendom did Islam pose such a threat to the ethnic spirit and identity of Western Christians.[4] Historically, the threat was against Christendom's territory, its institutions, its merchants, or individuals, etc. Even if subjugated by Muslims, the identity of the Christian remained intact, as the Muslim was experienced as the anti-identity of the Christian (Reeves 2000). The Muslim was perpetually portrayed as anti-Christian, and thus the identity of the Christian was internally strengthened by that juxtaposition. Now, wherein Muslims find themselves equal citizens to Christians and/or the ethnos-bound "legacy citizen" in Western democracies, the identity of the West becomes confused. As such, the West's political realization of the Enlightenment's universal values has devolved into a protracted identity crisis, a crisis that Western Muslims find themselves at the centre of.

Limits of Habermas' Translation Proviso

Looking at the growing social tensions within the democratic willed-communities of the West, critical theorist Jürgen Habermas followed liberal political theorist John Rawls and his argument for religious communities' public use of post-metaphysical reason (Habermas 2008; Hedrick 2010). Rawls, and later Habermas, suggested that Muslims within Western democracies had an imperative placed upon them by virtue of being equal citizens within a pluralistic constitutional state: they must "translate" the content of their religious tradition, their "closed semantic universe," into post-metaphysical reasoning, so that their arguments are "equally accessible to all persons" (Habermas 2008, 120). In other words, for Muslim citizens to contribute to the political will-formation of the democratic state without sacrificing their Islamic ideals, such ideals have to migrate from the depths of the Islamic tradition into language unencumbered by theology, soteriology, eschatology, etc., from which they originally derive. If a translation can be done, such Islamic ideals could enter secular-national discourses on an equal footing as ideas, notions, concepts, and ideals that emerge from secular sources.[5] This act of transforming religious semantics and semiotics into secular language is what Rawls and Habermas referred to as the "Translation Proviso" (Habermas 2008, 130). They both believed this translation of semantic and semiotic materials into religiously neutral language would help integrate Muslims into national discourse communities, particularly in western Europe and North America, as well as avoid "wars of religion and confessional disputes" (Habermas 2008, 120). For Habermas, the Muslim community is not expected to abandon their religious identity for a secular worldview or way of being. Rather, they could keep their traditions, values, cultural identities, etc., while at the same time using such material as the basis for their integration into the discourses of nations, albeit within secular form. By translating certain semantic elements of Islam, especially its moral-practical claims, Muslims engage fully in the "natural reason" that guides democratic debate in secular-pluralistic willed-communities (Byrd 2020a; Habermas 1984).

Among those who already accept Muslims as integral parts of their Western societies, such a "translation proviso" seems entirely appropriate, especially since Habermas also places upon the secular citizen a "mutual burden": the obligation to sincerely consider the input of the Muslim citizen, but also to understand that the faith of the Muslim remains valid—even appreciated—within the conditions of post-secular society. Such "open" citizens are not neophobic; they welcome newcomers to their society and see them as a social asset. However, there will always be those who remain skeptical of multi-culturalism and other forms of diversity. As such, Habermas calls for a "mutual learning process"—a form of mutual reciprocity meant to foster democratic discourse among equal citizens of different faiths and confessions. For the welcoming legacy citizen, this process is merely a tool to help integrate and assimilate new Muslim citizens into post-secular society. For the skeptic, it's a means of dissolving xenophobia. For those open to the input of non-legacy citizens, the secularization of Islamic values, principles, and ideals can find common ground with secular Enlightenment values, principles, and ideals and can work together to forward the legitimate needs of the national community in such a way that explicit religious values are not introjected into the secular polity, nor are they ignored. For the skeptic, the mutual learning process is a means by which they can assure themselves that religion has not penetrated the secular polity of their constitutional state. As such, through the "translation proviso," the democratic discourse remains *religiously neutral* yet open to the polyphony of citizens' voices.[6] In its essence, the translation proviso is an attempt to find a common language among citizens wherein they can find an overlapping consensus regarding national problems, challenges, and projects, without introducing the closed semantic universe of various religions, which would inevitably foreclose such a consensus.

Despite Habermas' optimism about the future of the multicultural and multi-confessional constitutional state, it also counts among its ranks those citizens who are not prepared to accept Muslims as somehow inherently belonging to the Western ethnosphere, those foreign to the legacy ethnoi, many of whom already attack the legitimacy of the *Willensgemeinschaft* and its grounding in the Enlightenment's universalism. Such critics perceive the translation of Islamic semantic and semiotic material into post-metaphysical language as being a stealth form of "Islamization" (Byrd 2020a, 268–273). They believe that the condition of *Überfremdung* (over-foreignization) will inevitably lead to the dysgenic amalgamation of ethnoi and cultures, and thus the destruction of legacy citizens' cultural, linguistic, and religious identity. It is thought that because legacy citizens of the democratic willed-states have already abandoned their pre-political foundations as a precondition for full membership within the nation, they lack cultural resources to defend traditional Western identities from being Islamized. As such, Habermas' translation proviso can be seen as a Trojan horse, meant to slip Islam into the national discourse via the camouflage of secular language. What appears on the surface to be "secular" argumentation is a "foreign" religion in disguise, with cultural imperatives and norms that contradict those of the modern secular democratic West. Pull back the veil of the "translation proviso" and the Islamic reality reappears.

Habermas' translation proviso, a "stealth" way of introducing Islam's moral-practical material into the political will-formation of the Western secular states, risks backfiring: it could make the Muslim community even more vulnerable to the idea that they are attempting to undermine the identity of the modern West. In other words, for far-right critics, not only is the West at risk of losing its *ethnic* identity via demographics—the "timebomb" of the prolific Muslim womb—but it is also at risk of losing its *cultural* inheritance, the Greco-Roman and Christian legacy, and its secular foundation.[7]

In the opinion of much of the far right, Muslim immigrants have found a common cause with a severe pathogen plaguing the modern West: white "ethnomasochism." Ethnomasochism is defined as a pathological "self-contempt" (*oikophobia*) born from a pathological sense of guilt, stemming from historical atrocities perpetrated upon people of colour by Europeans and Euro-Americans, most often through colonialism, imperialism, slavery, and genocide (Faye 2011, 136; Beckeld 2022). According to many on the far right, including the prominent intellectuals Guillaume Faye, Tomislav Sunic, and Michael O'Meara, by relentlessly denigrating the West, ethnomasochists seek to destroy it and its historical inheritance as a result of their misguided sense of compensation for past injustices. By turning racism inward, they devalue and decentre "white culture," thus paving the way for a multicultural geography that seeks to reconcile the descendants of history's white perpetrators with the descendants of their victims. In the process, ethnomasochists hope to alleviate the collective guilt they have wilfully appropriated for themselves by giving away their inheritance—the West in all its facets.

This form of "ethno-suicide" seeks to end the West as an exclusively white ethnosphere, turning it into something disconnected from Europe's indigenous ethnoi (Faye 2019). Additionally, as far-right French theorist Guillaume Faye writes, ethnomasochism is not only a sign of historical shame haunting the present, but also a sign that the West, especially Europe, has moved into its historical retirement, no longer having the civilizational energy to retain its position at the forefront of history. He writes,

> Ethnomasochism promotes a systematic apology for race-mixing and cosmopolitanism. Curiously, it denies Europeans the idea of an ethnic identity, which everyone else is accorded. They are obliged, thus, to mitigate themselves, while others, like Africans for example, are not...Ethnomasochism is nothing new in history. It's a symptom of a people too weary to live and perpetuate itself: an aging people ready to pass the baton to another. (Faye 2011, 136)

It is clear that there is an element of civilizational and ethnic self-loathing on the part of many legacy citizens in the West, especially on the political left. Whether that rises to the level of "ethno-suicide" or "white genocide" via intentional *Überfremdung* is questionable. However, the Islamophobia behind the idea of a "white genocide" through "over-foreignization" has merged with traditional Western anti-Semitism, producing a new and more insidious form of xenophobia: "Great Replacement Theory."

Le Grand Replacement 2.0

Renaud Camus' "Great Replacement Theory" has devolved into something much more vulgar than he originally articulated (and continues to articulate). While it is true that he argues against mass immigration to Europe and believes that the native European population is being intentionally diluted and/or "replaced" by Africans and Arabs, just as Europeans replaced Native Americans, he stops short of accusing the Jews of being behind "replacism" (Camus 2018, 117, 134). For centuries of European history, Jews were blamed for any disturbing changes in European society at large. In the twentieth century, Bolshevik Communism was likened to a Jewish plot to destroy Europe's religious heritage—a Jewish totalitarianism meant to impose equality of the Jew with the gentile.[8] Now, such anti-Semitic tropes have morphed into the idea that the anonymous Jew (*Der Jude*) is intentionally importing non-whites—predominantly Muslims—into the West as a way of diluting the white population's political, economic, and cultural power.[9] The more "diverse" the West is, the safer it is for Jews, and the safer it is for Jews, the more they can dominate all spheres of power. Thus, "white genocide" is the goal of the Jews in the West (Johnson 2018, 20). This anti-Semitic logic animated the alt right's chant "Jews will not replace us" in Charlottesville, Virginia, in August of 2017, during the deadly "Unite the Right" rally.[10]

What we see in the explicitly anti-Semitic version of the "Great Replacement Theory" is the marriage of traditional Western anti-Semitism (Jews as the nefarious force behind all social disruptions) and modern Islamophobia (Muslims are the foreign Others "invading" and "colonizing" the European ethnosphere) (Faye 2016). Understanding the pathological hatred for Jews and Muslims by so-called defenders of European/white identity helps us understand why Habermas' translation proviso, and its accompanying "mutual learning process," is so despised: it normalizes the presence of Muslims in the West by giving them a means through which Islamic concepts, values, and ideals can potentially enter the political will-formation alongside legacy citizens on an equal basis. Habermas' translation proviso, from an ultra-conservative perspective, is a way in which Islam and Muslims can secretly euthanize the residue of the *Volksgemeinschaft's* national culture as well as the universalist claims that legitimate the hated willed-community (Byrd 2020a, 268–273). Through the entrance of Islam into public discourse via secular language, the liberal-left "ethnomasochist" commits suicide both on the level of secularity (they let in explicitly religious voices, albeit stealthily) as well as on the level of traditional culture (they legitimate, normalize, and promote foreign cultures within an already decaying Western ethnosphere).

For white nationalists, neo-fascists, and other forms of Euro-supremacists, the only effective means to arrest this normalization of Islam and Muslims is to go to the extreme: *xenelasia*, or forced "remigration" of Muslims back to their own ethnospheres (or at least out of the Western ethnosphere).[11] This is presented as the "peaceful" option to genocide, the latter being completely unacceptable to speak of *publicly* after the Shoah, even in many far-right circles. If such a wholesale removal of the Muslim community is unachievable, a compromise condition by way of a complete marginalization of Muslim communities within Western states, so that their presence is tolerated but not integrated into the national identity, may be sought. However, the latter is a compromise; it does not achieve the purified "ethnostate" that is so desired by many on the far right (Johnson 2018, 95–103).

Against the Translation Proviso: Retreat into the National Geist as Perpetual Barrier

If Habermas' translation proviso allows Muslims in the West to enter into public will-formation on an equal basis with legacy citizens, then it can be seen legitimately as a challenge to the future of the West's "traditional" or "historic" identity, or at least how many on the far right conceptualize the West's "authentic" identity. By staying true to the democratic principle of equal participation of the citizenry in public discourse, and at the same time validating and absorbing Islamic moral-practical material into that public discourse, Habermas' translation proviso finds a way of diminishing the "Otherness" of Muslim communities in Western nations and includes the Muslim citizen as an inclusive *subject* within the national polity, not a feared *object* of political discourse. With the translation proviso, the obvious particularities of "foreign" ethnoi diminish in importance as semantic and semiotic materials from the Islamic tradition are translated into universally accessible reasoning in the public sphere. The far right's fear of "amalgamation" will indeed happen, but at an *intellectual level* via the public use of reasoning, through which the normalization and legitimization of the polyphonic nature of a multicultural, post-secular society occurs. With the normalization of the "Others" in the former democratic willed-community, cultural and ethnic amalgamation is inevitable as well, to some extent. Nevertheless, by successfully implementing the translation proviso, the Otherness of the Islamic community dissipates, and members of the *Ummah* (Muslim community) become integral elements within a more unified (although still diverse) citizenry. Nothing could be more catastrophic for those who have rejected the viability and desirability of the willed-community; the "inclusion of the Other" is exactly what they do not want.

Ultra-nationalists, conservatives, white supremacists, neo-fascists, and other far-right forces find themselves in a curious position in today's post-secular society. Since what they base their "authentic" (*Eigentlich*) identity on, the pre-political foundations of ethnos, are no longer what determines who is included in the demos, another means of excluding Muslims from the ethnic "nation" must be located that doesn't abandon the notion of ethnos but rather strengthens it. Here, we see a tendency to return to metaphysical solutions: Johann Gottfried Fichte's notion of the "national spirit," i.e., the re-establishment of the national spirit with the autochthonous *volk*. As conceptualized by Fichte, the corresponding spirit for each ethnic "nation" is not something that can be adopted via will. Rather, for the far right, the spirit of a people remains only within an authentic/ pure ethnic nation, and without that spirit, one is denied entry into the nation. Thus, while "Others" can become part of the demos in the post-secular society through the appropriate political foundations, and can even engage in ethnic miscegenation, they cannot wilfully enter into the spirit of a nation, which is tied to the original ethnos of the organic "nation." Only legacy citizens—those whose ethnicity is identical to the pre-political foundations of the nation, regardless of the political foundations—are carriers of the national spirit. Being that this spirit is metaphysical or, as Fichte says, often "hidden from their own eyes," it is not subject to materialist measurement, for it does not exist in the same way as race, ethnicity, or even legality does. Rather, it is an amorphous ethnos-derived metaphysical concept that can exclude the "non-identical" from the demos even when the "non-identical" is an equal citizen of the political demos (Adorno 1999, 362). This logic animates the claim that is often repeated by individuals on the far right: "You may be a legal *citizen* of this country, but you are not one of us." In this sense, the spirit of the people—its Geist—becomes a perpetual barrier for the Muslims in the West, for it is the product of the ethnic communities' cumulation of history, a history not shared by immigrants. They may ascend to the political foundations of the democratic state, but they lack the ethnic matrix of the pre-political foundations to be *of* the "nation" and its spirit. Again, just like the Jews before them, Muslims may be *homoiusius* (of similar substance) with legacy citizens, but they can never be *homousius* (of the same substance) with them. Therefore, the immigrant, refugee, or even Muslim citizen in the West is inherently *anatopic*; they are not racially inferior but rather residing in the "wrong place." Legal citizenship in the democratic state does not purchase their membership into the ethnos and its corresponding spirit, which claims to be, as Fichte claims, the "essence" of each nation. Without this essence, the Muslim in the West remains the "inherent alien," even if they can translate their semantic and semiotic materials from Islam into post-secular reasoning successfully.

As Muslims become an ever-present element of the demos within post-secular democratic states, there will be an increasing retreat into these forms of racist metaphysics by the far right, which will search for some way to justify the marginalization of Muslims. Even when Muslims successfully follow Habermas' translation proviso, and legacy citizens correspondingly fulfill the mutual burden of opening themselves up to the claims of Muslims, the impenetrable barrier of the national Geist will inevitably be elevated to national discourse as a means of reminding legacy citizens of their inherent separateness from their Muslim neighbours. As long as Muslims and non-Muslims in the West live in what Habermas calls "parallel societies" and do not thoroughly integrate and/or amalgamate, the stronger this claim will be, as the Muslim community will remain "foreign" to the majority even if such Muslims are equal citizens and active within the public sphere. In this condition, democratic "tolerance" becomes a willingness to accept the existence of the foreign Other in "our" midst; it is not acceptance of the Other as an integral part of who "we" are. To the degree that perceived foreignness remains, so too will the claim of different national spirits have legitimacy in parts of the citizenry. Through metapolitics, it is the goal of the far right to instill the idea in the native demos that the only true demos are that which is identical to the indigenous ethnos. The more this idea is restored, the harder it will be for the translation proviso to overcome the "Otherness" of Muslims in the West.

Da Capo:
Willensgemeinschaften

It is clear that we in the West have very little choice but to confront this particular problem. We cannot return to a retrotopian *Volksgemeinschaft* state wherein we resurrect a sense of "authenticity," "spirit," or *blut und boden* [blood and soil] connection of the past ethnically bound nation-states; the very thought of such an anachronistic reversal of the dialectic of history conjures up the most horrifying images of the Shoah (Byrd 2021). On the other hand, the growing presence of authoritarian populism, which calls for a palingenetic return to an imagined past, is increasingly a cause for concern, especially for ethnic minorities in the West. Such demagoguery has already seen its triumphs in numerous Western countries. From my perspective, Islam is an inherent part of the West and has been a part of the West—even if only as its shadow (in a Jungian sense)—for 1400 years. Yet for many, Islam remains the foreign "Other," if not the "inherent alien," both in ethnicity and in Geist. No explanation of Muslims' importance to Western nationals (in a utilitarian manner) will be enough to undo the entrenched feeling that Muslims exist as an existential threat, not only to those living in the West via terrorists but even to the dead. In other words, Muslims are not only a threat to the very identity of the living West but are seen as threatening to erase the inheritance bestowed upon the West by its Greco-Roman, Germanic, Christian, and Enlightenment predecessors.

The focus, from my perspective, should not be on the normalization of Muslims through discourse *about Muslims*, but rather, the normalization of the Western Enlightenment concept of *Willensgemeinschaft* among non-Muslims of the West, which is yet to be accepted in much of the population. It is not "the Muslim" who threatens modern Western identity—or a Western way-of-being-in-the-world—but rather the Westerners who cannot grasp the modern Enlightenment concept of the willed-community and yearn for the simplicity of an imagined former homogeneity: the ideology of Whitopia. Indeed, it is Muslims and other immigrants who make the very possibility of the promise of the Western Enlightenment realizable. Without integration of the "Other" and subsequent evaporation of the concept of the ethnos-bound Geist, the modern West cannot even fulfill its own Enlightenment promises to itself regarding *liberté, égalité, fraternité*. However, this fulfillment of universalistic promises is precisely what the Islamophobic far right will fight against in the post-secular societies of the West.

NOTES

1. Habermas reminds us that the term "nation" has its origins in the Roman goddess of birth and origin, *Natio*, suggesting that to belong to a given nation one must be born into that nation. This is to organically be the inheritor of that nation's sum cultural-historical matrix. As such, a "nation" is a collective of individuals who are of the "same descent, who are integrated geographically, in the form of settlements or neighborhoods, and culturally by their common language, customs, and traditions." However, such nations are not necessarily determined by polity. In other words, nations can exist without an exclusive state, such as the Kurdish nation that exists today. However, when a nation forms an exclusive state, they generally do so on the basis of their shared pre-political commonalities, thus creating the exclusive "nation-state." This "nation-state" recognizes itself symbiotically: it is a nation exteriorizing itself into an embodied state and a state-in-and-for the exclusive nation. The state, therefore, embodies the nation's particular matrix of ideals, values, and principles. See Habermas 1996, 494–495.
2. We will return to this issue shortly.

3. An important critic of the replaceability of ethnic communities is Renaud
    Camus, the theorist behind the "Great Replacement Theory." See Renaud
    Camus' 2018 book, *You Will Not Replace Us!*

4. We do have to be mindful that until the Protestant Reformation, most
    Europeans thought of themselves primarily as Christians, as opposed to
    belonging to a particular ethnos. Only with the rise of German national-
    ism, which pushed back against Catholicity, did Europeans really begin to
    think in ethnic/nationalist terms. Indeed, as religion began to decline in the
    Enlightenment, ethnic nationalism slowly began to reformulate how the
    nations of western and central Europe identified themselves. See Byrd 2020b.

5. Habermas takes it for granted that religion and theology can be translated
    into post-metaphysical reasoning, as he thinks that much of the West's
    philosophy, as well as its polity, has its primordial origins in religion.
    Indeed, he believes that religion is a source of meaning-material that
    secular modernity is in short supply of. Therefore, secular thinkers like
    himself must occasionally return to religion to replenish that which is
    running scarce: "philosophy must be ready to learn from theology, not only
    for functional reasons but also for substantial reasons." See Habermas and
    Ratzinger 2005, 44. Additionally, Habermas (2008, 131) writes, "Religious
    traditions have a special power to articulate moral intuitions, especially
    with regard to vulnerable forms of communal life. In corresponding politi-
    cal debates, this potential makes religious speech into a serious vehicle for
    possible truth contents, which can then be translated from the vocabulary
    of a particular religious community into a generally accessible language."

6. This form of religious neutrality has been formulated succinctly in the
    First Amendment to the Constitution of the United States, wherein
    it states, "Congress shall make no law respecting an establishment of
    religion, or prohibiting the free exercise thereof." The "establishment and
    prohibition" clause enshrines the idea that the government ought to (and
    will) remain neutral to religious claims and practices. Religious praxis
    will only be interfered with by the state if such practices violate positive
    law, such as human sacrifice. However, France's form of secularity, *laïcité*,
    diverges from the United States' form of religious "neutrality." French law
    holds that the state has the obligation to protect its citizenry from undue
    exposure to religion. Therefore, outward signs of religiosity, such as
    yarmulkes, crosses, and crucifixes, as well as hijabs, chadors, and niqabs,
    have been banned in public schools and other state institutions as being
    irreconcilable with French secularity.

7. This "loss of cultural inheritance" at the hands of secular modernity and multiculturalism reasoning was argued in a more rational discussion between Jürgen Habermas and Cardinal Joseph Ratzinger before the latter became Pope Benedict XVI. However, in 2006, Pope Benedict XVI caused quite a controversy in the Muslim world. In his Regensburg Lecture, entitled *Glaube, Vernunft un Universität. Erinnerungen und Reflexionen* [Faith, Reason, and the University: Memoirs and Reflections], he argued that Christianity was the religion of reason, contrary to Islam. It was the "de-Hellenization" of Christianity—the divorce of Christianity from reason—that made modern Christianity more like Islam: irrational, prone to violence, and totalitarian. Thus, for Pope Benedict XVI, intellectuals who undermine the Christian sources of the West make it easier for Islamization to occur. See Byrd 2020a, 238–246.

8. To be fair, Adolf Hitler also saw Christianity as the ancient "prototype" for modern Bolshevik Communism, as both operate on the basis of equality, which overturns the aristocratic law of nature. See Hitler 2000, 7, 51, 75, 78–79, 143, 146.

9. This was the primary motivator for Robert Gregory Bowers, the gunman in the 2018 "Tree of Life" Synagogue shooting in Pittsburgh, which left seven people dead, several of whom were Holocaust survivors. Bowers was convinced of a nefarious plot led by local Jews who were attempting to bring about a "white genocide" by aiding Muslim immigrants and refugees.

10. It is interesting to note that Renaud Camus argued against those at Charlottesville's 2017 "Unite the Right" rally, who chanted "Jews will not replace us." Camus argued, "It is not the Jews that are replacing you"; rather, Camus believes that Western Jews are also the victims of the "Great Replacement" and will most likely not survive it in Europe, due to the animus between Jews and Muslims (the replacers). Additionally, in my correspondence with Camus, he denied being an anti-Semite, although he does accept some of the critiques of Jewish billionaire George Soros that are usually espoused by anti-Semites. For a better understanding of Camus' stance on Jews, see his 1998 book, *You Will Not Replace Us!*, 166–168.

11. *Xenelasia* was a tradition practised by the ancient Spartans that has become popular among the far right as a "solution" to *Überfremdung*. It calls for the expulsion of those deemed "alien," and therefore injurious to the welfare of the native people, from the territories in which they have taken up residence. In this sense, *xenelasia* is a ritual cleansing of the ethnosphere

of all of those who would "pollute" the ethnosphere. It must also be noted that Niccolò Machiavelli also credited Sparta's practice of *xenelasia* as being one of the chief reasons it was able to create a long-lasting stable city-state, unlike other historical forces, especially the Roman Republic, which embraced a multiplicity of peoples and cultures within its borders and thus suffered from debilitating *disunitas* [disunity]. See Machiavelli 2020, 114. For a more in-depth understanding of the far right's fascination with ancient Sparta, see Cole 2019.

REFERENCES

Adorno, Theodor W. 1999. *Negative Dialectics*. Continuum.

Allen, Theodor W. 2012. *The Invention of the White Race: Volume 1: Racial Oppression and Social Control*. Verso.

Beckeld, Benedict. 2022. *Western Self-Contempt: Oikophobia in the Decline of Civilizations*. Cornell University Press.

Byrd, Dustin J. 2020a. *The Frankfurt School and the Dialectics of Religion: Translating Critical Faith into Critical Theory*. Ekpyrosis Press.

Byrd, Dustin J. 2020b. "Ethno-apotheosis and Bilderverbot: The Theo-Philosophical Basis for the Current Western Daseinkampf." *Islamic Perspective* 23: 1–28.

Byrd, Dustin J. 2021. "Palingenetic Ultra-Nationalist Christianity: History, Identity, and the Falsity of Peripeteic Dialectics." *Praktyka Teoretyczna* 4, no. 42: 39–64.

Camus, Renaud. 2018. *You Will Not Replace Us!* Chez l'auteur.

Cole, Myke. 2019. "The Sparta Fetish is a Cultural Cancer: The Myth of the Mighty Warrior-state Has Enchanted Societies for Thousands of Years. Now It Fuels a Global Fascist Movement." *New Republic*, August 1. https://newrepublic.com/article/154563/sparta-myth-rise-fascism-trumpism.

Evola, Julius. 2018. *The Myth of the Blood: The Genesis of Racialism*. Arktos Media.

Faye, Guillaume. 2011. *Why We Fight: Manifesto of the European Resistance*. Arktos Media.

Faye, Guillaume. 2016. *The Colonization of Europe*. Arktos Media.

Faye, Guillaume. 2019. *Ethnic Apocalypse: The Coming European Civil War*. Arktos Media.

Fichte, Johann Gottlieb. 2017. *Addresses to the German Nation*. Anodos Books.

Habermas, Jürgen. 1984. *The Theory of Communicative Action, Vol. 1: Reason and the Rationalization of Society.* Translated by Thomas McCarthy. Beacon Press.

Habermas, Jürgen. 1996. *Between Facts and Norms: Contributions to a Discourse Theory of Law and Democracy.* Translated by William Rehg. MIT Press.

Habermas, Jürgen. 2008. *Between Naturalism and Religion.* Polity Press.

Habermas, Jürgen, and Joseph Ratzinger. 2005. *The Dialectics of Secularization: On Reason and Religion.* Translated by Brian McNeil. Ignatius Press.

Hedrick, Todd. 2010. *Rawls and Habermas: Reason, Pluralism, and the Claims of Political Philosophy.* Stanford University Press.

Heidegger, Martin. 1962. *Being and Time.* Translated by John Macquarrie and Edward Robinson. Harper Perennial.

Hitler, Adolf. 2000. *Hitler's Table Talk: 1941–1944.* Translated by Norman Cameron and R.H. Steven. Enigma Books.

Johnson, Greg. 2018. *The White Nationalist Manifesto.* Counter-Currents Publishing.

Machiavelli, Niccolò. 2020. *The Prince.* Edited by Wayne A. Rebhorn. W.W. Norton.

Reeves, Minou. 2000. *Muhammad in Europe: A Thousand Years of Western Myth-Making.* NYU Press.

Schmitt, Carl. 1933. *Staat, Bewegung, Volk: Die Dreigliederung der politischen Einheit.* Hanseatische.

3

New French Islamophobia in a Post-secular France

ALAIN GABON

With different degrees of intensity depending on the country, Islamophobia has become one of the ideological backbones of the Western world. In France, it seems to enjoy a special status, and that country may currently be its main experimental laboratory, as best exemplified by the constant national debates around feminine Islamic clothing (the hijab, burqini, and other items of Islamic "modest fashion") over the past thirty years, from the first *affaires des voiles islamiques* of October 1989 (Bowen 2007; Scott 2007) to the September 2023 ban on abayas in public schools. Those affairs regularly throw the whole nation into convulsive episodes of national hysteria and moral panic over what is presented as existential threats to the Republic, France, and European-civilization-as-we-know-it. To understand the extent, depth, and gravity of French Islamophobia or Islamo-paranoia, to use the term of French sociologist of religions Raphaël Liogier (2012), one must take into account its main characteristics, without assuming those are exclusive to France.[1] This phenomenon is indeed widely shared across the entire Western world, often in similar forms and for similar reasons, as abundantly documented by independent and official data and statistics, detailed annual reports by NGOs, news and journalistic investigations, and academic scholarship (Lean 2017; Zempi and Awan 2021).

Main Characteristics

French Islamophobia displays four major characteristics: it has very deep historical roots and a multilayered structure; it is constantly reactivated, resignified, and enriched; it is mostly a top-down elite and state construct; and it is extensively theorized by France's political, media, intellectual, and artistic elites, who provide its intellectual alibis and justifications.

For the sake of nuance, let us say first that the history of the relations between Europe (France included) and Islam cannot be reduced to a permanent "clash of civilizations," a never-ending series of imperial confrontations, battles, conquests, competitions, and rivalries. Historians of Islam and the West insist on the need to avoid such simplistic and one-sided views. They emphasize instead the complexities of the interactions, including the permanent and rich exchanges, diplomatic and commercial relations, rapprochements, partnerships, political and strategic alliances (including military ones) as well as common cultures, tastes, and values (for example, trade). They focus on the many types of syncretism and hybridization that throughout history have resulted from the diverse and often contradictory encounters between the West and Islam (Fabre 2012). However, it is equally important to recognize the strength and virulence of the antagonistic reactions elicited in the "Christian West" by the birth of Islam in the seventh century and its subsequent expansion. From the two centuries of Crusades (1095–1291, initiated by a Frenchman, Pope Urban II) to the long and bloody colonial era—which for France only ended in 1962 with the independence of Algeria after a long and violent eight-year war—the conflicts, conquests, reconquests, invasions, raids, battles, razzias, and rivalries have been incessant and, more often than not, extremely brutal.

More importantly for our understanding of French Islamophobia, the conflictual and adversarial strand in the history of Islam and Europe has not only produced geopolitical and cultural frontiers—despite the fact those frontiers between the northwestern "Christian world" and the southeastern "Islamic world" were often penetrated, modified, or simply ignored (for example, by the merchant class)—but also created *mental maps and borders*, symbolic lines of demarcation, and epistemological barriers. Those symbolic frontiers have to this day been kept intact by fear, distrust, misperception, misunderstanding, and a sense of threat from Islam and Muslims. They are glaringly visible in the ways Muslims and their religion are excluded from definitions of French national identity and citizenship, kept outside the contours of Frenchness, as well explained, for example, in Roshan Arah Jahangeer's contribution to this volume (see Chapter 8). This in-group/out-group, Us versus Them mindset, consolidated by centuries of French imperial colonialism (Bancel, Blanchard, and Thomas 2017; Bancel, Blanchard, and Vergès 2006; Blanchard et al. 2014), constitutes the core of today's French Islamophobia—the real ideological and often subliminal frontier that keeps Muslims "Othered," excluded, perceived as foreigners or outsiders, and discriminated against in their own nation. Those mental borders can be seen, heard, and observed everywhere in French public discourse, state policies, media representations, and public opinion polls (Europe 1 2019). Islam is considered incompatible with life in France, very openly so and regardless of the fact that millions of devout and sincere Muslims prove otherwise every single day by living and practising their religion in peace and by being perfectly comfortable in a secular France. Still, as with other forms of racism, unjustified Islamophobic stereotypes and false perceptions trump facts and realities.

One example of French Islamophobia among the myriad one can easily find is the obsessional demonization of Turkish president Recep Tayyip Erdoğan as a prime enemy of France, if not an existential threat, which for years has been a perpetual theme in French media and politics. This unjustified anti-Erdoğan hysteria can best be understood as the latest manifestation of the old "fear of the Turk" and long Western fight against the Ottoman Empire from at least the fourteenth century (when the Ottomans crossed into Europe and the Balkans) to the early twentieth century (when the Ottoman Empire was defeated then partitioned by the Western powers after World War I in the 1920 Treaty of Sèvres). Those subliminal historical filiations sometimes become explicit in the numerous descriptions of Erdoğan as "the new sultan," an aspiring "Suleiman the Magnificent."

From Urban II's characterization of Turks as figures of the Antichrist to President Charles de Gaulle's infamous metaphor of French and Arabic people as similar to oil and vinegar, namely unable to mix (Fessou 2012),[2] Islam has for centuries been imagined as the great rival of the West, both frightening and necessary as a legitimizing principle in this "bloc-against-bloc," clash of civilization double essentialism. This scare rhetoric, antagonistic orientalist mindset, and negative, immensely hurtful stereotypes of Arabs and Muslims remain quite remarkably the exact same today regarding African immigrants and Islam in general. In today's France, those atavisms are cloaked in the rhetoric of national security, the "War on Terror," and the "fight against Islamism," which benefits from a very large, quasi-unanimous consensus. From the far right to the far left, the political class and the majority of the French population hardly bother anymore to differentiate between "Islam" and "Islamism," between Muslims and "Islamist extremists":

[Those] images of racial inferiority and enmity [have been] inherited from over a century of colonization… In their everyday dealings with the majority population, Maghrebis as a whole cannot escape the generally unstated and often unconscious but nonetheless potent legacy of the colonial era, which continues to color majority perceptions of minority groups… Such neo-colonial tendencies are apparent not only in everyday attitudes and behavior as well as in popular and mainstream cultural forms such as film, television, and comics, but also in the social and political institutions of contemporary France. (Hargreaves and McKinney 1998, 18–21)

This orientalist and neocolonial mindset continues to perceive Arabs (and associated populations like Berbers) and Muslims (first, second, or third generations, foreigners or citizens) with the eyes and minds of the old colonizers. Thus, the French are being told, Islam(ism) represents a mortal threat to our Republic that we cannot tolerate on our soil because it seeks to conquer and destroy us and wants to replace France and Europe with an Iranian or Saudi-style Islamist Republic. Because of their religion, Muslims are backward and archaic (they "oppress their women"), intolerant, rigid, inherently sectarian, insidious, untrustworthy and treacherous, resistant to democracy, always more or less fanatical, dangerous, heinous, and potentially violent, according to the well-entrenched "radicalization of Islam" myth (Gabon 2016). They are essentially foreign to secularism, Enlightened Reason, and gender equality, all things they neither understand nor are willing to accept because they remain stuck in their archaic, "medieval" religion. For all those reasons, Muslims are incompatible with life in our societies, incapable and unwilling to integrate, and unable to withstand criticism of their religion. Finally, deep down, whether they admit it like the "Islamists" do or conceal it through *taqiya* (the stereotype of the treacherous Muslims), they are fundamentally hostile to *L'Occident*, democracy, human rights, and the whole non-Muslim world, which they want to conquer and force into submission. After all, doesn't Islam mean "Submission"?

Those exclusionary, vilifying, and dehumanizing prejudices (Bridge Initiative Team 2018) have been elaborated since the very origins of Islam and have remained essentially unchanged since Urban II's Clermont speech. France thus still has to decolonize its dominant mentality and culture, a position articulated most forcefully by activist minority movements such as the Indigènes de la République.

The historical structure and foundations of French Islamophobia are not just deep and old, they are also multilayered: that mindset (a true episteme systematically constructed over centuries) is constantly reinscribed in new temporalities where each novel strata reactivates the previous ones, aggravates the stereotypes and paranoid fears, resignifies and enriches the Islamophobic edifice through the addition of new layers (e.g., new justifications like the "War on Terror") that both capitalize on previous ones and consolidate them, thus seemingly confirming the previous prejudices while solidifying the whole Islamophobic infrastructure. Those different temporalities that constitute the multilayered historical structure of French Islamophobia are not just mutually reinforcing, they also overlap. For example, while the periodization can differ according to analysts, the sequence of terrorist attacks from 9/11 to the 2015 Charlie Hebdo/Bataclan massacres occurred *during* the previous sequence, opened by the October 1989 headscarves affair, which started long before 9/11 and Mohammed Merah's first Jihadist murder on French soil in 2012. Contrary to what is sometimes said, the Twin Towers–Mohammed Merah–Charlie Hebdo–Bataclan sequence of Jihadist attacks did not produce French Islamophobia, which long predated them. They merely solidified old terrain, aggravated the situation, and exacerbated the fear of Islam and the resentment against Muslims by seemingly justifying those pre-existing hostile sentiments and negative stereotypes, in the "See? We told you Muslims are violent!" mode.

The last major feature of French Islamophobia is its rich and diverse theorization and justification by state elites and their various ideological agents. Here, too, a straight line can be drawn between today's perceptions of Islam and Muslims and the Pope's defence of the Catholic Church and fellow Christians during the Crusades, or the consistent conceptualization by major figures of the Republic, such as Jules Ferry,[3] of state racism through the colonialist mystique of *Mission Civilisatrice*. The exoticized orientalist iconography[4] and paternalist discourse of France's Civilizing Mission always served as a cover up for the far less glorious realities of brutal military conquest, land confiscation, enforced and legally codified inequality,[5] merciless exploitation of indigenous populations, and massacres of protesters and nationalist fighters until the 1960s and the Algerian war (Ginio and Sessions 2016). Today, the ideological and political justifications have changed: they are named "national security," the "War on Terror," the "Islamist threat," Islamist "separatism," the alleged "danger of Salafism" for social cohesion, the "defence of *laïcité* against radical Islam" or the preservation of "French mores," "values," and customs (ranging from *apéro-saucisson* to gender equality), all things supposedly endangered by a "foreign" religion. What is striking is how the stereotypes (Islam as an expansionist, hostile, anti-Western religion, etc.), the targeted and stigmatized populations, the unfounded fears, and fantasized threats (Gabon 2016), the whole episteme of mental, symbolic, and cultural representations at the heart of those ideological alibis remain fundamentally the same. Then and now, rather than a spontaneous, popular, grassroots-type racism, French Islamophobia has been a top-down construction. It is the elites of the nation—political, scientific, educational, philosophic, artistic (and religious, too, in the days of the Crusades)—who have always been the driving force behind the racist Otherization of Muslims (both French and foreign) and the propagation of contempt and distrust toward Islam. They have constructed Islam as the archenemy of Europe and its hostile inversion. In that multi-centennial imagination, Islam and Muslims are everything that Europe and Europeans are not, and vice versa. From the most influential European philosophers—such as humanists Erasmus and Michel de Montaigne, who are presented as the epitome of the French spirit and for whom the Turks were as powerful and bellicose as they were ignorant and devoid of culture—to nineteenth-century scientists, colonial imperialists like Jules Ferry, political thinkers like Ernest Renan, and major French political figures like Charles de Gaulle, France's ruling elites have viewed and constructed Islam as the complete negation of Europe: a dangerous and fanatical religion alien to science, closed to rational inquiry, and hostile to civil society (Dakhli 2012).

Today, in perfect historical continuity, there is constant media hysteria about the "Islamization" of Europe (Deltombe 2007); France's heads of state, including President Emmanuel Macron, give conspiracist speeches about an "Islamist hydra" that is supposedly about to swallow France; and top government members launch one witch hunt after another against "Islamo-leftists," Salafists," or teenage girls who wear the abaya (or anything that looks vaguely "Islamic") and for that only reason are publicly described as an existential menace and a "fundamentalist threat to the Republic." This relentless demonization of perfectly innocent and harmless groups is powerfully fuelled by the never-ending deluge of sensationalist books and high-profile media interventions from famed journalists and academics (Rougier 2020) about the allegedly "lost" or "conquered" (by Islam/ism) "territories of the Republic." It is further justified by the racist and Islamophobic declarations of acclaimed mediatized artists such as novelists Kamel Daoud[6] (2016) and Michel Houellebecq (2015).[7]

Root Causes

In addition to the "culture of antagonism" (to use Géraud Poumarèdes' expression) that has structured relationships between Islam and the West since the emergence of that religion, other historical French characteristics help explain the virulence of today's Islamophobia. First, one can mention the mystique and absolutism of the French state. Whether in its pre-Revolutionary monarchist form or its various Republican incarnations, the French state has always been intolerant and wary of "intermediary bodies," or *les corps intermédiaires*, religions included.[8] The August 24, 2021, "anti-separatism" law, which dramatically restricts the autonomy of associations, is therefore not a rupture or a novelty but an aggravation of a long and well-established historical trend, fully within the DNA of French state authoritarianism.[9] Second, rather than secularism, which implies separation of state and religion as two autonomous realms, a much longer and often stronger tradition of Gallicanism dating back to the Middle Ages has always tried to control and shape religions.[10] Third is widespread anticlericalism that continues to consider religion the antithesis of reason, if not an outdated relic. This anticlerical mindset has itself a quadruple origin: the emergence of atheist philosophies in the seventeenth century; the strong strand of anticlericalism in Enlightenment philosophy; the bloody struggle of French Revolutionaries against the Catholic Church; and the 1905 laws on the separation of churches and the state, following a long and fierce fight against a Catholic Church that did not want to lose its privileges. Finally, as a fourth factor explaining the virulence of today's French Islamophobia, the dramatic secularization (here, in the sense of decline of religious faith and practice) and de-Catholicization of French culture between the 1960s and the 1990s has produced one of the most atheist and irreligious populations in the world.[11] France, "The First Daughter of the Catholic Church" during the Middle Ages, has now largely lost not just its appreciation for religion but its understanding of the religious experience itself, including its own, though now largely past majority religious experience and, even more so, the "imported" "foreign" minority religion of Islam. Evidently, none of those structural cultural characteristics could offer a favourable terrain for the deployment of Islam.

New French Islamophobia

Overdetermined by the long-term root causes outlined above, with their various temporalities in which French Islamophobia is imbricated (a bit like Russian dolls), the latest Islamophobic sequence inaugurated by the first headscarves affair of October 1989 has mobilized a truly mind-blowing array of methods, both conscious and unconscious—as explained earlier, Islamophobia has for centuries been so pervasive among the majority French population, including its ruling elites, that it should sadly be considered second nature. We only have space here to briefly mention a few prominent techniques, most of which are glaringly visible to any observer of French society.

Construction of an Imaginary and Essentialized "Bogeyman Islam"

This occurs through media, politicians, public intellectuals, and artists representing Islam and Muslims as a problem (Deltombe 2007), an existential threat, or at best a "challenge to the Republic," "our way of life," and "Western civilization" itself. This constant problematization of the presence of Islam and Muslims in France is a form of permanent harassment, lived as such by most French Muslims. It maintains an atmosphere of suspicion, fear, and distrust against their religion and them as people through the creation of false or dramatically exaggerated dangers related to Islam or "Islamism." This anti-Muslim hysterical threat inflation is disseminated through countless news stories, alarming magazine covers and headlines, sensationalist books, constant political hype, and incendiary public debates on the Jihadist or Islamist threat, the "radicalization of the Muslim youth," headscarves, burkinis and other modest fashion, halal menus in public schools, Islamist "separatism," "Islamoleftism," and more. There is literally not a single month without such episodes of moral panic and hysteria, often about feminine Islamic clothing. As a result, Muslims are kept in a permanent state of tension and stigmatization.

Conspiracist Pathologization of Islamic Normality

Here, perfectly normal phenomena and natural transformations of Western societies—spontaneous, organic shifts in the environment due to demographics and immigration, like the transformation of urban space and neighbourhoods, the presence of halal butcher shops, Islamic clothing in the streets, a mosque next to a Catholic church, etc.—are presented in typical "Islamization of Europe" conspiracist paranoia as signs of stealth Jihadism and evidence of a global ideological project of conquest whose goal is to replace Europe by a vast Islamic caliphate. In such scare rhetoric, justified by a steady stream of poorly researched works from mediatized academics such as Gilles Kepel, Bernard Rougier, and more recently Florence Bergeaud-Blackler, normal and harmless cultural change becomes evidence of a concerted, deliberate, and intentional invasion, of a hostile "Islamist" takeover of France and Europe piloted and coordinated from abroad by the usual suspects (usually Saudi Arabia, Turkey, or Qatar). Those high-profile academics, whose enormous media surface is inversely proportional to the quality and integrity of their works,[12] contribute powerfully to the stigmatization of Islam and Muslims by lending their university titles and credentials to largely Islamophobic media and governments, with whom they are always keen to collaborate and help design repressive policies (Rougier 2020).[13]

The Securitization of Islam and Muslims

The imaginary Islam and Muslim population described above is essentially a fantasy. Nonetheless, those false perceptions and symbolic representations end up producing concrete social and political consequences that are themselves very real. What Jocelyne Cesari (2018) has called the "securitization" of Muslims—exceptional political measures of a usually repressive type, like increased military presence and police controls and systematic surveillance of mosques, implemented by governments outside the rule of law and often in violation of

it—stems from the perception of Islam as a threat. This pushes governments left, right, and centre to treat that religion and its practitioners
as primarily an "at-risk" population and a national security menace.
This state of exception is justified by the invocation of the need to preserve the security of citizens against Jihadism and protect the Republic
against an "Islamist" conquest. The dramatic mutation and expansion
of the post-9/11 War on Terror into a vaguely defined "war on Islamism"
represents a major development in the relations between France and
Muslims that is now creeping into every area of life, to the point many
non-Muslims are now negatively affected, not as the designated targets
but as the collateral damage of those political operations. This new
atavism with old roots is influencing and shaping public policies and
law, such as the recent bill against "Islamist separatism" or the Law to
Strengthen the Respect of the Principles of the Republic[14] (see Jahangeer
in Chapter 8 of this book; also République française 2021), but also
administrative routine, public debates, media, cultural production, and
French academic and intellectual life, as seen in the recent debates on
"Islamo-leftists" who are supposedly taking over France's entire school
system, research, and universities.

Falsification and Weaponization of French Laicity for Islamophobic Purposes

In order to cover up those Islamophobic enterprises that are now
causing Muslims to face a pervasive atmosphere of discrimination, a
number of blatant lies are being spread (either out of ignorance and
confusion or more cynically and deliberately) about French *laïcité* and
the famous law of 1905 on the separation of churches and state. Two of
those fallacies stand out. The first, heard everywhere and usually with
no rectification, is that France is "a secular country" or "a secular society." This is factually false: France is not a secular society, it *has a secular
state*, which is completely different. Namely, religious neutrality applies
only to the state and its official representatives, government workers,

and civil servants such as public school teachers and administrators, judges, elected officials, and government members. But until the March 15, 2004, law banning "ostensible" religious signs, symbols, and clothing from public schools, French *laïcité* in its religious neutrality aspect was *never meant to apply to civil society and the population itself*, which would have violated their constitutionally guaranteed freedom of religion. The extension to categories of the population such as school children of the obligation of religious neutrality and religious invisibility represents a grave falsification of French secularism[15] and a severe violation of both the text and the spirit of the 1905 law (Baubérot 2014). The second fallacy is the often-repeated notion that in France, "religion is a private matter" to be practised at home, in private, or in places of worship. This is also blatantly false on both legal and cultural grounds. French as well as European law (the latter being a part of the former) clearly and explicitly allow not just private and individual religious practice but *public as well as collective* freedom to practise one's religion, with others and in public (European Court of Human Rights 2022). Culturally, it is also shockingly false to claim that religious practice in France is or should be limited to "the private sphere." Masses are public events broadcasted on public state television and radio channels; church bells can be heard daily in countless cities and villages; processions of saints and public religious gatherings like the Popes' visits or Catholic youth days are themselves mass public events; Jehovah's Witnesses proselytizing door-to-door in their recognizable outfits have been a common sight for decades, and so on and so forth. Countless similar examples can easily be found to debunk this falsehood of "religion belonging to the private sphere, not the public one." It is for Islam and Islam only that religious practice in France is deemed "strictly private," in a glaring double standard.

Since October 1989, French *laïcité* has thus increasingly been turned into what it was never intended to be: a tool to attack the constitutional liberties of Muslims in France and their right to equal treatment of their religion. This falsified, profoundly illiberal and authoritarian pseudo *laïcité* is no longer the liberal, benign, democratic, egalitarian, and emancipatory secularism it was in the 1905 law, but a radically corrupted, falsified, and weaponized type of un-secular or post-secular, counterfeit *laïcité*.

"House Negro versus Field Negro"

In reference to Malcolm X's famous 1963 speech (Riverbends Channel 2013), this classic yet effective divide-and-conquer strategy, easily observable everywhere in French media and politics, selects the "good," "moderate," legitimate "Muslims of the Republic" (the pro-governmental or quietist ones), then pits them against the critical ones, often directly—so, for example, in television debates of X versus Y that play out like boxing. The former are promoted, celebrated, and paraded everywhere by politicians and media as models for other Muslims to emulate. Their support, quietism, or political docility and acquiescence to the Powers That Be is generously rewarded in the form of appointments on government and official commissions, lucratively paid official "reports" (on *laïcité*, etc.), programs on state TV and radio channels, and more. The latter—the bad Muslims who will not be silenced and keep opening their mouths to criticize the government on its pro-Israeli positions and other issues—become publicly vilified as "radicals," "extremists," and "Islamists." They now increasingly see their organizations simply shut down through mere executive or local administrative orders, while their leaders get sued (sometimes expelled, too, if they are foreigners or dual citizens) for "Islamist separatism" or "incitement to hatred" against the Republic.[16]

Islamic Exceptionalism, Double Standards, Differentialist Treatment of Islam and Muslims

Here, too, there are countless examples, but we can single out a fairly recent one. In 2021, President Emmanuel Macron and Interior Minister Gérald Darmanin launched their "Charter of the Principles of Islam" initiative (Grande Mosquée de Paris 2021) with the goal of defining and regulating not just the structure of the representation of Muslims in France and the internal functioning of mosques but even the Islamic creed and theology itself. They then tried to force Muslim organizations and mosques to sign it, openly threatening with state repression anyone who refused. Only Islam was subjected to such a treatment, because unlike Catholicism or Judaism it is perceived as a threat to be controlled from above. None of the other religions were asked to sign such "charters" and oaths to respect the principles, laws, and values of the French Republic.

The Macron Years

Although Emmanuel Macron was first elected in 2017 on the promise of an inclusive and open society, presenting himself as an antidote to the bigotry of Marine Le Pen, seven years later and after Macron's 2022 re-election, the situation of Muslims in France is actually a lot worse than it was back in 2017.

Under Macron, state Islamophobia has become far more legally entrenched, judicialized, and politically as well as administratively systematized (CAGE 2022). It is now also undergoing a systemic double process of *horizontal expansion* and *vertical penetration*. On one hand, more civic groups (associations of all kinds, including sports clubs) and private-sector entities (e.g., private businesses)—which, according to French *laïcité*, should not be concerned by such obligations—are now themselves being incorporated in the regime of religious neutrality (République française 2021, Titre IER Chapitre Ier Article 1). Concretely, that means no more freedom of religion, religious clothing, prayers during work time, etc. for employees or association members. On the other hand, state control, restrictions, and repression of religious freedom penetrates deeper and deeper into the private lives of Muslims (and other collateral victims of such laws), including family life and educational choices like home-schooling or private Islamic schools (République française 2021, Titre IER Chapitre V Section 1).

Three new repressive trends and methods have also dramatically coalesced as a direct result of legislative enterprises like the August 24, 2021, Law to Strengthen the Respect of the Principles of the Republic, a major Macron initiative often presented as an epitomic symbol of his first term. First and second among those methods of repression: *collective punishment* and *guilt by association*, by which the proven or simply presumed guilt of one member of an association or organization (mosques are particularly targeted) can be extended to the totality of the association and group (République française 2021, Titre IER Chapitre II Article 16). This has now become routine in France and is well documented by the chilling 2022 CAGE report. Now, an entire mosque of thousands of Muslims, including its sociocultural activities and Arabic classes, can easily be shut down through mere local administrative decision because of one post by one member on the mosque's Facebook page or Twitter account that will be deemed "heinous" by the local mayor or prefect. The French sections of the annual European Islamophobia Reports (Najib 2022) and Islamic associations like CAGE (2022) have documented hundreds of such occurrences. In today's France, such repression is actually a source of pride and leverage by politicians with presidential ambitions. Thus, in September 2021, Interior Minister Gérald Darmanin publicly bragged of personally shutting down 650 "places frequented by fundamentalists,"[17] including mosques, Islamic publishing houses, and charities, as well as human rights and anti-discrimination organizations like the Collective Against Islamophobia—actions that have been vocally denounced by Amnesty International (2020), Human Rights Watch, and more. Such methods, used to dismantle and ban any Islamic organization or mosque labelled "fundamentalist," "Salafist," "Islamist," or "separatist" by any local official on the flimsiest of evidence or with no evidence at all, have now become routine.

The third trend: the ever-worsening *criminalization of thought, creed, and belief,* another red line the Macron government is now also casually crossing. For example, the Charter of the Principles of Islam, a Macron-Darmanin operation, explicitly demands that French Muslims formally recognize the superiority of French laws and the Republic (itself a mere political form) over their own faith. This is a clear violation of freedom of consciousness not demanded from any other religious believer, most notably Catholics—who, to this day, refuse to recognize the legitimacy of laws such as those for same-sex marriage or even abortion yet are never accused of "fundamentalism or 'separatism'" and certainly not persecuted the way Muslims are. The Charter also declares that mosques cannot have any political agenda or engage in any political or ideological activity or discourse, and they must ban a more-than-vaguely defined "political Islam," including the Muslim Brotherhood, Salafism, Wahhabism, and the Tabligh (FranceMaghreb2 2021). This criminalization of thought, political opinion, activism, and religious belief—only when it comes to Muslims—clearly constitutes a massive violation of freedom of consciousness and has been abundantly denounced as such both nationally and internationally. To take another example, in the Darmanin executive decrees banning Islamic associations like the Collective Against Islamophobia and Coordination Against Racism and Islamophobia, the "evidence" of "incitement to hatred and violence" invoked for shutting down those organizations includes the following: "cultivating the suspicion that Islamophobia exists in French society," "using the expression 'institutionalized Islamophobia,'" and "comparing the French military interventions in Mali, Libya and Somalia to the terrorist attacks that took place on French soil" (Darmanin 2021).

There is a dual goal to this all-out offensive and neocolonial management of Islam and Muslims, the cornerstones of which are the August 24, 2021, law and the Systematic Obstruction policy (CAG 2020). First, it aims to produce a quietist, docile, obedient, passive "French Islam" that would be entirely controlled by the state itself, from its internal organization to its cadres (imams, etc.) and now even its doctrine and articles of faith—something even the colonial administrators of France's imperial Muslim colonies did not seek to do. Quite amazingly, France under Macron is therefore exceeding and surpassing their historical zeal. Second, those policies try to strip French Muslims of the possibility of organizing themselves autonomously, outside the reach and control of the state.

Conclusion:
A Neocolonial and Post-secular France

French state Islamophobia has now reached the level of genuine persecution. Muslims are increasingly treated as second-class citizens and kept in a hostile neocolonial situation in their own country, while France itself can be said to be in a post-secular situation. When it comes to Islam and Muslims, there is no more separation of church and state. All three major pillars of French *laïcité* and the 1905 law— freedom of religion, strict equality of treatment of all religions, and separation of churches and state including non-interference of the state in matters of religious doctrine—have been systematically ignored, lost to the hostile majority perception that the dangerous, extremist religion of Islam and its suspicious practitioners need to be controlled, reshaped, and re-educated in the grand historical tradition of France's Civilizing Mission.

NOTES

1. For example, see Chapter 7 in this volume for Zeinab Diab's analysis of Quebec's Law 21, much of which could actually be applied to France without changing a word.

2. "Have you seen the Muslims with their turbans and their djellabas? You can see that they are not French. Try to mix oil and vinegar. Shake the bottle. After a moment they separate again. The Arabs are Arabs, the French are French. Do you think that the French can absorb ten million Muslims who will tomorrow be twenty million and after tomorrow forty? If we carry out integration, if all the Berbers and Arabs of Algeria were regarded as French, how would one stop them from coming to settle on the mainland where the standards of living are so much higher? My village would no longer be called Colombey-les-deux-Églises [the two churches] but Colombey-the-two-mosques." (My translation)

3. To this day, Jules Ferry remains one of the most revered and celebrated figures of the French Republic as founder of the "free, secular, mandatory" public school system. His name is on countless streets, avenues, public squares, and schools throughout France. When one remembers that he proudly declared that "inferior races," including conquered Muslim populations, were in need of "civilization" by the "superior races," it is hardly surprising that the French public school system became in October 1989 the first and main arena of that new French Islamophobia, when Muslim schoolgirls were expelled from their school (illegally, as it turned out later) for refusing to remove their hijabs and be "civilized" and "enlightened" by the Republic.

4. Most famously, Eugène Delacroix's paintings.

5. Through differential colonial law and "indigenous codes," Muslim colonial subjects were systematically stripped of the Republic's equal rights despite the fact those were supposed to be "universal." French Universalism always was, and remains, relative.

6. In his famous column in *Le Monde*, Daoud first described Arab men, all of them, as psychologically deformed sexual perverts and potential rapists, then squarely attributed that collective perversion and sexual threat to Islam. This unsurprisingly lent him great acclaim and media fame as a "courageous" intellectual who is not afraid of telling "the truth."

7. His 2015 novel *Submission* and his uninhibited public declarations on "Islam, the stupidest religion on earth" gave Islamophobia the legitimacy of France's most famous, most widely read, and most globally celebrated novelist.

8. Historically, the French state has always been suspicious, hostile, and repressive of intermediary bodies and competing identities and loyalties (ethnic, religious, regional, or national). It usually seeks to either eliminate, reduce, control, and at best coerce those *corps intermédiaires* seen as potential rivals for the loyalty of the French.

9. See Chapter 8 in this volume for Roshan Arah Jahangeer's analysis of that law, which is perfectly congruent with my own perspective.

10. The constant celebration of "French-style *laïcité*" or *laïcité à la française* systematically ignores the fact that in France, it is actually state authorities who decide what constitutes a religion versus a sect and therefore select which creeds can be allowed to exist on French soil and which ones are banned (like, for example, the Church of Scientology). That task, a major and far-reaching one, is the prerogative of a quasi-confidential inter-ministerial corps named MIVILUDES. It is therefore doubtful that France ever was the secular Republic she imagines herself to be, given that the very definition of what "a religion" is has remained the prerogative of a small group of top civil servants or *hauts fonctionnaires* under the direct supervision of the interior minister.

11. The data differs according to the sources, but France is usually listed as the fourth most atheist country in the world and the first by far in Europe (Haski 2016) with nearly 30 percent of the population declaring themselves "convinced atheists" and another 34 percent "without religion" (Wike 2016).

12. See Bergeaud-Blackler 2023 and Dazey 2024. On Bernard Rougier, see Bonnefoy 2020.

13. Rougier's bestselling book on the "Islamist conquest" of French Muslims was not surprisingly praised by those politicians from the far right to the left who themselves had for years developed a similar discourse. In his pamphlet disguised as academic research, the presence on the same street of a halal butcher shop, an Islamic library, and a mosque is presented as a deliberately constructed "Islamist ecosystem" that is itself part of a grand plan to indoctrinate the Muslim population and cut them off from mainstream France, rather than perfectly normal signs of the presence of a large Muslim population in that neighbourhood. In this aggressively hostile vision and oriented (mis)readings of social phenomena related to Islam, normal developments and organic change become recoded as an existential menace: the signs of an "Islamist conquest." This conspiracist mindset is actually not far from that of Eric Zemmour and his Eurabia and Great Replacement fantasies. At the very least, they objectively serve and fuel his heinous rhetoric.

14. Almost all the articles of that law originated in incendiary public debates and controversies against various aspects of Islam in France, such as the supposed threat of indoctrination of Muslim children by Islamic private schools or their own parents when they choose home-schooling. This false perception that Muslim parents home-school their children to better indoctrinate them into "fundamentalist" and "extremist" forms of Islam such as Salafism has now led the government and Parliament to dramatically restrict home-schooling for all, to the point of rendering it almost impossible, while also severely tightening the control of private (read: Islamic) schools. In the process, it is actually Catholic families who are suffering from this in greater numbers.

15. For more on this, see Chapter 8 in this volume by Roshan Arah Jahangeer.

16. The caricatural version of this dichotomy operated by the state and media between the good and the bad Muslims is best illustrated by the opposition between Drancy Imam Hassan Chalghoumi (or Islamic intellectual Ghaled Bencheik) and Tariq Ramadan.

17. A remarkable declaration and policy, since "fundamentalism" is not even a crime in French law.

REFERENCES

Amnesty International. 2020. "France: Shutting Down Anti-Racist Organisations Risks Freedom." November 20. https://www.amnesty.org/en/latest/press-release/2020/11/france-shutting-down-antiracist-organisation-risks-freedoms/.

Bancel, Nicolas, Pascal Blanchard, and Dominic Thomas, eds. 2017. *The Cultural Legacy in France. Fracture, Rupture, and Apartheid*. Indiana University Press.

Bancel, Nicolas, Pascal Blanchard, and Françoise Vergès. 2006. *La République coloniale*. Fayard.

Baubérot, Jean. 2014. *La laïcité falsifiée*. La Découverte.

Bergeaud-Blackler, Florence. 2023. *Le frérisme et ses réseaux*. Odile Jacob.

Blanchard, Pascal, Sandrine Lemaire, Nicolas Bancel, and Dominic Thomas, eds. 2014. *Colonial Culture in France since the Revolution*. Indiana University Press.

Bonnefoy, Laurent. 2020. "Idées toutes faites sur 'les territoires conquis de l'islamisme.'" *Orient XXI*, February 10.

Bowen, John. 2007. *Why the French Don't Like Headscarves: Islam, the State, and Public Space*. Princeton University Press.

Bridge Initiative Team. 2018. "Factsheet: Common Anti-Muslim Tropes." Georgetown University, December 4. https://bridge.georgetown.edu/research/factsheet-common-anti-muslim-tropes-2/.

CAGE. 2022. *"We Are Beginning to Spread Terror": The State-Sponsored Persecution of Muslims in France*. March 2. https://www.cage.ngo/articles/we-are-beginning-to-spread-terror-the-state-sponsored-persecution-of-muslims-in-france.

Cesari, Jocelyne. 2018. "Securitization of Islam and Religious Freedom." Berkley Center For Religion, Peace, and World Affairs (Georgetown University), September 13. https://berkleycenter.georgetown.edu/posts/securitization-of-islam-and-religious-freedom.

Dakhli, Leila. 2012. "Communs contemporains et malentendus présents: itinéraires de compréhension aux XIXème et XXème siècles." In *L'Europe et l'Islam. La Liberté ou la peur?*, edited by Thierry Fabre. Éditions Parenthèses.

Daoud, Kamel. 2016. "Cologne, lieu de fantasmes." *Le Monde*, January 29. https://www.lemonde.fr/idees/article/2016/01/31/cologne-lieu-de-fantasmes_4856694_3232.html.

Darmanin, Gérald (@GDarmanin). 2021. "Gérald Darmanin Twitter post." Twitter, October 20, 2021, 12:26 p.m: "L'association 'Coordination contre le racisme et l'islamophobie' a été dissoute en conseil des ministres, conformément aux instructions du Président de la République. Comme le détaille le décret que j'ai présenté, elle appelait à la haine, à la violence et à la discrimination: https://t.co/5giwOcQEfC" / Twitter.

Dazey, Margot. 2024. "Enquêter sur des mouvements islamistes. Enjeux conceptuels, méthodologiques et épistémologiques d'une approche centrée sur l'idéologie." *Revue des mondes musulmans et de la Méditerranée* 155, no. 1.

Deltombe, Thomas. 2007. *L'Islam imaginaire. La construction médiatique de l'islamophobie en France, 1975–2005*. La Découverte.

Europe 1. 2019. "61% des français pensent que 'l'islam est incompatible avec les valeurs de la société française.'" October 27. https://www.europe1.fr/societe/selon-un-sondage-ifop-pour-le-journal-du-dimanche-78-des-francais-jugent-la-laicite-menacee-3927717.

European Court of Human Rights. 2022. *Guide on Article 9 of the European Convention on Human Rights. Freedom of Thought, Conscience and Religion.* Updated August 31. https://ks.echr.coe.int/documents/d/echr-ks/guide_art_9_eng.

Fabre, Thierry, ed. 2012. *L'Europe et l'islam, la liberté ou la peur? Rencontres d'Averroès 18.* Parenthèses Editions.

Fessou, Didier. 2012. "L'Huile et le vinaigre." *Le Soleil numérique* (blog), January 29.

FranceMaghreb2. 2021. "Charte des principes du conseil national des imams: le texte intégral." January 18. https://www.francemaghreb2.fr/news/charte-des-principes-du-conseil-national-des-imams-le-texte-integral-21574.

Gabon, Alain. 2016. "The Twin Myth of the Western 'Jihadist Threat' and 'Islamic Radicalisation.'" *Cordoba Papers* 4, no. 1: 3–26. http://thecordobafoundation.com/publications/arches/cordoba-papers-the-twin-myths-of-the-western-jihadist-threat-and-islamic-radicalisation/.

Ginio, Ruth, and Jennifer Sessions. 2016. "French Colonial Rule." *Oxford Bibliographies*, February 25. DOI: 10.1093/OBO/9780199846733-0029.

Grande Mosquée de Paris. 2021. *Charte des principes pour l'islam de France.* January 20. https://cdnuploads.aa.com.tr/uploads/userFiles/a0375fc1-552e-4508-bc69-6dc1b8417822/Charte-des-principes-17.01.2021-1-.pdf.

Hargreaves, Alex G., and Mark McKinney. 1998. "Introduction: The Post-Colonial Problematic in France." In *Post-Colonial Cultures in France*, edited by Alex G. Hargreaves and Mark McKinney. Routledge.

Haski, Pierre. 2016. "La Carte de l'athéisme dans le monde: la France numéro 4." *L'Obs* 18, November 21.

Houellebecq, Michel. 2015. *Soumission.* Flammarion.

Lean, Nathan. 2017. *The Islamophobia Industry: How the Right Manufactures Hatred of Muslims.* Pluto Press.

Liogier, Raphaël. 2012. *Le mythe de l'islamisation: Essai sur une obsession collective.* Seuil.

Najib, Kawtar. 2022. "France." In *European Islamophobia Report 2021*, edited by Enes Bayrakli and Farid Hafez. https://islamophobiareport.com/islamophobiareport-2022.pdf.

République française. 2021. "LOI n° 2021–1109 du 24 août 2021 confortant le respect des principes de la République." August 25. https://www.legifrance.gouv.fr/jorf/id/JORFTEXT000043964778.

Riverbends Channel. 2013. "Malcolm X: The House Negro and the Field
   Negro (1963)." YouTube. February 7. https://www.youtube.com/
   watch?v=jf7rsCAfQCo.

Rougier, Bernard. 2020. *Les Territoires conquis de l'islamisme.* PUF.

Scott, Joan Wallach. 2007. *The Politics of the Veil.* Princeton University Press.

Wike, Richard. 2016. "5 Ways Americans and Europeans Are Different." Pew
   Research Center, April 19. https://www.pewresearch.org/short-reads/
   2016/04/19/5-ways-americans-and-europeans-are-different/.

Zempi, Irene, and Imran Awan. 2021. *The Routledge International Handbook of
   Islamophobia.* Routledge.

4

The Best Muslims Are the Ones Who Leave

Neoliberalism and the Limits of Accommodation

JINAN BASTAKI

Islamophobia does not exist in a vacuum, and throughout the ages, it has been justified in different ways. As Grosfoguel (2012, 13) notes, the inferiorization of Muslims and other non-European "Others" took different forms throughout the centuries: from "people with the 'wrong religion' (imperial difference) into the inferior 'savages and primitives' of 'people without civilization' (colonial difference)." Within the current context of hegemonic neoliberalism, Muslims are generally portrayed as unfit for neoliberal subjectivities. Muslims—whether at home or abroad—are racialized and seen as inferior due to their cultural and religious practices; thus, they need some sort of intervention by neoliberalism.

However, this same neoliberalism not only tolerates but welcomes Muslims when large amounts of capital are involved. Using three significant examples—the granting of visa waivers for citizens of Gulf

Arab states to travel to the UK and the EU, the accommodation of their values and practices, and the so-called "Muslim ban" by the Trump administration—this chapter demonstrates that at the intersection of Islamophobia, neoliberalism, and nationalism, "foreign" Muslims with capital—with all their peculiarities that are problematized in the place they are temporarily visiting—can be accommodated and even embraced, since they typify the borderless movement of capital and, on the surface, colourblind nature of the neoliberal order. However, contrary to claims of multicultural neoliberalism, this does not dismantle racism but, rather, helps maintain it. These Muslims come from states that have peacefully accepted neoliberal hegemony and they bring their capital and they leave. Hence, they make no demands for structural change. Indeed, Islamophobic discourse can continue to be used by neoliberals, nationalists, and neoliberal nationalists when convenient and to further their aims, particularly against racialized subjects already failed by global capitalism, while at the same time appearing to welcome these same racialized subjects.

This chapter first sketches out the theoretical framework for the intersection of neoliberalism, Islamophobia, and nationalism. Then, through the examples described above, it explains the practical manifestation of these intersections. Finally, it explores the limits of acceptance within the neoliberal framework and the wider implications.

Islamophobia, the Muslim Other, and Neoliberalism

There is a long history of constructing Muslims as the Other (Green 2019; Allen 2016; Grosfoguel and Mielants 2006). Indeed, the "Orient" more broadly has served as Europe's most repeated image of the Other, and ideas about the Orient reiterate the latter's superiority over oriental backwardness, whatever form that took (Said 1979). Countries as varied as Egypt or Iraq, Morocco, or Turkey, as well as their people, are essentialized in such a way to justify imperialism and colonialism and to serve as a contrast to the West. As biological racism became largely unacceptable, it was replaced by cultural racism, which focuses on the supposed cultural inferiority of a group of people—in this case, because of their Islam—but essentializes them in the same way that biological arguments do. Indeed, Muslims in different countries are overwhelmingly associated with non-European national origins, such as being Bangladeshi or Pakistani in the UK, or North African in France (Grosfoguel 2012). Through this racialization, Muslims around the world are viewed as a uniform group, holding innate characteristics (Carr 2021).

The racialization and problematization of Muslims—Islamophobia—can be manifested in different ways. It may be explicit or implicit in certain laws (Kahn 2010; Hagopian 2004), or through discrimination in different sectors (Bartkoski et al. 2018; Brüß 2008). It can be at a popular level and manifested either in overt actions (Kielinger and Paterson 2013; Organization for Security and Co-operation in Europe n.d.; Bakht 2022) or in subtleties that under-lie everyday interactions through microaggressions and prejudices (Abid et al 2021; Bakali 2016; Steele et al. 2015). It can be, and often is, perpetuated by the media, which can both mirror and influence popular opinion as well as politicians (Saeed 2007; Saleem et al. 2017; Ahmed and Matthes 2017; Shaver et al. 2017).

More recently, some have situated anti-Muslim bias and marginalization within the framework of the hegemonic neoliberal-ism that emerged after the 1970s (Carr 2021; Waikar 2018; Kabel 2014). Neoliberalism is not simply about economic policies that promote financial and market liberalization, deregulation, and privatization. Rather, as Wendy Brown notes, it is a "governing rationality" that changes every human sphere "according to a specific image of the economic" (Brown 2015, 9–10). In the neoliberal imaginary, neoliberal policies grant freedom and opportunity to all, and racism is reduced to individual tendencies as opposed to a structural system (Davis 2007).

For those who have reaped the benefits of neoliberalism, it is due to individual merit, and failure to attain these benefits must be linked to lack of hard work (Davison and Shire 2015). Yet the global economy is far from neutral. The effects of neoliberalism are unequal, and this can be seen in how they affect different racialized communities (Markell 2017). It is embedded in the history of racism, as Davison and Shire explain, since "the operations of the market are always underpinned by unequal power structures" (2015, 83), race being an important one. Insofar as neoliberalism is a phase of capitalism, and "capitalism *is* racial capitalism," it produces, exploits, and moves through "relations of severe inequality among human groups" (Melamed 2015, 77). Indeed, early proponents of neoliberalism were opposed to any ethnic projects that called for government intervention to progress equality (Kymlicka 2013). The later embrace of multiculturalism came in order to create "a cosmopolitan market actor who can compete effectively across state boundaries" (Kymlicka 2013, 111), yet anyone displaced by neoliberalism is portrayed "as handicapped by their own monoculturalism and other historic-cultural deficiencies" (Melamed 2011, 1). Neoliberalism does not only result in racial inequality, it reinforces the existing racial structure of society (Roberts and Mahtani 2010). As Melamed notes,

> terms of privilege accrue to individuals and groups, such as *multicultural, reasonable, feminist,* and *law-abiding,* that make them appear fit for neoliberal subjectivity, while others are stigmatized as *monocultural, irrational, regressive, patriarchal,* or *criminal* and ruled out. Such individualization camouflages the structural and material relations positioning persons within modes of production and structures of governance. (Melamed 2011, 152, original emphasis)

Indeed, this is why nationalism—a racialized notion of who belongs to the nation and who does not—and neoliberalism also make for not-so-strange bedfellows. While neoliberals can utilize nationalist discourse for legitimacy in order to scapegoat the Other for the failings of neoliberalism and the inequality that it reinforces, neoliberals also rely on nationalism to further the neoliberal agenda by opposing international regimes that interfere with free-market principles "to advocate in favour of national fiscal and regulatory sovereignty" (Harmes 2012, 72). The racism of the far right does not generally rely on overt "blood and soil" racism but complements neoliberal racism in its focus on "cultural or behavioral, rather than purely physiological traits" (Davidson and Saull 2017, 715).

How does this relate to Muslims and Islamophobia? Muslims, as racialized subjects and quintessential threatening outsiders, are conceptualized as adversative to neoliberal values (Waikar 2018). Muslims are portrayed as the uncivilized Other abroad, in order to justify neoliberal intervention. Muslims are also subjected to social programs designed to deradicalize them to instill values congruent with the neoliberal project, and they are reduced to the binary of the "good" and the "bad" Muslim. "Good" Muslims are generally secular, Westernized, and liberal—the perfect fit for a neoliberal society— whereas "bad" Muslims are the opposite (Carr 2021). Outward markers of Muslimness are a reminder of group affiliations that are in opposition to the neoliberal ideal. Hence, Islamic practices are problematized and can be restricted domestically. Insofar as citizens in liberal democracies have a say in the laws and mobilize to impose their political will, these perceptions of Muslims lead to institutionalizing (or reinforcing institutional) discrimination against Muslims who fail to integrate into the neoliberal order. For example, in a referendum in 2021, Swiss voters voted to ban the niqab, despite the fact that only 21 to 37 women in total actually wore a niqab; both the Parliament and executive council were against the referendum; and, due to COVID-19, face masks in shops, restaurants, cultural venues, and other public settings and events were mandatory at the time of the vote (Oltermann 2021).

Many neoliberal nation-states have actively regulated migrant groups and excluded those who are seen as economically undesirable (Lueck, Due, and Augoustinos 2015). But what happens when an "economically desirable" migrant looks like the undesirable, problematic Muslim?

The Neoliberal Exception: Accommodating Muslim Capital

This section will examine the intersection of neoliberalism and Islamophobia with reference to three main incidents. The first is the waiving of visa requirements for citizens of some Gulf Arab states by the Schengen countries and the UK. This situation was chosen because it reflects the institutional level of neoliberal-Islamophobic logic, where certain Muslims are privileged despite persistent inferiorization by governments. The second demonstrates neoliberal accommodation for wealthy Muslim tourists in places that receive high numbers of them, such as London and Munich. This is, again, despite the fact that those same accommodations incite intense criticism and debate when they are made for Muslim citizens. Finally, we will examine US President Donald Trump's 2015 comments about a "complete shut-down of Muslims" coupled with the countries chosen as part of the ban, and the concurrent measures taken against popular airlines from Arab countries, such as Emirates. This incident was chosen because it exposes the flimsiness of the welcoming of Muslims in the neoliberal order, as well as neoliberalism's relationship with Islamophobic nationalism.

The aim of this section is to show that foreign Muslims are not only tolerated but are even welcomed when they bring vast capital, particularly when their stay is temporary and purely or largely related to the capital that they bring. This fits squarely with the neoliberal ethos that the markets are "colourblind" and that neoliberalism is the answer to racism. However, it is precisely the temporary nature of their stay that means that Islamophobic stereotypes need not be dismantled and, indeed, can continue to be perpetuated, since Muslim tourists make no demands upon public institutions. However, once there is interference in profit-making, Islamophobic tropes are used to fuel racist nationalism and refuse entry.

The Visa Waiver

In 2014, citizens from four Gulf Arab states—the UAE, Qatar, Oman, and Kuwait—were permitted to travel to the UK with an electronic visa waiver document, as opposed to having to apply for a visa beforehand, which allowed them to visit the UK for up to six months without a visa (Gower 2015). In June 2022, it was announced that visa restrictions for UAE and other Gulf state passport holders would be lifted in 2023, meaning that they would be given visa-free access. The reason was largely economic: £1.2 billion was injected into the UK economy in 2012 by tourists from Gulf Cooperation Council countries. It was reported that those tourists spent an average of £3,417 per person per visit, which is significantly above the spending of nationals from other countries (UK Government 2021). The decision to grant waivers was made under the Conservative and Liberal Democrat coalition government, which had pursued more restrictive policies for non-European immigration. For example, they had introduced measures to limit the number of visas available to skilled workers with a job offer, reintroduced visa interviews, and limited international students' rights to work and bring family members to the UK. They also closed the post-study work visa program and replaced it with more limited provisions; they likewise legislated for the Immigration Act 2014, which was intended to make it easier to remove people who had been denied permission to stay in the UK (by reducing the scope to appeal and simplifying the removal process) and to create a more "hostile environment" for people living in the UK without valid immigration status, among others (Gower 2015). This same Conservative government has faced many accusations of Islamophobia.

In 2016, Conservative candidate Zac Goldsmith's campaign for mayor of London against Labour candidate Sadiq Khan was overtly Islamophobic. Goldsmith accused Khan of having associations with alleged extremists (Booth 2016). Then-Prime Minister David Cameron linked Mayor Khan to Suliman Gani, who was accused of supporting ISIL (which was untrue, and many conservative candidates had shared political platforms with him). Cameron had to later apologize for the slur, and former defence secretary Michael Fallon had to both apologize and pay compensation for making similar remarks (Stewart 2016). Indeed, Cameron's rhetoric has been regarded as orientalist and Islamophobic when speaking about British Muslims. A £20 million scheme was announced in 2016 to teach Muslim women English in an effort to combat segregation and extremism. The proposal and its promotional materials portrayed Muslim women as "linguistically deficient, culturally suppressed and visibly alien" (Habib 2016). But such Islamophobia is not limited to individual Conservative Party MPs and candidates. A survey published in 2019 found that the majority of Conservative Party members thought that Islam was a threat to the British way of life (Mairs 2019). Yet, it was the same Conservative Party that opened the doors to citizens of Gulf Arab states—when they benefit the economy and, more crucially, they do not stay.

On February 17, 2014, the European Parliament voted by majority to exempt Emirati nationals from the requirement of a visa for short-stay visits to countries in the Schengen Area. Of the 577 EU representatives present, 523 voted in favour of the decision, a large majority. In May of 2015, the UAE and EU signed the Schengen Area visa waiver agreement, and the final step was taken in December of 2015, when 537 of 667 European Parliament members voted in favour (European Parliament 2015). The UAE became the first Arab and Muslim-majority country to be granted visa-free access to the Schengen countries.

However, overall, Europeans view Islam as incompatible with the West (*Economist* 2015). Across the board, Muslims and Islam were regarded unfavourably in European countries, including France, Germany, Sweden, and the Netherlands (Abdelkader 2017). In the run-up to the Brexit referendum in 2016, one of the dominant discourses in the UK was that Brexit would stop Muslim immigration, even though the UK was leaving the EU—not exactly a Muslim-majority continent (Evolvi 2019). There are recorded instances of hate crimes against Muslims in many European countries during the time period the visa waivers were granted and, in the UK, particularly after Brexit. For example, in 2013, 226 anti-Muslim hate crimes were recorded in France, an increase of 11.3 percent from the previous year. In the UK, from July 2014 to July 2015, there were more than 800 anti-Muslim bias incidents in London—*multicultural London*—alone. After Brexit, there was a spike in hate crimes (TellMAMA 2017). Leaders of the extremist National Socialist Underground in Germany were on trial for the murders of ten people, primarily of Turkish heritage, between 2000 and 2007 (Abdelkader 2017). In 2013 in Sweden, there were approximately 300 reported anti-Muslim hate crimes, and most hate crimes targeted women who were visibly Muslim or communal property such as mosques (US State Department 2014). Furthermore, the institutional denial of public services to refugees from Muslim-majority countries (during the period of passing these laws, it was mainly Syrians) relied not only on the notion that public services would be overwhelmed (Parker 2015; Wilmott 2017), which can and is applied to any group of refugees and migrants, but specifically on Islamophobic prejudices focusing on threats of terrorism (Matar 2017; Rettberg and Gajjala 2016). As Wilson and Mavelli (2016, 1–2) note:

> The concurrent rise of mass displacement and violent extremism (stereotypically associated with Islam), has resulted in a complicated entanglement where "refugee" equals "Muslim" and "Muslim" equals "terrorist" in public discourse and consciousness. This is contributing to the belief that all refugees are potential

terrorists, prompting narrow policy responses primarily concerned with security rather than solidarity and humanitarianism.

Despite this, the visa-waiver agreement for the UAE was passed with an overwhelming majority at the European Parliament. The relevant part of the rapporteur's justification for granting Emiratis visa-free, short-stay travel is encapsulated in the following two sentences:

> In 2014, around 230 000 Emiratis travelled to Europe, mainly for purposes of *business or luxury tourism...* Moreover, the UAE does *not present any risk of clandestine immigration* or *threat to public policy or security.* (Gabriel 2015, emphasis added)

Before examining the specific iterations of the different party members, it is worth noting the political orientation of the voting parties. The Alliance of Liberals and Democrats for Europe (ALDE) party is liberal centrist. The Progressive Alliance of Socialists and Democrats (S&D) is centre-left in orientation, while the European People's Party (EPP) is centre-right and liberal-conservative in orientation. GUE/NGL represents the left in the European Parliament (EP) and is composed of left-wing and far-left members.[1] Europe of Nations and Freedom represents the far right and is anti-immigration. The European Conservatives and Reformists (ECR) is a centre-right political group that is anti-federalist and right-wing. The Europe of Freedom and Direct Democracy (EFDD) was a Eurosceptic and populist political group. Finally, Non-Inscrits (NI) are members of the European Parliament who do not belong to one of the recognized political groups.

GUE/NGL members either abstained or voted against the agreement due to the human rights record of the UAE, with the majority abstaining. With the exception of a few from the far-left party and some NIs, who cited the human rights record, it was the far right and anti-immigration parties that voted against. The discourse centred on the threat of so-called Islamic terrorism and increased flow of refugees. This is despite the fact that many recognized that, for the UAE in particular, there was no threat of illegal immigration nor any security concerns. For example, Marine LePen, the notorious French far-right member of the EP, stated:

> I voted against the EU-UAE short-stay visa waiver agreement. According to Ms. Gabriel's report, the country in question poses no threat either in terms of irregular migration, or in terms of security and public order. Regarding mobility, confidence in visa applicants is reportedly high, with the visa refusal rate being relatively low. Visa liberalization simplifies travel conditions. However, we have a duty to ask ourselves whether it is appropriate to conclude visa waiver agreements at a time when *the risk of terrorist attacks is real* and when the European Union has lost all immigration control. (European Parliament 2015, emphasis added)

In terms of those who voted for, however, the majority were from the ALDE (liberal centrist), S&D (centre-left), and EPP (centre-right), with some votes from EFDD and ECR. Indeed, the bulk of those voting for the agreement cited trade between the countries, the number of Emiratis travelling for luxury tourism, as well as the number of Europeans residing in and visiting the UAE. Some representatives added the following points:

> Hugues Bayet (S&D): The rapporteur considers that the UAE does not present any risk *related to illegal immigration, public order or security* and has provided the European institutions with

useful information in this regard. In addition, they issue biometric passports to their
citizens.

Andrea Bocskor (EPP), in writing: With regard to
mobility, the available data show a high
degree of reliability for visa applicants, with
few rejected applications. The country poses
*no threat to either irregular migration or security
and public order.*

Fabio Massimo Castaldo (EFDD): Furthermore, the
UAE does not pose a threat either in terms
of *irregular migration or in terms of security and
public order.* I therefore voted in favour.

Brice Hortefeux (EPP): This country is an essential
commercial and strategic partner for France,
especially on the military level, since it hosts
a French military base on its territory. *The
migration risk for this country, whose GDP per
capita is equivalent to that of France, is very low.*
(European Parliament 2015, emphasis added)

While the benefit of luxury tourism from the UAE to Europe was
unanimously agreed upon, it was additionally emphasized that
migration and security risks are both low. The generally visibly Arab
Muslims coming from the UAE would not be staying—they would
bring their capital and then leave. They are welcome to assert markers
of their Muslimness as long as that is related to their capital and their
temporary stay. Islamophobic stereotypes can be downplayed or even
ignored. To quote Grosfoguel (2012, 15):

The so-called neutrality of the West is contradicted
when Muslims affirm their practices and identities in
the public sphere and when they make claims against

discrimination in education or the labor market as citizens with equal rights within Western states.

There is no threat from Emiratis choosing to become citizens of Europe or using visa-free travel to do so. Allowing them access that is not available to others is because, unlike the stereotypical "bad" Muslims of the default Islamophobic imaginary—easily associated with violence and backwards practices, tainting the civilized European landscape—*these* Muslims pose a low terrorism threat. Hence, and as will be further discussed in the next section, accommodating their cultural and religious idiosyncrasies is a temporary measure that can increase capital and, at the same time, ostensibly affirm the values of multiculturalism, liberalism, and tolerance.

The Neoliberal Multicultural City

Observant Muslims who bring vast capital also have needs particular to their faith: prayer spaces, halal food, and possibly places that respect the particular needs of Muslim women, such as separate wellness areas. Accommodating these Muslim practices has been the subject of controversy in various European countries. We will examine two of the most public disputes: halal food in the UK and separate spaces for women in Germany. These incidents were chosen because they were quite high-profile and can clearly be juxtaposed with the measures taken to welcome other Muslims.

Halal Food in London
In London, which is generally considered very multicultural and diverse, there are many Arab, Turkish, Persian, Malaysian, and South Asian restaurants serving halal meat. Additionally, some mainstream chains serve halal chicken. Most famously, a controversy erupted in May 2014 regarding the chain restaurant Pizza Express, which was "discovered" to be serving halal chicken by *The Sun* tabloid, and other tabloids and papers followed suit in commenting on the issue (Davies 2014; Bold

2014). One might assume that this was simply sensationalization of an issue by one popular tabloid. However, it resulted in mainstream commentary (Henley 2014) and the problematization of the serving of halal meat, with then-deputy prime minister Nick Clegg weighing in on the matter (Murphy 2014). A Twitter campaign, #boycottpizzaexpress, revealed explicit Islamophobic undertones (Taylor 2014).

At the same time, if one visits the high-end restaurants of Mayfair, one will find many halal options on the menu. Kai, a Michelin-starred restaurant no less, offers halal chicken. China Tang and Cut, both part of the upscale Dorchester Collection hotels owned by the Sultan of Brunei, offer halal choices. The main menu at Novikov, an upmarket Mayfair restaurant owned by a Russian businessman, clearly labels halal items, which turns out to be most of the dishes. Aside from being out of reach for most regular people, including London's native Muslim population—who, on average, are socio-economically less well off (Muslim Council of Britain 2011)[2]—these establishments cater to the specific profile of the wealthy Arab Muslim tourist.

Generally, most people are not mindful about the slaughter of their food, unless there is some high-profile media controversy that brings to the fore issues of animal welfare. The killing of animals for food is something most people prefer not to know, and removing animal slaughter from public view was part of the European civilizing process (Lever 2019). As Schlegelmilch and colleagues show, animosity towards Muslims is what negatively impacts the purchase of halal products by other segments of society (Schlegelmilch, Khan, and Hair 2016). They show that while some businesses wish to attract the Muslim consumer base by having halal offerings, they need to understand that it may negatively impact the consumers who are hostile to Muslims. Indeed, Lever argues that the controversy around halal slaughter is linked to the increasing visibility of Muslim immigrants and "to wider anxieties about immigration and integration"; that "the slaughter practice of *outsiders* is often seen as cruel, barbaric and inhumane, as very often, are the *outsiders* themselves" (Lever 2019, 891, emphasis in text). Indeed, this is why halal food at, for example, Pakistani restaurants in the UK has not been controversial, since it is within a racialized community space and does not encroach upon the mainstream. When some upscale Mayfair restaurants cater to Muslim tourists, it does not touch upon issues of immigration, integration or "national values" and hence is not threatening in the same way. Islamophobia can remain for the citizens, while profit-making exceptions are made for the temporary visitors with capital.

Women-only Swimming Pools in Germany

The Othering of Muslims can more clearly be seen in the battle for Muslim women's bodies. Muslim women who veil become the centre of attention and are viewed as being in particular need of saving, even if violently (Brayson 2019; Najib and Hopkins 2020; Abu-Lughod 2002). In Germany, similar to other European countries, separate hours for Muslim swimmers at public pools, or women-only pools, and wearing the burkini have been subject to controversy. One study found that 10 percent of public pools provide separate swimming hours for women (Michalowski and Behrendt 2020). Some women-only pools have been around for over a century, and they give women "the freedom of being able to walk around partially or completely naked without the male gaze" (The Local Germany 2017). Yet, in Regensburg, Germany, a public pool banned the wearing of the burkini after one Muslim woman wore it to a women-only pool in the city. The mayor justified this, saying, "This also contradicts the fundamental ideas of integration and mutual understanding, which [are] always being discussed in many towns" (Malm 2016). Moreover, when a women-only private gym opened in Cologne in April 2007, German media depicted it as an example of Muslim segregation, despite being a private facility open to all women (Shavit and Wiesenbach 2012). Yet in the summer months in Munich, some international luxury hotels have been providing the same for their international Muslim patrons. Le Meridien and the Sofitel, both five-star hotels in prime locations and frequented by many tourists from Gulf Arab states, have provided women-only days and/or hours at the spa and pool to cater to their clients.[3] This was not advertised on their website. Profitability aside, this is within a context where the practices of Muslim women have been problematized in Germany, not simply in public facilities, but private ones as well.

When Muslim women are citizens, liberal feminism expects and sometimes even demands that they exercise their "freedom" and "choice" by looking like the Western feminine subject (Sheth 2022). Indeed, when they are not citizens, military interventions are justified in order to save Muslim women, usually using images of Muslim women wearing the full face veil as the ultimate symbol of their subjugation, ignoring other forms of oppressions that may be a direct result of foreign intervention (Hirschkind and Mahmood 2002). Such is the relationship with Muslim women who veil. Yet, when Muslim women are temporary visitors, bringing vast capital with them as they frequent seemingly cosmopolitan cities, accommodations for their veiling practices and needs are less controversial.

Neoliberal multiculturalism tolerates these differences until they interfere with profit-making.

When Capital is Threatened

At the end of 2015, Donald Trump called for a "total and complete shut-down of Muslims entering the United States" (Taylor 2015). This statement came after the San Bernadino shootings by a Muslim couple, one of whom was a US citizen and the other in the country legally as his spouse. After winning the election, then-President Trump issued an executive order on January 28, 2017, blocking refugees and travellers with passports from seven Muslim-majority countries for a period of ninety days: Iran, Iraq, Libya, Somalia, Sudan, Syria, and Yemen. Though the order was initially blocked by the lower courts, the

US Supreme Court upheld an amended list of states in the ban: Iran, Libya, Somalia, Syria, Yemen, and North Korea as well as political officials from Venezuela. The ban was expanded in 2020 to include more countries in Africa and Asia, including Nigeria, Eritrea, Myanmar, and Kyrgyzstan, while Sudan and Tanzania would no longer be allowed to participate in the Diversity Visa lottery. President Trump used xenophobic and racist language against different non-white groups— calling Mexican immigrants criminals and rapists, African nations "shithole" countries—and he emphasized Islamophobic stereotypes to justify the ban (Waikar 2018). The numbers of refugees to be admitted was also slashed by about 80 percent, exemplifying the connection between neoliberal, nationalistic, and Islamophobic rhetoric to justify the exclusion of asylum seekers (Lueck, Due, and Augoustinos 2015). In 2020, Trump warned supporters at a rally in Minnesota (a state that had already elected a former refugee from Somalia, Representative Ilhan Omar) that voting for Biden would result in "a 700 percent increase in the importation of refugees from the most dangerous places in the world, including Yemen, Syria, and Somalia...Opening the floodgates to radical Islamic terrorists" (Packer 2020).

What is evident from Trump's list of banned countries are their shared economic and ethnic profiles: largely poor, Global South states, home to the stereotypical "undesirable" immigrant. Furthermore, it is particularly telling that Muslim-majority Arab Gulf states are glaringly absent from the list of banned countries despite the call for a "total and complete" ban against Muslims. It can be argued that this reflects political alliances that are more important than convenient Islamophobia. However, in March of 2017, citing security concerns and threats of terrorist infiltration (BBC News 2017a), the US banned electronic devices larger than a mobile phone from cabin luggage on flights of nine airlines[4] from ten Middle Eastern airports[5] that were active partners in the coalition against ISIS (BBC News 2017a). The International Air Transport Association (IATA) disputed the effectiveness of this ban as a security measure (BBC News 2017b).

While some saw this as another iteration of the Muslim ban (Al-Qassemi 2017), others viewed the measures as simply a pretext "to stifle competition from Gulf airlines and to encourage US-bound passengers to fly on American carriers" (Kurzman 2017). Indeed, while the electronic device ban seems to be the antithesis of neoliberal economic policies, the domestic US airlines that had flagged the issue did not use protectionist rhetoric but neoliberal rationale: according to them, Gulf states were unfairly subsidizing state-owned carriers (Shepardson and Wise 2017). These airlines were accused of not participating in a true free-market, neoliberal system. Yet, as Davidson notes, "Capitalism is based on competition, but capitalists want competition to take place on their terms; they do not want to suffer the consequences if they lose" (Davidson 2008, 36). Hence, it was easy to rely on Islamophobic tropes to support the ban. Trump, as many have observed, could focus on racist, nationalist, and anti-neoliberal discourse, winning the hearts of his electoral base at home, while pushing for further domestic deregulation, lowering of taxes, and dismantling of welfare. As Cozzolino (2018, 69) observed:

> It is a populist capitalization of the structural contradictions of neoliberalism and of the crisis of legitimation of the traditional political elites, and, at the same time, a strengthening of those (neoliberal) patterns which have determined economic imbalances and social unrest—yet, intertwined with new nationalist elements.

While Muslims may be accommodated based on the wealth that they bring in to a country, the limits of that accommodation become apparent when capital is threatened. To drum up support for restrictions, one need not solely rely on neoliberal justifications, though these will feature, but existing stereotypes about Muslims that have not been dismantled by the privilege they have received in certain areas and spheres. Indeed, the privileges are perhaps meant to be exceptional, for some Muslims and not others, based on the flow of capital that they facilitate and how well they fit into the neoliberal order.

Conclusion

Islamophobia in many Western, non-Muslim-majority countries has a deep history and is reproduced in different ways and in different spheres, particularly after the events of 9/11. But there have always been exceptions, particularly when the exceptions benefit capitalist order and neoliberal logic. Within the framework of neoliberalism, Islamophobic tropes are reproduced to cement the identity of the Other by portraying Muslims as culturally inferior and unfit for the neoliberal order, justifying foreign intervention and domestic restrictions. Yet this is not so for all Muslims. While the binary of the "good Muslim, bad Muslim" posits that the "good Muslim" is secular and Western, shedding the most overt, uncomfortable aspects of their Muslim observance, the wealthy, foreign, mobile "good Muslim" need not do so.[6] As Grosfoguel (2012, 15) observes,

> In the case of the Anglo-American world, multicul-
> turalism and diversity operates to conceal White
> Supremacy. The racial minorities are allowed to
> celebrate their history, carnival and identity as long
> as they leave intact the white supremacy racial/ethnic
> hierarchy of the status quo.

This "good" Muslim is not forced to erase the outward markers of their Muslim identity and religious observance; on the contrary, they are welcomed and celebrated. Granting wealthy, foreign Muslims the privilege of access and accommodation for their religious practice benefits the neoliberal order and does not disrupt it. It has the appearance of true, middle-class cosmopolitanism that welcomes certain types of differences but does nothing to affect structural change from within. Indeed, this allows for keeping Islamophobic tropes intact, and these can still potentially be used to justify intervention—whether domestically or internationally—when Muslims "step out of line."

NOTES

1. Confederal Group of the European United Left/Nordic Green Left
2. In a 2011 census, it was found that almost half of the Muslim population lives in the most deprived areas, and a high percentage of Muslim households rely on social housing. See Muslim Council of Britain (blog), "British Muslims in Numbers: Census Analysis," https://mcb.org.uk/report/british-muslims-in-numbers/.
3. This was ascertained through personal visits by the author in 2013, as well as a more recent study of the guest reviews of the hotels. "Sofitel Munich Bayerpost Hotel," https://www.agoda.com/sofitel-munich-bayerpost-hotel/hotel/munich-de.html; August 2, 2016, review: "A very nice hotel with great rooms and a fantastic location. The spa, however, cannot be beat. It is amazing and because they work to cater to a muslim guest population, the spa was only for women from 10pm–midnight. My wife and two older teenage girls LOVED it."
4. Emirates, Etihad Airways, Qatar Airways, Turkish Airlines, Saudia, Royal Jordanian, Kuwait Airways, EgyptAir, and Royal Air Maroc.
5. Egypt, Morocco, Jordan, the United Arab Emirates, Saudi Arabia, Kuwait, Qatar, and Turkey.
6. As Melamed shows, global neoliberal multiculturalism requires certain cultural and economic criteria. See Jodi Melamed, *Represent and Destroy: Rationalizing Violence in the New Racial Capitalism* (University of Minnesota Press, 2011).

REFERENCES

Abdelkader, Engy. 2017. "A Comparative Analysis of European Islamophobia: France, UK, Germany, Netherlands, and Sweden." *UCLA Journal of Islamic and Near Eastern Law* 16, no. 1: 29–63.

Abid, Abubakar, Maheen Farooqi, and James Zou. 2021. "Persistent Anti-Muslim Bias in Large Language Models." In *Proceedings of the 2021 AAAI/ACM Conference on AI, Ethics, and Society*, 298–306.

Abu-Lughod, Lila. 2002. "Do Muslim Women Really Need Saving? Anthropological Reflections on Cultural Relativism and Its Others." *American Anthropologist* 104, no. 3: 783–790.

Ahmed, Saifuddin, and Jörg Matthes. 2017. "Media Representation of Muslims and Islam from 2000 to 2015: A Meta-Analysis." *International Communication Gazette* 79, no. 3: 219–244.

Allen, Chris. 2016. *Islamophobia*. Routledge.

Al-Qassemi, Sultan Sooud. 2017. "Trump's Laptop Ban Targets Gulf Airlines." Middle East Institute. March 22. https://www.mei.edu/publications/trumps-laptop-ban-targets-gulf-airlines.

Bakali, Naved. 2016. *Islamophobia: Understanding Anti-Muslim Racism through the Lived Experiences of Muslim Youth, Vol. 5*. Springer.

Bakht, Natasha. 2022. "Niqab Bans Boost Hate Crimes against Muslims and Legalize Islamophobia." *The Conversation*, May 25. https://theconversation.com/niqab-bans-boost-hate-crimes-against-muslims-and-legalize-islamophobia-podcast-180012.

Bartkoski, Timothy, Ellen Lynch, Chelsea Witt, and Cort Rudolph. 2018. "A Meta-Analysis of Hiring Discrimination against Muslims and Arabs." *Personnel Assessment and Decisions* 4, no. 2: 1.

BBC News. 2017a. "Flight Ban on Laptops 'Sparked by IS Threat.'" March 22. https://www.bbc.com/news/world-us-canada-39348615.

BBC News. 2017b. "Laptop Cabin Ban 'Ineffective' Says IATA." March 28. https://www.bbc.com/news/business-39425532.

Bold, Ben. 2014. "UK Supermarket Shoppers Unknowingly Eating Halal Meat." *Campaign Live*, May 8. https://www.campaignlive.co.uk/article/uk-supermarket-shoppers-unknowingly-eating-halal-meat/1293385?utm_source=website&utm_medium=social.

Booth, Robert. 2016. "Tories Step up Attempts to Link Sadiq Khan to Extremists." *The Guardian*, April 20. https://www.theguardian.com/politics/2016/apr/20/tory-claims-sadiq-khan-alleged-links-extremists.

Brayson, Kimberley. 2019. "Of Bodies and Burkinis: Institutional Islamophobia, Islamic Dress, and the Colonial Condition." *Journal of Law and Society* 46, no. 1: 55–82.

Brown, Wendy. 2015. *Undoing the Demos: Neoliberalism's Stealth Revolution.* MIT Press.

Brüß, Joachim. 2008. "Experiences of Discrimination Reported by Turkish, Moroccan and Bangladeshi Muslims in Three European Cities." *Journal of Ethnic and Migration Studies* 34, no. 6: 875–894. https://doi.org/10.1080/13691830802211166.

Carr, James. 2021. "Islamophobia, Neoliberalism, and the Muslim 'Other.'" *Insight Turkey* 23, no. 2: 83–106.

Cozzolino, Adriano. 2018. "Trumpism as Nationalist Neoliberalism: A Critical Enquiry into Donald Trump's Political Economy." *Interdisciplinary Political Studies* 4, no. 1: 47–73.

Davidson, Neil. 2008. "Nations and Neoliberalism." *Variant* 32: 36–38.

Davidson, Neil, and Richard Saull. 2017. "Neoliberalism and the Far-Right: A Contradictory Embrace." *Critical Sociology* 43, no. 4–5: 707–724.

Davies, Emily. 2014. "Pizza Express Reveal All the Chicken They Use Is Halal." *Daily Mail Online*, May 7. https://www.dailymail.co.uk/news/article-2622052/Pizza-Express-reveal-chicken-use-halal-dont-tell-customers-unless-ask-staff.html.

Davis, Dana-Ain. 2007. "Narrating the Mute: Racializing and Racism in a Neoliberal Moment." *Souls* 9, no. 4: 346–360.

Davison, Sally, and George Shire. 2015. "Race, Migration and Neoliberalism." *Soundings* 59 (Spring): 81–95.

Economist. 2015. "Islam in Europe," January 7. https://www.economist.com/graphic-detail/2015/01/07/islam-in-europe.

European Parliament. 2015. "United Arab Emirates Agreement: Short-Stay Visa Waiver—Results of Votes in Parliament—2015/0062(NLE) — A8-0324/2015." Legislative Observatory, December 15. https://oeil.secure.europarl.europa.eu/oeil/popups/sda.do?id=26380&l=en.

Evolvi, Giulia. 2019. "#Islamexit: Islamophobia and Twitter after Brexit." *LSE Blogs* (blog). February 28. https://blogs.lse.ac.uk/brexit/2019/02/28/islamexit-islamophobia-and-twitter-after-brexit/.

Gabriel, Mariya. 2015. "Recommendation on the Draft Council Decision on the Conclusion, on Behalf of the European Union, of the Agreement between the European Union and the United Arab Emirates on the Short-Stay Visa Waiver | A8-0324/2015 |." European Parliament, November 16. https://www.europarl.europa.eu/doceo/document/A-8-2015-0324_EN.html.

Gower, Melanie. 2015. "Immigration and Asylum: Changes Made by the Coalition Government 2010–2015." SN/HA/5829. UK Home Office.

Green, Todd H. 2019. *The Fear of Islam: An Introduction to Islamophobia in the West.* 2nd edition. Fortress Press.

Grosfoguel, Ramon. 2012. "The Multiple Faces of Islamophobia." *Islamophobia Studies Journal* 1, no. 1: 9–33.

Grosfoguel, Ramon, and Eric Mielants. 2006. "The Long-Duree Entanglement between Islamophobia and Racism in the Modern/Colonial Capitalist/ Patriarchal World-System." *Human Architecture: Journal of the Sociology of Self-Knowledge* 1 (Fall): 1–12.

Habib, Sadia. 2016. "David Cameron Should Celebrate Muslim Women, Not Strip Them of Their Identity." *The Conversation*, January 21. http:// theconversation.com/david-cameron-should-celebrate-muslim-women-not-strip-them-of-their-identity-53347

Hagopian, Elaine C. 2004. *Civil Rights In Peril: The Targeting of Arabs and Muslims.* Pluto Press.

Harmes, Adam. 2012. "The Rise of Neoliberal Nationalism." *Review of International Political Economy* 19, no. 1: 59–86.

Henley, Jon. 2014. "Which Restaurant Chains Have Gone Halal—and Why?" *The Guardian*, May 7. https://www.theguardian.com/lifeandstyle/2014/ may/07/halal-meat-restaurant-menus-humane-slaughter.

Hirschkind, Charles, and Saba Mahmood. 2002. "Feminism, the Taliban, and Politics of Counter-Insurgency." *Anthropological Quarterly* 75, no. 2: 339–354.

Kabel, Ahmed. 2014. "The Islamophobic-Neoliberal-Educational Complex." *Islamophobia Studies Journal* 2, no. 2: 58–75.

Kahn, Robert A. 2010. "Are Muslims the New Catholics-Europe's Headscarf Laws in Comparative Historical Perspective." *Duke Journal of Comparative and International Law* 21: 567.

Kielinger, Vicky, and Susan Paterson. 2013. "Hate Crimes against London's Muslim Communities: An Analysis of Incidents Recorded by the Metropolitan Police Service 2005–2012." London: Metropolitan Police Service.

Kurzman, Charles. 2017. "Trump's Muslim Laptop Ban." *POLITICO*, April 4. https://www.politico.com/magazine/story/2017/04/trumps-muslim-laptop-ban-214984.

Kymlicka, Will. 2013. "Neoliberal Multiculturalism." In *Social Resilience in the Neoliberal Era*, edited by Peter Hall and Michèle Lamont. Cambridge University Press.

Lever, John. 2019. "Halal Meat and Religious Slaughter: From Spatial Concealment to Social Controversy—Breaching the Boundaries of the Permissible?" *Environment and Planning C: Politics and Space* 37, no. 5: 889–907. https://doi.org/10.1177/2399654418813267.

Lueck, Kerstin, Clemence Due, and Martha Augoustinos. 2015. "Neoliberalism and Nationalism: Representations of Asylum Seekers in the Australian Mainstream News Media." *Discourse & Society* 26, no. 5: 608–629.

Mairs, Nicholas. 2019. "Most Tory Members Believe Islam Is 'a Threat to British Way of Life,' Poll Finds." *Politics Home*, July 8. https://www.politicshome.com/news/article/most-tory-members-believe-islam-is-a-threat-to-british-way-of-life-poll-finds.

Malm, Sara. 2016. "German Swimming Pool Bans the BURQINI after Women Complained." *Daily Mail Online*, June 10. https://www.dailymail.co.uk/news/article-3634754/German-swimming-pool-bans-BURQINI-women-complained-saw-Muslim-bather-wearing-one.html.

Markell, Patchen. 2017. "Neoliberalism's Uneven Revolution: Reflections on Wendy Brown's Undoing the Demos." *Theory & Event* 20, no. 2: 520–527.

Matar, Dina. 2017. "Media Coverage of the Migration Crisis in Europe: A Confused and Polarized Narrative." *IEMed Mediterranean Yearbook*, 292–295.

Melamed, Jodi. 2011. *Represent and Destroy: Rationalizing Violence in the New Racial Capitalism*. University of Minnesota Press.

Melamed, Jodi. 2015. "Racial Capitalism." *Critical Ethnic Studies* 1, no. 1: 76–85.

Michalowski, Ines, and Max Behrendt. 2020. "The Accommodation of Muslim Body Practices in German Public Swimming Pools." *Ethnic and Racial Studies* 43, no, 11: 2080–2098. https://doi.org/10.1080/01419870.2020.1770827.

Murphy, Joe. 2014. "Nick Clegg: I'll Eat Halal, But It Should Be Clearly Labelled." *Evening Standard*, May 8. https://www.standard.co.uk/news/politics/nick-clegg-i-ll-eat-halal-but-it-should-be-clearly-labelled-9337259.html.

Najib, Kawtar, and Peter Hopkins. 2020. "Where Does Islamophobia Take Place and Who Is Involved? Reflections from Paris and London." *Social & Cultural Geography* 21, no. 4: 458–478.

Oltermann, Philip. 2021. "Switzerland to Ban Wearing of Burqa and Niqab in Public Places." *The Guardian*, March 7. https://www.theguardian.com/world/2021/mar/07/switzerland-on-course-to-ban-wearing-of-burqa-and-niqab-in-public-places.

Organization for Security and Co-operation in Europe. n.d. "Anti-Muslim Hate Crime." OSCE Office for Democratic Institutions and

Human Rights. Accessed June 1, 2022. https://hatecrime.osce.org/
anti-muslim-hate-crime.

Packer, George. 2020. "Donald Trump's Refugee Policy Is Bureaucratic
Sadism." *The Atlantic*, October 24. https://www.theatlantic.com/
ideas/archive/2020/10/donald-trumps-refugee-policy-is-bureaucratic-
sadism/616840/.

Parker, Samuel. 2015. "'Unwanted Invaders': The Representation of Refugees
and Asylum Seekers in the UK and Australian Print Media." *ESharp* 23,
no. 1: 1–21.

Rettberg, Jill Walker, and Radhika Gajjala. 2016. "Terrorists or Cowards:
Negative Portrayals of Male Syrian Refugees in Social Media."
Feminist Media Studies 16, no. 1: 178–181.

Roberts, David J., and Minelle Mahtani. 2010. "Neoliberalizing Race, Racing
Neoliberalism: Placing 'Race' in Neoliberal Discourses." *Antipode* 42,
no. 2: 248–257.

Saeed, Amir. 2007. "Media, Racism and Islamophobia: The Representation of
Islam and Muslims in the Media." *Sociology Compass* 1, no. 2: 443–462.

Said, Edward W. 1979. *Orientalism*. Vintage.

Saleem, Muniba, Sara Prot, Craig A. Anderson, and Anthony F. Lemieux. 2017.
"Exposure to Muslims in Media and Support for Public Policies
Harming Muslims." *Communication Research* 44, no. 6: 841–869.

Schlegelmilch, Bodo B., Mubbsher Munawar Khan, and Joe F. Hair. 2016. "Halal
Endorsements: Stirring Controversy or Gaining New Customers?"
International Marketing Review 33, no. 1: 156–174.

Shaver, John H., Chris G. Sibley, Danny Osborne, and Joseph Bulbulia. 2017.
"News Exposure Predicts Anti-Muslim Prejudice." *PloS One* 12,
no. 3: e0174606.

Shavit, Uriya, and Frederic Wiesenbach. 2012. "An 'Integrating Enclave': The
Case of Al-Hayat, Germany's First Islamic Fitness Center for Women
in Cologne." *Journal of Muslim Minority Affairs* 32, no. 1: 47–61.

Shepardson, David, and Alana Wise. 2017. "Trump Administration Holds Talks
with Airlines, Keeps Pressure on Gulf Carriers." *Reuters*, December 12.
https://www.reuters.com/article/us-usa-airlines-gulf-idUSKBN1E62O8.

Sheth, Falguni A. 2022. "Anxieties of Liberalism: Secularism, Feminism, and
Suitable Muslim Women." In *Unruly Women: Race, Neocolonialism, and
the Hijab*, edited by Falguni A. Sheth. Oxford: Oxford University Press.

Steele, Rachel R., Michael T. Parker, and Brian Lickel. 2015. "Bias within Because
of Threat from Outside: The Effects of an External Call for Terrorism

on Anti-Muslim Attitudes in the United States." *Social Psychological and Personality Science* 6, no. 2: 193–200.

Stewart, Heather. 2016. "David Cameron Apologises after Saying Ex-Imam 'Supported Islamic State.'" *The Guardian*, May 11. https://www.theguardian.com/politics/2016/may/11/david-cameron-apologises-after-saying-ex-imam-supported-islamic-state.

Taylor, Adam. 2014. "Inside Britain's Big, Dumb Halal Pizza Scandal." *Washington Post*, May 8. https://www.washingtonpost.com/news/worldviews/wp/2014/05/08/inside-britains-big-dumb-halal-pizza-scandal/.

Taylor, Jessica. 2015. "Trump Calls For 'Total And Complete Shutdown Of Muslims Entering' US." *NPR*, December 7. https://www.npr.org/2015/12/07/458836388/trump-calls-for-total-and-complete-shutdown-of-muslims-entering-u-s.

TellMAMA. 2017. "How Race and Religious Public Order Offences Rose after EU Vote." *TELL MAMA* (blog), May 3. https://tellmamauk.org/how-race-and-religious-public-order-offences-rose-after-eu-vote/.

The Local Germany. 2017. "Hundreds Sign Petition to Kick Male Staff out of Historic Women-Only Baths." *The Local Germany* (blog), July 4. https://www.thelocal.de/20170704/hundreds-sign-petition-to-kick-men-out-of-historic-women-only-baths/.

UK Government. n.d. "New Visa Waiver Scheme for Qatar, Oman, the UAE and Kuwait." GOV.UK. Accessed November 10, 2021. https://www.gov.uk/government/news/new-visa-waiver-scheme-for-qatar-oman-the-uae-and-kuwait.

US State Department. 2014. "International Religious Freedom Report: Sweden." http://www.state.gov/j/drl/rls/irf/religiousfreedom/index.htm.

Waikar, Prashant. 2018. "Reading Islamophobia in Hegemonic Neoliberalism Through a Discourse Analysis of Donald Trump's Narratives." *Journal of Muslim Minority Affairs* 38, no. 2: 153–178.

Wilmott, Annabelle Cathryn. 2017. "The Politics of Photography: Visual Depictions of Syrian Refugees in UK Online Media." *Visual Communication Quarterly* 24, no. 2: 67–82.

Wilson, Erin K., and Luca Mavelli. 2016. "'Good Muslim/Bad Muslim' and 'Good Refugee/Bad Refugee' Narratives Are Shaping European Responses to the Refugee Crisis." *Religion and the Public Sphere*, December 6. http://eprints.lse.ac.uk/76440/.

II

Law, Gender, and
Secular Translations

5

Religiosity as a Threat

Muslims in Japan and Denmark

SAUL J. TAKAHASHI

Within academic and policy circles, there
is ongoing debate regarding post-secularism and how traditionally
secular states should deal with what is portrayed as an increased
prominence of religion in the public sphere.[1] The assumption that
religion had disappeared from public debate has been somewhat
unproven, and some have cast doubt on the concept of post-secularism
itself (see Schaafsma 2015; Molendijk 2015). I submit that, regardless
of whether religion has indeed become a stronger social and political
force in today's world, the fact that this debate is taking place indicates
the anxiety with which many commentators and policymakers (especially in "advanced," industrialized countries) view religion. Muslim
religiosity has increasingly been viewed as a threat in many countries,
not only to national security in a traditional, state-centric sense but
to national culture and the very fabric of society. Within this context,

protection of the rights of Muslims warrants greater attention. This chapter shall use the framework of the international law of human rights in examining the situation in two avowedly secular states, Japan and Denmark.

International Human Rights Law

Modern international human rights law is itself based largely on liberal values. It clearly envisions a secular society where no particular religion is given special preference by the government, and religion is a matter of personal choice. The founding document of international human rights law, the Universal Declaration of Human Rights (UDHR), states in Article 18: "Everyone has the right to freedom of thought, conscience and religion; this right includes freedom to change his religion or belief, and freedom, either alone or in community with others and in public or private, to manifest his religion or belief in teaching, practice, worship and observance." Freedom of religion is reiterated in legally binding form in several international human rights treaties, in particular the International Covenant on Civil and Political Rights (ICCPR). After essentially repeating the aforementioned UDHR provision in Article 18(1), the ICCPR goes on to state that "(2) No one shall be subject to coercion which would impair his freedom to have or to adopt a religion or belief of his choice." During the drafting of the ICCPR, it was stressed that "coercion" need not be physical but also includes other, more subtle forms of "guiding" persons to a particular religion, such as through legal privileges or other incentives (Nowak 2005, 416).

Many—though not all—articles of the ICCPR contain provisions stipulating when rights may be subject to limitations—for example, on grounds such as the protection of national security, public health, or morals. Article 18(1), regarding the internal beliefs and conscience of the individual (*forum interum*), is not subject to any limitations. Article 18(2), *forum externum*, does contain grounds for limitation, stating that the right to manifest one's religion "may be subject only to such limitations as are prescribed by law and are necessary to protect public safety, order, health, or morals or the fundamental rights and freedoms of others." It is particularly noteworthy that national security, a justification for limitation found in most other ICCPR articles, is not included as a reason that states can limit the exercise of religious beliefs—another issue on which there was significant debate during the drafting of the treaty (Nowak 2005). Indeed, freedom of religion is held to be so fundamental that, as stipulated in Article 4 of the ICCPR, states must ensure that right, even during a state of emergency where the existence of the state itself is endangered.

Islamophobia as the Global Norm

In particular, since the terror attacks on New York on September 11, 2001, and the advent of the so-called global War on Terror (GWOT), Muslims have been widely labelled as potential terrorists and threats to national security, with minority Muslim communities in many countries viewed as a potential fifth column. Governments have targeted Muslim communities for special law enforcement measures, surveillance, and questionable "counter radicalization programs" (see Ismael and Rippin 2010; Poynting and Morgan 2012; Tyrer 2013; American Civil Liberties Union 2017; Bazian 2017; Beydoun 2018; Zempi and Awan 2019; Bayrakli and Hafez 2021). Mosques and religious institutions have been forcibly closed under sweeping government counterterrorism powers (see CAGE 2022), and some countries have even adopted laws and policies aimed at stripping the citizenship of Muslims suspected of engaging in terrorism—in the words of some critics, a modern return to banishment (Carey 2018).

These measures have been based on the profiling of all Muslims as a terrorist threat, a practice that international and other human rights organizations have stressed on many occasions violates international human rights standards (Ruteere 2015; United Nations 2010). Though current practices would theoretically appear to constitute religious, as opposed to racial, profiling, Scheinin, the UN Human Rights Council special rapporteur on the promotion and protection of human rights and fundamental freedoms while countering terrorism, noted that "in practice, most terrorist profiles use ethnic appearance and national origin as proxies for religion, as religious affiliation is normally not readily identifiable (and in any case easy to conceal)" (Scheinin 2007, 13). Nonetheless, the prohibition on discrimination in international law applies equally to profiling based on race or religion.

The targeting of Muslim populations has taken place within a broad international trend of securitization, with the need to ensure security held as the ultimate and overarching objective by which all policies are judged. Shalhoub-Kevorkian (2015) has created the term "security theology" to describe this phenomenon, arguing that security has become an absolute value to be pursued above any and all other objectives, under any and all circumstances. Tyrer (2013) notes how societies have been grasped by a climate of fear, with a vicious cycle created whereby excessive steps against purported terrorist threats simply add to more fear.

However, measures taken by governments have been justified not only on the basis of combatting terrorism, but also by the purported need to protect the dominant culture. The era of the GWOT has been characterized by the "clash of civilizations" narrative popularized by Samuel Huntington (1993). Muslim countries (and "Islam" itself) are portrayed by governments and media outlets as barbaric, backward, and the enemy of (Western, European) civilization (see Sayyid and Vakil 2010; Morey and Yaqin 2011; Bracke and Aguilar 2020). Muslim-minority communities are portrayed as inherently abusive toward women and sexual minorities, intolerant of freedom of expression, and generally incapable (or unwilling) to embrace enlightened European values. "Parallel societies" are said to exist in areas where large concentrations of Muslim minorities live: societies where liberal values and human rights are subjects of disdain, women are oppressed, free speech is ignored, and the police dare not tread (so-called "no-go zones").

Through this process of framing the Muslim Other, a binary is created whereby *we* are held (subtly or overtly) to be the exact opposite—a process elucidated by Said (1978). Contrary to the uncivilized, savage Muslim, *we* are civilized, rational, and liberal (except when we are not). *We* respect women's rights and the freedom of expression, and *we* are always peaceful (except when we are bombing other countries to "protect democracy"). Within this discourse, opposition to Islam is portrayed not as a discriminatory attitude but "the litmus test for authentic liberalism and 'Europeanness'" (Birt 2010, 118). The situation in France, where both trends have reached alarming proportions, is so severe that at least one prominent NGO has stated that it amounts to persecution (CAGE 2022; see also Chapter 8 by Jahangeer and Chapter 3 by Gabon in this book).

Of course, the two trends (treating Muslims as a security threat and as a threat to Western culture) are not mutually exclusive. In either case, however, it must be stressed that it is the religiosity of Muslims that is at the heart of the Othering. It is the devotion of Muslims and the manifestation of their beliefs that, in the minds of policymakers and society at large, marks them as different and threatening in (and to) secular society.

Freedom of Religion in Japan and Denmark

Though geographically and socially distant, Japan and Denmark each have a strong and longstanding dominant narrative of being ethnically and culturally homogeneous, one that is repeated time and again throughout public discourse. Like all narratives that have a mutually reinforcing relationship with national myths, whether the portrayal is accurate is hardly relevant: "What does matter is how they graft over to the existing myths and identities of the population, even if they are pure fancy...Rather than a concern with objective truth, the reality created through such fantasy lies simply in the coherence of the story itself" (Hinck et al. 2020, 135). For a short period, from the country's modernization to the end of World War II, Shinto, the Japanese indigenous religion, was designated as the national religion. Many commentators note that the bullish, nationalistic version of Shinto promoted by the government during this time had little to do with the original, peaceful, nature-worshiping version (see Sakamoto 1994). In any case, postwar Japan is a constitutionally secular state, with constitutional protections for the freedom of religion, no national religion, and with a clear separation between religion and public institutions. Most Japanese are areligious, with 62 percent stating in 2018 that they had no particular religious affiliation (Kobayashi 2019, 53). Religion is largely considered a personal matter in Japan, belonging solely in the private sphere, and many view organized religion with ambivalence, if not downright suspicion.

As in Japan, freedom of religion is clearly protected in the 1849 Constitution of Denmark. At the same time, the Constitution ensures a privileged position for the Evangelical Lutheran Church, designating it as the national church and mandating support by the state. The bulk of the church's budget comes from state grants and voluntary church taxes (Nielsen 2012; US Department of State 2021). According to the European Values Survey of 2017, 54 percent of Danes self-identify as religious—the same percentage as in Germany but significantly higher than Sweden (27 percent) and Norway (37 percent). At the same time, only 19 percent of Danes say religion is "very or quite important in their lives," a figure far lower than any of the other three neighbouring countries; and the percentage of respondents who believe that religious beliefs should be taught at home is also relatively low, at 4 percent (though 5 percent of Swedish respondents also stated the same) (Atlas of European Values 2017).

Historically, both Japan and Denmark had limited numbers of Muslim residents until significant migration took place in the postwar era. Muslims in Denmark consist mainly of migrant labourers from predominantly Muslim countries who arrived in the 1970s and refugees from the 1980s onwards, and their descendants (see Nielsen 2012). An estimated 4 to 5 percent of the population is Muslim. Japan has had migration from predominantly Muslim countries only from the 1990s, though mainly due to the country's highly restrictive attitude towards immigration. The proportion of Muslims within the wider Japanese population remains less significant than in Denmark, at an estimated 0.17 percent. In Japan, roughly 10 percent of Muslims—2,000—are estimated to be converts from the indigenous population (Tanada 2019, 1), whereas in Denmark that number is estimated at 2,000 to 5,000 (Ministry of Foreign Affairs of Denmark n.d.). No official collection of religious affiliation is conducted in either country, meaning all these numbers are estimates at best.

Islamic Religiosity Framed as a Security Threat in Japan

In October 2010, a large internet leak of internal police documents showed that the Japanese police had been engaging in blanket surveillance of all foreign national Muslims (residents and visitors) since at least 2004. Every foreign national or foreign-born Muslim in Japan was treated as a possible terrorist risk and was the subject of pervasive surveillance, with information gathered not only on employment or immigration status but also political views and levels of religious devotion. Mosques were deemed to be potential "terrorist infrastructure" and were systematically surveilled, often 24/7 from neighbouring apartments rented by the police specifically for this purpose. Persons going in and out of mosques and Muslim-owned businesses were followed, with detailed information collected and stored in a police database. In one document from 2008, the police say they had gathered surveillance data on 72,000 persons (Tokyo Chiho Saibansho 2014).

In addition to the entire Muslim community, there was also further surveillance of "high-risk" persons. While (very vague) security concerns were one factor in the assessment of whether a particular person was "high risk," religious devotion was also a pronounced red flag, with adherence to Islamic religious principles a clear (in the eyes of the police) indicator of increased tendencies toward terrorism. As noted by this author in a previous publication, "observations are made [throughout the police documents] regarding the level of religious devotion of targeted individuals and the mosques (if any) they attend regularly" (Takahashi 2018, 198). Individuals who "consistently engage in prayer and other religious rituals" or who "refrain from alcohol and non-halal food" are openly treated as potential terror threats (Tokyo Chiho Saibansho 2014).

One Moroccan was treated as a potential risk because he "started to pray and attend Friday prayers...after his first daughter was born." The police found him to be dangerous enough to interview his (Japanese) ex-wife several times, and they asked her pointed questions about his religious observance. The report elaborates in menacing tones that, according to his ex-wife, when they first met he "did not go to the mosque and drank alcohol...[However, after] marrying, his religious devotion became extremely strong...It was after he received a prayer carpet from his mother that his Islamic colours became very strong." An interview report of another Moroccan national highlights that he attends Arabic classes with his children; and yet another report, of an Algerian, states that his computer showed "frequent access to Islamic religious audio files" (Dai-san Shokan Henshuubu 2010, 63, 67, 73).

Media Treatment of Surveillance and Court Judgment

Almost immediately after the leak, the mainstream media started to disseminate a narrative that was highly critical of the police—but for being unable to secure the information collected through the surveillance, not for the surveillance itself. The ineptitude of the police in being unable to prevent the leak had led to the damaging of Japan's credibility in the eyes of so-called "security partners" (e.g., the United States)—a major sin in postwar Japan. While some press reports raised concerns that privacy had been violated, this was held to be solely because of the poor information security practices of the police—it was the leak that was the problem, not the surveillance itself. Fundamental questions about the surveillance itself, certainly questions related to human rights, were simply not raised.

A literature survey by the author shows that, from right-leaning newspapers to left-of-centre publications, 74 percent of articles (including leader articles) tacitly—and in some cases openly—supported the blanket surveillance of Muslims. Only 4 percent of articles raised fundamental human rights-based concerns with the surveillance—and *all* of those were published in late 2013 or early 2014, after which the case had, for all practical purposes, been closed, and during which time there was fierce public debate regarding two government bills that would allow heightened surveillance of the citizenry. Cynically put, it was only once people realized that Japanese citizens (and not just foreign nationals) could also be subject to rights abuses that surveillance became an issue.

In late 2010, a group of Muslims who had been surveilled (and whose personal information had been included in the leaked documents) sued for compensation from the government, arguing the surveillance had violated their rights to non-discrimination and to freedom of religion. In its judgment, delivered in January 2014 (and subsequently confirmed on appeal by the Supreme Court), the Japanese judiciary adopted without any reservation the narrative disseminated by the media, dismissing any human rights–based concerns.

At the outset of the judgment, the court immediately decided that generalized surveillance of Muslims was "a necessary measure to prevent international terrorism" (Tokyo Chiho Saibansho 2014), essentially ruling out any argument that the surveillance had been violative of human rights. As part of their (somewhat spurious) reasoning to justify this assessment, the court cites the 2004 case of Lionel Dumont, a suspected senior Al Qaeda officer who had been in Japan between 2002 and 2003. There is no connection, direct or indirect, between the Dumont case and the surveillance, but the court stated pointedly that Dumont was "a devout Muslim. He never failed to pray five times a day, and frequented mosques" (Tokyo Chiho Saibansho 2014). The unsaid yet clear implications of the court's logic are that adherence to Islamic scriptures must be an indicator of being a terrorist—that is, not all Muslims may be terrorists, but all terrorists are Muslims (see Takahashi 2018). Indeed, the court even juxtaposes Dumont's true life as a (suspected) religious extremist and terrorist with the façade he maintained while in Japan of a "serious Frenchman quietly going about his work" (Tokyo Chiho Saibansho 2014). There is no indication as to why being a "serious Frenchman" is inherently incompatible with being a devout Muslim; like many other elements in its judgment, the court appears to think it is simply self-evident.

The religiosity of Muslims, therefore, was a clear factor in the court's reasoning. Indeed, this logic appears elsewhere in the judgment, where the court states that surveillance is necessary because "To ascertain whether a particular individual is a peaceful Muslim or a terrorist affiliated with Islamist radicals, one has no alternative but to assess external factors, such as how much he participates in religious ceremonies or education activities" (Tokyo Chiho Saibansho 2014). In other words, religious devotion (or at least participation in religious activities) is, to the court, an important indicator that one is affiliated with a terrorist organization.

Regarding the violation of freedom of religion, the court summarily dismissed the argument of the victims with extremely questionable reasoning, stating there could only be a violation if the government had openly banned Islam, forcibly closed down all religious facilities, and arrested Muslims because of their faith. Since that had not been the case, the court asserted, "even supposing difficulties were caused regarding some religious matters, such difficulties would be of an indirect and unintended nature" (Tokyo Chiho Saibansho 2014) and therefore were perfectly acceptable. Such a narrow definition of the right to freedom of religion is clearly not warranted by international human rights standards.[2] The court then relied on circular logic, returning to its initial statement that the surveillance was necessary and asserting that "[g]iven that [the surveillance] was a necessary and inevitable measure to prevent terrorism, there is no violation of [human] rights" (Tokyo Chiho Saibansho 2014).

International human rights treaty organizations (committees that monitor application of human rights treaties and make recommendations to state parties on strengthening human rights) were critical of the surveillance, stating they were "concerned about reports of surveillance activities of Muslims...which may amount to ethnic profiling. The Committee considers systematic collection of security information about individuals, solely on the basis of their belonging to an ethnic or ethno-religious group, a serious form of discrimination" (Committee on the Elimination of Racial Discrimination 2014, 9; see also Human Rights Committee 2014). Like most of the recommendations of human rights treaty organizations over the years, these concerns were largely ignored by Japanese authorities. To this day, official discourse on issues related to security is dominated by the notion that Islamic extremism is the predominant threat to global peace and stability, that Japan is also threatened by Islamist terrorism, and, by extension, that Muslims are to be viewed with general suspicion. In official parlance, terrorism—international terrorism in particular—is associated heavily (or is practically synonymous) with Islamic groups (see Keisatsucho 2020).

Japan also has its share of academics acting as Islamophobic commentators. For example, the publications of bestselling author Akari Iiyama are full of unsubstantiated claims, such as the notion that the Quran requires Muslims to kill all nonbelievers, including Japanese, and that "Conquering the world is the obligation of all Muslims" (Iiyama 2018, 81). Iiyama claims that Islam is fundamentally incompatible with democracy, alleging that all Muslims supported the killing in France of cartoonists and editors who published satirical cartoons of the Prophet Muhammad and that there is no possibility for freedom of religion or expression in Islam.

Muslims Framed as a Threat to Danish Culture

In Denmark, openly discriminatory attitudes against Muslims, and Islam itself, have continued throughout recent years in government policy, the media, and popular discourse. Ozcan and Bangert note that the sheer "concept of Islam and the mentioning of Muslims [has been] presented as in contradiction with the unity of Danish society" (2019, 258). One public opinion survey conducted in 2019 indicated that at least one in four Danes strongly or at least partially agreed that Muslim migrants should be deported from the country (Ozcan and Bangert 2019, 232).

These attitudes have been solidified through numerous moral panics that clearly target Muslims and the open display of their religious faith. In 2018, a law was passed requiring persons obtaining Danish citizenship to shake the hand of the government official at the ceremony, in a "less than implicit assumption" (Vinding 2020, 54) that Muslims refrain from shaking hands with members of the opposite sex. In 2018, the government adopted a law imposing substantial fines on women who wear the Muslim full face veil in public (the "burka ban"), even though only an estimated 100 to 200 women in the country wear such face coverings (Ozcan and Bangert 2019, 269).[3]

As noted above by Scheinin, religious discrimination is often used as—or at least becomes—a proxy for racial discrimination. Key in the Danish context is the concept of "non-Western" residents, an official statistical categorization used in Danish law and policy. In Danish immigration law, a migrant is classified as having come from a "non-Western" country if their country of origin is any besides a European Union member state, Switzerland, the United Kingdom, Andorra, Iceland, Lichtenstein, Monaco, Norway, San Marino, the Vatican State, the United States, Canada, Australia, or New Zealand. As noted by the Open Society Justice Initiative (OSJI, 2021, 6), these "Western" countries have no geographical coherence and have only "one common characteristic: all have majority populations which are perceived to be white." In addition, perhaps uniquely in Denmark, *descendants* of migrants from "non-Western" countries are also labelled as such, *even if they have Danish citizenship.* The only way to have the "non-Western" label removed is if the person is born in Denmark *and* if at least one of their parents is (or later becomes) a Danish citizen. In theory, therefore, the label could remain in perpetuity.

In Danish discourse, the "non-Western" label is widely used as a euphemism for "Muslim." In recent years, the labelling has become even more overt, with the creation in December 2020 of the new statistical category of MENAPT (Middle East, North Africa, Pakistan and Turkey)[4] to be distinguished from other "non-Western" countries. As also noted by the OSJI, the twenty-four MENAPT countries have no geographical coherence, with the only common factor being that they are all Muslim-majority countries. For example, "Eritrea and Ethiopia (*not predominantly Muslim*) are not on the list, though they are geographically placed between Egypt, Somalia and Djibouti (*predominantly Muslim*), which are on the list" (emphasis in original) (European Website on Integration 2021). There is no attempt on the part of the government to hide the discriminatory intent of the new category: the Danish immigration minister is quoted as saying, "Fundamentally... we in Denmark don't really have problems with people from Latin

America and the Far East. We have problems with people from the Middle East and North Africa" (The Local 2020).

Muslim "Ghettos" and "Parallel Societies"

Perhaps unsurprisingly, Danish policies in recent years have been based on a consistent and fundamental problematization of migrants from "non-Western" countries. A brutal example of this is the assortment of legal amendments and policies known collectively as the "ghetto" policies—nakedly prejudiced policies that Ozcan and Bangert (2019) argue are indicative of Denmark's slide from a democracy to an ethnocracy. Since 2010, areas in Danish cities with over 1,000 residents that fulfill several criteria, such as high unemployment and a high crime rate, have been officially designated as "ghettos." In 2018, the government announced that an area would only qualify as a "ghetto" if over half of its residents were from "non-Western" countries, making the ethnic and religious composition of the area the defining criterion (Danish Economics and Interior Ministry 2019, 111). Upon introducing the bill, the immigration minister stated, "I think we might as well be straight-forward and say that there are problems...that originate from, and that also relate to, the way some Muslims have chosen to practice their religion...We should not stand for it" (Vinding 2020, 96).

Though the government changed the "ghetto" terminology in 2021, the policies—and statements surrounding their implementation—still openly target "non-Western" migrants as a problem to be solved. Indeed, in March 2021, the government announced a policy goal that aimed towards having no more than 30 percent of "ghetto" residents from a "non-Western" background (*Guardian* 2021). Under the "ghetto" laws, daycare attendance is mandatory for twenty-five hours per week for all "non-Western" children of "ghetto" residents from the time they turn one year of age, in a purported effort to teach the children Danish values. Parents who do not enrol their children in daycare (branded by the government as "parents in parallel societies that do not take responsibility" for their children) are deprived of child care benefits (Danish Economics and Interior Ministry 2019, 25), which could result in what has been called "devastating effects" for the family (Mandates of the Special Rapporteur 2020, 3).

Ghetto residents are also prohibited from taking their children on "forced re-education trips." Though vague, the apparent intent of the law is to prevent children of "non-Western" backgrounds from spending extended periods of time in their "country of origin," during which time they could be resocialized in problematic, "non-Western" behaviour. Parents who attempt such trips are subject to reductions in child care benefits and even imprisonment, as such travel "exposes the child's health and development to grave danger" (Danish Economics and Interior Ministry 2019). Finally, the measures allow for "enhanced punishment zones," under which criminal penalties can be doubled within "ghettos." Other measures that were proposed by the government but were rejected included a curfew of 8:00 p.m. in all "ghettos" and the fitting of electronic ankle bracelets on all juvenile residents (Ozcan and Bangert 2019, 269).

The objective of the "ghetto" policies is to eradicate "ghettos" by the year 2030, with this to be accomplished, if necessary, by demolishing housing units and dispersing residents. Since a concentration of Muslim residents is the defining factor in a particular area being designated a "ghetto," this would, in effect, result in forced evictions and demolitions targeting Muslims. There is currently an ongoing court case in Copenhagen regarding the sale (and subsequent demolition) of apartments in the "ghetto" of Mjolnerparken, which is expected to provide a clear judgment on the legality of the "ghetto" policies. On October 16, 2020, three UN Human Rights Council special rapporteurs submitted an urgent appeal to the Danish government, requesting that it halt the sale until a judgment had been delivered. In their appeal, the special rapporteurs condemned the "ghetto" policies, calling them "incompatible with Denmark's commitments to equality, inclusivity, and tolerance" and "inconsistent with Denmark's international human rights obligations, particularly to combat racial discrimination" (Mandates of the Special Rapporteur 2020, 5).

A notable feature of the discourse is, as pointed to earlier, the repeated emphasis on the notion that people from "non-Western" countries are creating "parallel societies," where primitive religious norms are the law of the land and rules and European values are shunned. In no government statement is "parallel society" defined in any concrete way; indeed, even the government admits that it is "difficult to identify with great precision" and that any "statistics are subject to inherent uncertainty" (Danish Economics and Interior Ministry 2019, 10). Vinding (2020, 96) also calls the notion of "parallel societies" a "widely held political fiction." Nevertheless, the government contends that "parallel societies" constitute a "threat to our modern society, a place where freedom, democracy, equality and tolerance are not accepted as fundamental values, and where rights and duties do not go together." The government furthermore emphasizes that it must eradicate "parallel societies" so that "Denmark shall be Denmark again" (Danish Government 2018, 5).

Recently, the somewhat overlapping notion of "social control" has also been stressed in official discourse, according to which Muslim families purportedly exert inappropriate control over their children's lives, restricting their freedom and personal development. To give an emblematic example of the notions underpinning what is understood as "social control," in October 2020, the integration minister "urged Muslim community leaders to endorse premarital sex" (Hassani 2021, 248).

Conclusion

In Japan, Islamophobic discourse has centred on portraying Muslims as potential terrorists and a threat to national security. In Denmark, on the other hand, the discourse has tended to focus on culture, with

Muslims painted as incapable of adjusting to Western values and, therefore, threatening the social fabric of the country. In both countries, however, the religiosity of Muslims is portrayed as a key factor in them being allegedly dangerous to society. Muslims who might partake in religious rituals once or twice a year but, on the whole, do not take their beliefs seriously are held to be "good" Muslims; whereas "bad" Muslims are religiously observant, overt in their religious displays in public spaces, and generally portrayed as tending toward radicalization and terrorism. Human rights treaty organizations and other human rights organizations have criticized the measures taken by both governments, but their concerns have largely fallen on deaf ears.

It is an open question whether religion has truly entered the public space in a more overt way in institutionally secular countries and what that means for those countries. What is clear is that not all religions are viewed equally: Islam is viewed as uniquely inclined toward terrorism and distinctively barbaric and backward. Openly discriminatory policies that violate international norms are being advanced in many countries, of which the two in this paper are examples. Any debate on post-secularism and the impact of increased religiosity in society should be cognizant of the importance of protecting human rights—in particular, international norms on the freedom of religion.

NOTES

1. The research for this paper was funded in part by the Japan Society for the Promotion of Science ("Kaken"), grant number JP19K23166. Parts of the paper build on Saul Takahashi, "Muslim Surveillance in Japan: A Narrative Based on Trivialization," *Islamophobia Studies Journal* 4, no. 2 (Spring 2018): 195–209; and "The Ummah: Guardian of Muslims in an Age of Weakened Citizenship Rights," *Journal of Islam and the Contemporary World* 14, no. 2 (2021): 1–26.

2. Japanese courts have generally not given adequate consideration to international human rights standards, attempting to interpret them as identical to

the Japanese Constitution and Japanese precedents. See, for example, Shin 2013.

3. Andreassen (2013, 220) has criticized these discourses using a feminist lens, stating that "[a]pparently...a woman can only be a fully included member of Danish society and the welfare system if she is bodily available for the male gaze and the male touch." See also Hervik 2011.

4. The twenty-four countries are: Syria, Kuwait, Libya, Saudi Arabia, Lebanon, Somalia, Iraq, Qatar, Sudan, Bahrain, Djibouti, Jordan, Algeria, United Arab Emirates, Tunisia, Egypt, Morocco, Iran, Yemen, Mauretania, Oman, Afghanistan, Pakistan, and Turkey. See European Commission 2020.

REFERENCES

American Civil Liberties Union. 2017. "Raza v. City of New York—Legal Challenge to NYPD Muslim Surveillance Program." https://www.aclu.org/cases/raza-v-city-new-york-legal-challenge-nypd-muslim-surveillance-program.

Andreassen, Rika. 2013. "Take Off That Veil and Give Me Access to Your Body: An Analysis of Danish Debates about Muslim Women's Head and Body Covering." In *Gender, Migration and Categorisation: Making Distinctions between Migrants in Western Countries, 1945–2010*, edited by Deirdre M.M. Moloney and Marlou Schrover. Amsterdam University Press.

Atlas of European Values. 2017. "European Values Survey." EValue. www.atlasofeuropeanvalues.eu. Accessed May 23, 2022.

Bayrakli, Enes, and Farid Hafez, eds. 2021. *European Islamophobia Report 2020*. Istanbul: Leopold Weiss Institute. https://www.islamophobiareport.com/EIR_2020.pdf

Bazian, Hatem. 2017. *Annotations on Race, Colonialism, Islamophobia, Islam, and Palestine*. Amrit.

Beydoun, Khaled. 2018. *American Islamophobia: Understanding the Roots and Rise of Fear*. University of California Press.

Birt, Yahya. 2010. "Governing Muslims after 9/11." In *Thinking through Islamophobia: Global Perspectives*, edited by Salman Sayyid and AbdoolKarim Vakil. Hurst.

Bracke, Sarah, and Luis Manuel Hernández Aguilar. 2020. "'They Love Death as We Love Life': The 'Muslim Question' and the Biopolitics of Replacement," *British Journal of Sociology* 71, no. 4: 680–701.

CAGE. 2022. *We Are Beginning to Spread Terror: The State-Sponsored Persecution of Muslims in France.* March 2. https://www.cage.ngo/articles/ we-are-beginning-to-spread-terror-the-state-sponsored-persecution- of-muslims-in-france.

Carey, Brian. 2018. "Against the Right to Revoke Citizenship." *Citizenship Studies* 22, no. 8: 897–911.

Committee on the Elimination of Racial Discrimination. 2014. "Concluding Observations on the Combined Seventh to Ninth Periodic Reports of Japan." CERD/C/JPN/CO/7–9, August 26. Geneva: United Nations.

Dai-san Shokan Henshuubu. 2010. *Ryuushutsu kou-an tero joiuhou zen de-ta: isuramu kyouto iko-ru terorisuto nanoka? [Leaked Public Security Terror Information, Complete Data: are All Muslims Terrorists?].* Dai-san Shokan.

Danish Economics and Interior Ministry. 2019. *Redegørelse om parallelsamfund [Statement on Parallel Societies].* Copenhagen.

Danish Government. 2018. *Ét Danmark uden Parallelsamfund [One Denmark without Parallel Societies].* Copenhagen.

European Commission. 2020. "Denmark: New Statistics Category for Migrants from Muslim Countries." December 11. https://ec.europa.eu/migrant- integration/news/denmark-new-statistics-category-migrants-muslim- countries_en.

European Website on Integration. 2020. "Denmark: New Statistics Category for Migrants from Muslim Countries." December 11. European Commission. https://ec.europa.eu/migrant-integration/news/ denmark-new-statistics-category-migrants-muslim-countries_en.

Guardian. 2021. "Denmark Plans to Limit 'Non-Western' Residents in Disadvantaged Areas." March 17. https://www.theguardian.com/ world/2021/mar/17/denmark-plans-to-limit-non-western-residents- in-disadvantaged-areas.

Hassani, Amani. 2021. "Denmark." In *European Islamophobia Report 2020*, edited by Enes Bayrakli and Farid Hafez. Leopold Weiss Institute. https:// www.islamophobiareport.com/EIR_2020.pdf.

Hervik, Peter. 2011. *The Annoying Difference: The Emergence of Danish Neonationalism, Neoracism, and Populism in the Post-1989 World.* Berghan.

Hinck, Robert S., Skye C. Cooley, and Randolph Kluver. 2020. *Global Media and Strategic Narratives of Contested Democracy: Chinese, Russian, and Arabic Media Narratives of the US Presidential Election.* Routledge.

Human Rights Committee. 2014. "Concluding Observations on the Sixth Periodic Report of Japan." CCPR/C/JPN/CO/6, August 20. United Nations.

Huntington, Samuel P. 1993. "The Clash of Civilizations?" *Foreign Affairs* 72 no. 3: 22–49.

Iiyama, Akari. 2018. *Isura-mukyou no ronri* [*The Logic of Islam*]. Shincho Shinsho.

Ismael, Tareq Y., and Andrew Rippin, eds. 2010. *Islam in the Eyes of the West: Images and Realities in an Age of Terror*. Routledge.

Keisatsucho [National Police Agency]. 2020. "Kyokusa bouryoku shuudan no genjou tou" ["Radical Left Violent Organizations: Current Situation"]. January. Tokyo.

Kobayashi, Toshiyuki. 2019. "Nihonjin no shuukyouteki ishiki ha dou kawatta ka" ["How Japanese Religious Attitudes and Actions Have Changed"]. *Housou kenkyuu to chousa* [*Research of News Reporting*]. NHK.

Mandates of the Special Rapporteur. 2020. "Urgent Appeal to Denmark," UA DNK 3/2020, October 16. United Nations.

Ministry of Foreign Affairs of Denmark. n.d. "Muslims in Denmark." https:// libanon.um.dk/en/about-us/aboutdenmark/muslimsdenmark. Accessed January 10, 2023.

Molendijk, Arie. L. 2015. "In Pursuit of the Postsecular." *International Journal of Philosophy and Theology* 76, no. 2: 100–115.

Morey, Peter, and Amina Yaqin. 2011. *Framing Muslims: Stereotyping and Representation*. Harvard University Press.

Nielsen, Jorgen S. 2012. *Islam in Denmark: The Challenge of Diversity*. Lexington Books.

Nowak, Manfred. 2005. *UN Covenant on Civil and Political Rights: CCPR Commentary*. 2nd revised edition. NP Engel.

Open Society Justice Initiative. 2021. "Request to the Committee on the Elimination of Racial Discrimination for the Early Warning and Urgent Action Procedure in Respect of a Proposed Expansion of Denmark's 'Ghetto Package.'" July. Copenhagen.

Ozcan, Sibel, and Zeynep Bangert. 2019. "Islamophobia in Denmark: National Report 2018." In *European Islamophobia Report 2018*, edited by Enes Bayrakli and Farid Hafez. Istanbul: Leopold Weiss Institute. https:// www.islamophobiareport.com/EIR_2018.pdf.

Poynting, Scott, and George Morgan. 2012. *Global Islamophobia: Muslims and Moral Panic in the West*. Routledge.

Ruteere, Mutuma. 2015. "Report of Special Rapporteur on Contemporary Forms of Racism, Racial Discrimination, Xenophobia and Related Intolerance." A/HRC/29/46, April 19. Geneva: United Nations.

Said, Edward W. 1979. *Orientalism*. Pantheon Books.

Sakamoto, Koremaru. 1994. *Kokka shinto keisei katei no kenkyuu [Creating Shinto as National Religion: A Study]*. Iwanami Shoten.

Sayyid, Salman, and AbdoolKarim Vakil. 2010. *Thinking through Islamophobia: Global Perspectives*. Hurst.

Schaafsma, Petruschka. 2015. "Making Sense of the Postsecular: Theological Explorations of a Critical Concept." *International Journal of Philosophy and Theology* 76, no. 2: 91–99.

Scheinin, Martin. 2007. "Implementation of General Assembly Resolution 60/251 of 15 March 2006 entitled 'Human Rights Council,' Report of Special Rapporteur on the Promotion and Protection of Human Rights and Fundamental Freedoms while Countering Terrorism." A/HRC/4/2. United Nations.

Shalhoub-Kevorkian, Nadera. 2015. *Security Theology, Surveillance and the Politics of Fear*. Cambridge University Press.

Shin, Hebon. 2013. *International Human Rights Law: Dynamism of International Standards and Coordination with Domestic Law*. Shinzan-sha.

Takahashi, Saul. 2018. "Muslim Surveillance in Japan: A Narrative Based on Trivialization." *Islamophobia Studies Journal* 4, no. 2: 195–209.

Takahashi, Saul. 2021. "The Ummah: Guardian of Muslims in an Age of Weakened Citizenship Rights." *Journal of Islam and the Contemporary World* 14, no. 2: 1–26.

Tanada, Hirofumi. 2019. "Nihon ni okeru isuarm: kyousei no tame no kadai" ["Islam in Japan: What Needs to be Done for Coexistence"]. June 21. Tokyo. https://www.spf.org/global-data/user132/islam_japan/islamseminer_text.pdf?20190729125939. Accessed January 10, 2023.

The Local. 2020. "Denmark to Classify Immigrants from Muslim Countries Separately in Crime Statistics." December 14. Copenhagen. https://www.thelocal.dk/20201214/denmark-to-classify-muslim-countries-separately-in-official-statistics/. Accessed January 10, 2023.

Tokyo Chiho Saibansho [Tokyo District Court]. 2014. 2011 case nos. 15750, 32072, 3266, LEX/DB 25517582.

Tyrer, David. 2013. *The Politics of Islamophobia: Race, Power and Fantasy*. Pluto Press.

United Nations. 2010. "Durban Review Conference: Outcome Document." https://www.ohchr.org/en/publications/reference-publications/durban-review-conference-outcome-document.

US Department of State. 2021. "2020 Report on International Religious Freedom: Denmark." May 12. Washington, DC. https://www.state.gov/reports/2020-report-on-international-religious-freedom/denmark/.

Vinding, Niels Valdemar. 2020. *Annotated Legal Documents on Islam in Europe: Denmark*. Brill.

Zempi, Irene, and Imran Awan, eds. 2019. *The Routledge International Handbook of Islamophobia*. Routledge.

6

Muslim Women, Trials, and Terror under the UAPA in India

AREESHA KHAN

In this chapter, I analyze four case studies that
explore Muslim women's responses to their male relatives' incarceration
in India's war on terrorism. I examine how India's anti-terror laws that
target Muslim men have an effect far beyond the men themselves. The
public act of the state charging Muslim men with draconian anti-terror
laws codifies the subversion of the provision of arrest over the presumption of innocence until proven guilty, and through these arrests, the
Indian state marks boundaries of who is included and excluded from
equal treatment. These arrests also impose many hardships on Muslim
men and their families. For example, their low conviction rates result
in long trials that can stretch twenty or more years. The arrests of men
who are in most cases sole breadwinners also leads to the economic dis-
empowerment of their families. The arrests not only have an economic
impact but also social ramifications, creating a sense of familial loss.

Women from these families interact with the public sphere while the state enters their private lives, blurring the line between personal and public for them. Using the concepts of the public sphere (Habermas 1964), resistance, and vulnerability (Butler et al. 2016), I provide case studies of how religion is instrumental for all the Muslim women whose male relatives have been targeted by the state.

I engage with the concepts of "public" and "private" at various levels. At one level, the public sphere becomes central to resistance, as it is where individuals may assemble en masse and where communication between public institutions and individuals happens. The public sphere was conceptualized with the development of the modern nation-state as its powerful administrative apparatus grew along the lines of modern capitalism. So, the idea of the "public sphere" tends to evolve with the shifting nature of the state. According to Habermas (1964), the public sphere is a space where civil society comes together and forms public opinions, and it becomes a sphere of interaction with the state. The opposite of public is private, the distinction of which is crucial in feminist discourse. It is also key to secularism— gendered spheres of the public are considered secular and male, and the private is considered religious and female (Scott 2017). I examine Muslim women's resistance, which, as formulated by Judith Butler et al. (2016), is where subjects rely on mobilizing vulnerability as a form of agency against a secular patriarchal public sphere. I take the idea of post-secularism and attempt to explain the nature of Indian state and Muslim women's engagement with the public sphere regarding their assertions of religion and the process of seeking justice in India. The chapter problematizes the idea of secular India, the public sphere, and the post-secular society by investigating Muslim women's reactions to the incarceration of their male relatives.

Indian Muslim Women

Muslims are a minority community in India. They comprised 14.2 percent of the total population in the 2011 census done by the government. The socioeconomic realities of Indian Muslims are marred with marginalization and restricted upward mobility, owing to structural inaccessibility to educational and political institutions. The characterization of Muslims as the Other in India is imposed and reimposed through global and national media, and it is covertly and overtly peddled by the Hindu nationalist agenda. The community's marginalization is also owed to global stereotyping of the Muslim identity as "orthodox" and "backward," which shifts the onus of the community's marginalization and its "non-progress" onto the community itself and their religion. Such narratives also typify the gender question among Muslims by presenting Muslim women as an ahistorical victim Other (Jamil 2017).

All the images and narratives of "backwardness" and "orthodoxy" are assembled and used to foster prejudice and violence against Muslims. Since the 1980s Muslim family and personal law, concerning family, marriage, and inheritance, has been used to further marginalize Muslims and the socioeconomic status of the community in broader Indian society. Hindu communalists' obsession with Muslim personal law led to the appropriation of the Uniform Civil Code's formation (Hasan and Menon 2004), which was initially praised by feminist groups for promoting gender justice. The debates around Muslim family and personal law essentialized Muslims and Islam and denied the agency of Muslim women by promoting that it is Islam and Muslim men who oppress Muslim women. In contrast, it is posited that secularism is the guarantor of gender equality and freedom to Muslim women. Notwithstanding the patriarchal nature of Muslim families, most of the essentialized stereotypes are intended to Other the community; what goes unnoticed are issues of inaccessibility and mobility as well as the risks of violence and vulnerability that the community continues to face in supposedly secular Indian society. These issues are highlighted not only in the structural absence of Muslims from public and private institutions, but also in Muslims' day-to-day lives and activities, ranging from their livelihood to their habitation across rural and urban spaces.

In India, Muslim Othering is historically marked by the 1947 India-Pakistan partition at the end of British rule, which placed Muslims' loyalty to the state of India under perpetual scrutiny, endangering their claims to equal citizenship. Still, what goes unobserved and unstated is that when such dominant narratives are in play around one's identity, there is no passive acceptance. Instead, there is resistance to it—which entails a long list of actions, from the way Muslims navigate spaces that are very much defined by the past and present of communal violence and the way they mediate their everyday in the public domain. These mediations also include negotiating with the secular state and resistance to its actions and laws. One such act of resistance is against the entrapping of Muslims in India under terrorism and anti-terrorism charges, as discussed in the next section.

Summarized History of Indian Terrorism Laws and Litigations

The Unlawful Activities (Prevention) Act (UAPA) was passed in 1967. Following this, passed in 1987, was the Terrorist and Disruptive Activities (Prevention) Act (TADA), which was intended to counter what the Indian state labelled as "terrorist" activities, particularly against the backdrop of the Punjab's Sikh separatist Khalsa movement. The TADA was repealed in 1995 by the Indian Parliament on the grounds of violating human rights. It was succeeded by the Prevention of Terrorist Activities Act (POTA) in 2002, which lapsed in 2004. At that point, the UAPA became longstanding legislation; it was amended three more times, in 2008, 2012, and 2019. With each amendment, the UAPA became more rigid. This was especially true for the 2019 amendment, which gave power to the central government to designate individuals as terrorists. The UAPA is one of the ways the Indian state criminalizes citizens and stigmatizes and excludes them from society.

In the year 2020, 4,021 terrorism-related cases were pending from 2019 under the UAPA, and 796 cases were registered in 2020. The total number of cases pending investigation was 4,817. Of those cases, only 297 were investigated and had sufficient evidence to proceed with prosecution. The police dismissed 726 cases. The total number of cases that went through full trials in 2020 was 2,642, and fourteen cases were abated by the courts (NCRB 2020, 853–863). There was a high rate of cases pending or halted at both the investigation and trial stages. According to data compiled by the National Crime Records Bureau (NCRB), the conviction rate under the UAPA between 2015 and 2019 was below 2 percent. The 2008 amendment to the UAPA added Section 43D (5), regarding bail. It states that a person accused under the UAPA cannot be granted bail until the court has assessed their guilt, based on the charge sheet of the National Investigation Agency.[1] Following a hearing and the public prosecutor's application submission, if there are grounds to believe that the case is prima facie true, then the court can deny bail to the accused.

Given the difficulty of securing bail and the lengthy duration taken for charge sheet preparation, investigation, and trial litigation, the process can take as long as twenty-plus years. In what follows, I focus on the implications for the Muslim men who have been arrested under the UAPA and are facing terrorism trials in Indian courts. How does it affect the women in their families, and how do the women cope amid the years their male family members are languishing in jail? The accusations and incarcerations demonstrate the direct (public) action of an institution on the personal (private) lives of citizens, marking the entry of the state (a public entity) into the gendered lives of women and the institution of family (private entities). In this way, the supposedly secular Indian state blurs and collapses its self-distinction between public and the private as it attempts to exert power over and exclude minority religious groups using anti-terrorism laws.

Methodology

My research consists of qualitative case studies that document Muslim women's reactions and resistance amid the prosecution and incarceration of their male family members. Resistance becomes part of their everyday lives when they have to convince the public of their male family members' innocence. I have attempted to record the vulnerabilities involved in this process and women's interactions within the public sphere by observing the methods they use to mobilize support and humanize their male family members. Four case studies are discussed here: Nargis Saifi, Khalid Saifi's spouse; Rehannath, Siddique Kappan's[2] spouse; Soufiya Maudani, Abdul Nassar Maudani's[3] spouse, and Biyummah, Zakariyah's mother. Secondary data sources include news articles, investigative reports, and books covering terrorism trials. Primary data was collected through interviews with Nargis Saifi and Rehannath, who are currently engaging publicly as wives of men under terror charges. The women in my study are under public scrutiny as mothers or wives of men looked upon as "criminals" or "terrorists" in the public sphere.

Muslim Men and Terrorism Charges

In December 2001, just over two months after 9/11, Surat City police arrested 127 men from ten different provinces. They were targeted under several sections of the UAPA for their affiliation with a banned organization called the Students Islamic Movement of India (SIMI).[4] On March 7, 2021, they were all acquitted of terrorism charges after twenty years of being under trial. Jamia Teachers' Solidarity

Association (2013) compiled a report titled "Framed, Damned and Acquitted: Dossiers of a Very Special Cell," documenting sixteen such cases, in which those arrested by the Delhi Special Cell[5] were accused of being operatives and agents of terrorist organizations. They were charged with the heinous crimes of war against the state, criminal conspiracy, sedition, planning and causing bomb blasts, training of terrorists, keeping a collection of arms, ammunition, and explosives, and the transfer of funds for terrorist activities. However, between 1992 and 2012, many of the accused in those cases were acquitted by the courts. The association's report records the comments of judges in their final judgment and demonstrates how so-called evidence was tampered with and fabricated by the police and the prosecution. For example, Mohammad Amir Khan was entrapped for twenty bomb detonations that took place between December 1996 and December 1997 in Delhi, Rohtak, Sonepat, and Ghaziabad. He was acquitted of all charges after fourteen years of imprisonment.

The four cases that I examine here are currently going through trials in the courts. The first case I discuss is that of Abdul Nasser Maudani, who is a fifty-six-year-old leader of the People's Democratic Party in Kerala. Maudani was accused of involvement in the 1998 Coimbatore blasts and was acquitted following nine and a half years on trial. In 1998, he was arrested and remanded to judicial custody in Crime No. 151/98 for alleged offences under Indian Penal Code (IPC) Sections 120B (criminal conspiracy), 147 (rioting), 148 (using an armed weapon for rioting), 307 (shooting with intention to kill), among other charges, and under various sections of the Explosive Substances Act. He was acquitted of all those charges in 2007. In 2008, he was again accused of detonating the Bangalore serial blasts, for which he has been under trial for the last thirteen years. Second, Zakariyah is a thirty-two-year-old native of Parappanangadi, near Malappuram, Kerala. He was arrested in 2009 by the Karnataka police, who accused him of "providing technical support" for the Bangalore blasts of 2008 in which Maudani was accused. Third, Khalid Saifi is accused of being a co-conspirator in communal violence that took place in northeast Delhi in 2020. He is charged under several sections of the UAPA for terrorist activity and conspiracy. Fourth and finally is Siddique Kappan. Uttar Pradesh (UP) police accused Kappan of conspiring to instigate violence and disruption of the peace in the Hathras district of Uttar Pradesh. According to the First Information Report filed against him by the UP police, he is charged under Sections 124A (sedition), 153A (promoting enmity), and 295A (deliberate and malicious acts intended to outrage religious feelings) of the IPC, in addition to provisions of the UAPA and the Information Technology Act.

Anti-terror laws have historically been used by the Indian state against dissenting and marginalized classes of people whose political and religious ideas are perceived as a threat to the integrity and sovereignty of the Indian nation-state. The Indian state invokes anti-terror laws on Muslims and charges them with terrorist conspiracies because they suspect Muslims in India are connected to Islamic countries.

Women's Vulnerabilities Resulting from the Incarceration of Male Family Members

The Indian state's war on terror and its anti-terror practices, such as incarceration, target urban and rural poor and working-class communities and even marginalized middle-class and minority communities. This targeting and resulting incarceration have deeply gendered effects. It affects men of minority or racialized religious communities—not just as racial-ethnic communities but specifically as *men*. According to Black feminists Appell and Davis (2011), the incarceration of men acutely impacts families. After enduring a long trial, the accused, upon acquittal, testifies to their ordeal and the pain of social exclusion. Their personal tragedy and stigma are not something borne by them as individuals alone but by their entire family.

In one of his public speeches that was recorded for a documentary, Abdul Nasr Maudani said:

> I was put in prison continuously for four years without [being permitted] to see my dear wife Soufiya. Who can give compensation for my suffering? Salahuddin Ayoobi [Maudani's son] learned to walk and talk on the prison premises. (Sasi 2014)

In one speech, Maudani speaks about his and his wife Soufiya's trauma:

> What have they done to my wife, who is an ordinary homemaker? She has suffered for ten years. She was on the verge of a mental breakdown. We have not talked about this in public. (Sasi 2014)

His statements describe some of the ways incarceration has impacts far beyond the lives of individuals, exceeding the period of a person's captivity and acquittal (Sasi 2014). Nargis, whose husband is Khalid Saifi, gives an account of probing by her family and neighbours as to whether she would shop at the market. They warned that the police would be keeping an eye on her. She bristled at the warnings and said, "Let them check, what will they see, what am I going to do? Let them come and check my bag and find *aloo-pyaaz* [potatoes and onions] kept in it." She appears to be fed up with continuous warnings from her family that she is being watched, and after all, she is just going to buy groceries for her home. Her response to her family shows the way she tackles such comments and questions that come her way. She resists patriarchal familial dynamics, which keeps her wary of her situation, but as Khalid's wife, she also resists the institutional injustice and police surveillance inflicted upon her. In this way, women's very small day-to-day acts of learning and familial interactions should be understood as a form of resistance. Like these and other Muslim women, families of incarcerated Muslim men also share in experiences of trauma when their husbands, sons, brothers, or other family members are accused of terrorism and imprisoned. My study respondents, like Rehannath and Nargis, whose husbands are in prison, expressed feelings of unhappiness and longing for their partner's return. Rehannath articulates how she feels about Siddique's absence:

> Like one losing their strength, my strength has been snatched away. The difficulties of his absence, depression. Life is just moving forward without me. It doesn't feel like living anymore, there is no hope, I don't know how to convey it...it's a difficult situation.

There is an uninterrupted feeling of emptiness and loneliness, as Nargis shares:

> Without him, there was constant fear and anxiety and especially the lockdown was horrible. When everything including the streets was deserted, so was our home and my heart. Everything around me was scary and I had so many questions. When will this end? When will things get better? How long are we going to be apart? Will we ever get justice or not? There are no answers to the questions that I have, who shall I ask?

On one hand, women like Nargis and Rehannath shared these feelings in the absence of their husbands; on the other hand, there are mothers like Biyummah, who find themselves swinging back and forth between questions, worries, hope, and hopelessness. Biyummah has challenged the UAPA, and its amendment acts in the Supreme Court, by filing a petition under Article 32,[6] seeking a writ of mandamus finding that these acts violate fundamental rights enshrined under Articles 14[7] and 21[8] of the Constitution of India.

These Muslim women pose not only an institutional challenge but also an informal challenge to the sovereign power of the state, as demonstrated by Rehannath, who wrote in the comments of a Facebook post by Kerala's incumbent chief minister (CM). The CM's post condemned the molestation of two nuns on a train at Jhansi, Uttar Pradesh. In her comment, Rehannath wrote that the post reeks of the CM's double standards since he chose to be completely silent when her husband was framed and charged by the Uttar Pradesh government and police. Social media has thus become instrumental to the resistance of some young women, like Nargis and Rehannath, who frequently engage with people on such forums and post about their visits to the police station and share their memories. They share about personal life experiences and moments that they have shared with their male family members. Women have posted personal memories, such as a picture from their marriage anniversary celebration. Nargis felt that through such posts, she could convey to the public that Khalid is simply a social worker and a family man. She says, "I want to show people this side of him as well." This is one of the ways Nargis attempts to humanize her husband, despite his criminalization and dehumanization by the media and the court of public opinion. Similarly, when talking about her spouse, acknowledging the difference between her husband's life and her own, Rehannath details the differences between Siddique's and her likes and dislikes (Maktoob 2020a). Shared experiences and resistance bring the women together in solidarity with sympathetic groups and communities to form a cohesive social network. However, at the same time, it also brings them closer to abuse and harassment. Nargis shared such incidences as well, saying:

> People are of both types. If there are good, there are
> bad too. You have seen that there was an entire media
> trial. However, if people knew them, they would know
> that he is not like that. People write bad things too.
> Initially, I was scared, people used to write very bad

things when I used to post from his [Khalid's] Twitter
account. Once I had put a picture of my daughter,
there were so many bad things said about her, so many
abuses and accusations of being "anti-national" and
"terrorists" and "jihadi."

Such comments add to the mental trauma she is already suffering.
This trauma has been repeatedly talked about by these women as well
as by incarcerated men like Maudani (Sasi 2014). But it does not stop
here. The public conscience is built on the police's fabrication of the
cases and by public hysteria.

Women like Soufiya Maudani also face direct trauma. Kerala
police pressed charges against Soufiya for committing violent acts.
She was accused in the 2005 Tamil Nadu state bus-burning incident in
Kalamassery. The police thought that Soufiya, knowing the plight of
her husband in the Coimbatore jail, wanted to send a strong message to
the Tamil Nadu government. Hence, in her process of resisting, Soufiya
has become a target of public condemnation. She is viewed as having
been manipulated by her husband to commit disruptive acts and violence. In the eyes of the public, she has become a threat.

However, the Indian state's incarceration of Muslim men
leaves their women family members vulnerable in multiple ways.
Time and again, Muslim women are confronted by and warned about
the state's machinery, which has targeted the men in their families to
exclude them from society but which the women resist by humanizing their men in public. As Black feminists have explained in studies
of African American women's experiences of their men's incarceration, Afrocentricity is about expanding the humanizing motif in all
aspects of society and is a self-conscious struggle to empower women
and men (Harvell 2010). Women in my study do the same by bringing
their personalities and religious identities to the public sphere, by
sharing their emotions and feelings, and by talking about their male
family members' personal lives. Their resistance is extended to all

their interactions and daily existence. This resistance is invisibilized, as it appears to be an individual's struggle. However, these individuals are part of the broader targeting and incarceration of marginalized communities in India. Since their inception, India's terrorism laws have been a tool that the state has wielded against minorities and marginalized communities, demarcating who is included and excluded. In this political situation, Muslims are essentialized—that is, racialized—and individuals' presumption of innocence is inverted. This is what Muslim women challenge and resist in the public sphere. Their resistance to the incarceration of Muslim men under the UAPA includes the challenges posed in courts, their posts and comments on social media, their management of familial pressures, and their response to state surveillance.

Their means of resistance, in its physical manifestations, stems from the community-building and support garnered by the women. Notably, these women derive their sense of justice from their understanding of Islam—from what religion and God have taught them about justice. Nargis repeatedly emphasized the role of religion in helping her to have faith and stay sane in times of personal desolation. Biyummah, in an interview with Maktoob (2020b) says that there is a *sarkar* above all the *sarkars* (there is a government above all the governments, referring to God) that will bring justice one day. Referring to her belief in God, whose system is above all the systems of the government, Biyummah explained her belief that He will deliver justice for her son and herself. Through her religion, she asserts her faith in the justice system of the state. When Biyummah talks of the greater justice and Nargis references the Quran and says that she believes her husband has completed a sunnah-e-Yousuf,[9] they invoke religion and God in seeking ultimate justice, but they rely on the justice that they seek from the judiciary. These religious assertions are made by women, in this case vis-à-vis the secular state or in the secular public sphere, suggesting that an overlap and not-so-clear boundaries between the religious private and the secular public.

In the Public Sphere

The resistance of these women in India to the criminalization of their male family members needs to be situated within a much broader context. A number of the Muslim women who have been affected by the incarceration of their men resulting from terrorism trials under the UAPA have responded by dissecting their personal lives and bringing that to the public. Much study has been devoted to various forms of resistance, and there have been attempts to restore respect for devalued or neglected forms of it (Abu Lughod 1990). Even though the colonial undercurrent of benevolence toward Muslim women (and narratives of "saving" them) has remained and, in fact, continues to be very actively practised by the secular Indian state, statist feminism fixes Muslim women in a similar colonial perception. Muslim women are considered docile cultural or social beings who are divorced from politics (Malik 2018), thus putting the agency of Muslim women in doubt.

With differences among Muslim women in culture, nation, region, practice, and belief, the complexities differ and hence taper the contextualization or interpretation of their presence within the framework of feminist theory. Indian Muslim women across regions of India carry different experiences that are informed by their local cultural, social, political, and religious milieus. These differences thread the lines of identity for a Muslim woman. As demonstrated by Rehannath, Nargis, Biyummah, and Soufiya, the women variously utilize their agency, build communities with other women and activists, and mobilize themselves to fight injustice. Their action and participation in protests to deal with legal affairs have allowed them to receive support from organizations. Their resistance work has allowed them entry to the public sphere, and through their fight for justice, they have also been able to garner support from the community in times of financial crisis and deal with their legal, social, and emotional turmoil.

The public sphere, as defined by Habermas, becomes central to these women's resistance as it is the sphere where these women engage with the so-called secular state, where they collectivize and interact. The value of the public sphere, rooted in civil society, lies in the claim that there are concerns important to all citizens and that the state or any other powerful organization is in place to serve the collective interests of ordinary people (Calhoun et al. 2011). The public differs in definition and intent from the private sphere, and anything that is not public becomes private. Joan Scott (2017) explains that women were assigned to the private, feminine sphere as part of the modern secular project. However, this public-private dichotomy has been debated and interrogated by the women's movement and feminist researchers who, while examining the patriarchal aspects of private-public spheres, overlooked the secular underpinning of this distinction that relegated women to the private sphere (Scott 2017). Nevertheless, the disintegration and crossing of boundaries have been the central themes of the discourse concerning private and public spheres (Wischermann and Mueller 2004). At the juncture of feminist theory and political practice, the discourse seems to dissolve the boundaries between the spheres. This could involve characterizing the private as political or claiming that the personal is political too, thus creating alternative public spheres or disintegrating the private.

This deconstruction of the public-private dichotomy in feminist theory helps to critique and dislocate the codes assigned to the public and the private as male and female. Feminist historians in the 1970s and 1980s sought a double perspective; on one hand, they were critiquing the notions of the private sphere as a "women's realm" and claimed that the marking of the public and private is based on patriarchal power structures. On the other hand, as the historiography was reconstructed, there were many instances of women crossing the boundaries and through numerous examples, it was illustrated women were not always excluded from the public sphere (Wischermann and Mueller 2004). While the public sphere is a space of interaction, the idea of women's resistance cannot be captured and understood solely by studying large-scale collective insurrections or small-scale local movements. Similarly, Muslim women's resistance to the Indian state needs to be understood in this context, where their reactions to families and social media, and solidarity with each other, are also forms of resistance where they bring their personal lives to the public, collapsing the private-public binary that supposedly is the hallmark of secular state.

Muslim women's personal and religious selves are physically present in the public and secular sphere as they take part in protests and press conferences, attend court trials, and go to the police station and prisons to meet their male family members. When they physically enter the public sphere, they bring their personal sphere with them, including their beliefs, religion, and emotions. As the distinction between the private and the public fades and their private identities become part of the public sphere, the distinction between the religious and secular also blurs. Despite blurring the distinction and gaining public recognition, these women continue to suffer.

Secular and Post-secular India

The use of the UAPA on a religious minority is an example of racialized targeting that raises questions about the nature of the Indian state. Is the Indian state a secular state or has it ever been secular? The distinctiveness of Indian secularism for intervention or refraining from interfering in religion is based upon the values or rights in question that are supposed to be protected or advanced (Bhargava 2013). However, claims that the Indian state was ever secular have been refuted. There is criticism that the Indian Constitution has been found to be Hindu-tainted. The constitutional debates of the 1940s highlight the Hindu bias of the Indian nationalist movement and the Constitution, and institutionalized Hindu communalism is very prevalent (Singh 2005). Colonialism has played a part in this institutionalization. The nature of modern liberal secularism instituted in India by the British made it possible for the politicization of Hindutva in the state structures. British colonialism transplanted European liberal secularism in India, which resulted in the rise of conflicts between Hindus and minority religious groups. This European model of state formation and institutional practices disposed religion to politicization (Bose 2009). This feature made the Hindu right invincible once it established the majority and came to power in 2014. This is how Indian state secularism has become mixed with Hindu communalism.

As a result of the supposed resurgence of religions in the public sphere, Habermas developed post-secularism as a conceptual tool to explain the coexistence of religious communities in ever-increasing secularizing environments (Mozumder 2011). The proposition was that both religious and secular communities will learn from each other. However, before religion enters the public sphere, it has to undergo a process that Habermas calls translation for it to become worthy of acceptance (Habermas 2008). The filtering that Habermas speaks of for making religion sound neutral in the public sphere gives precedence to secularism. However, according to Talal Asad, traditional theories of secularism fail to explain the role of religion in contemporary societies (Mozumder 2011) because, despite claims of secularism, the religious agency of the state exists and continues to shape the public sphere, as evidenced in India. When the Muslim women in my case studies seek justice from the secular judiciary/state while invoking their religious beliefs and agency, this becomes a particular post-secular moment. However, these women become a part of the secular public sphere when exchanges happen between the two. The question arises: is this interaction, where women assert their religion in the secular public sphere, indeed post-secular, or is it a response to the post-secularization of the Indian polity and society wherein the Hindu right wing has established a populist regime?

There is a need to deconstruct the normative presupposition of the secular over the religious and the unavoidable separation of religion from the state and the public sphere (Mozumder 2011), which are both patriarchal. It impairs us from understanding the nuance of the bias of the Indian Hindu state. It should also be noted that although the state is said to have Hindu bias, Hinduism is not a homogenous category and Hindu society is deeply divided along caste lines. Therefore, such bias is that of the patriarchal-based forward-caste Hindus. Whether the Indian state is secular is debatable, especially with the rise of Hindutva in the state apparatus and the way it continues to target Muslim men with anti-terror laws, bolstered by the US-led War on Terror. It is difficult to disentangle religion from the Indian state.

Although the Hindu right's cultural majoritarianism criticizes the centre-left parties as pseudo-secular parties (Gudavarthy 2021), it does not criticize the idea of secularism itself but argues that tolerance, a hallmark of modern liberal secularism, has worked against the interest of the majority community and in favour of minority communities (Gudavarthy 2021).

A final question that arises and that must be addressed here is the rise of the Hindutva regime, which has become associated with the state and that views Muslims as suspect and violent, resulting in societal and economic discrimination against them. Muslims suffer from routinized violence and discrimination from the state and the public. However, these practices have not emerged out of the blue, since Hindutva (or the Hindu right) came to power, but existed even under the centre-left regimes that came before. All that the Hindu right has done is to take hold of the popular imagination and cultivate the narrative of "historical injury." This narrative is built over Muslims who have been a ruling elite in the past with a sizeable middle-class population that migrated to Pakistan during partition, and where Urdu is an official language in many parts of the country (Gudavarthy 2021). This has led to hatred and prejudice against, along with a deep sense of historical injury felt by, Muslims and led to an organized political process of Othering them.

Is this Islamophobia? Ajay Gudavarthy (2021) argues that a phobia is categorized as fear of the unknown, and fear of this "alien" or concrete Other "Muslim" is termed Islamophobia. This categorization is more fit for countries of Europe and North America, where phobia of Muslims is built out of their depiction as an unknown variable prone to militancy and violence. However, violence against Muslims in India is not borne out of fear of the unknown, since here the histories of both Hindus and Muslims are entangled and cannot be unknown or unimaginable in concrete social terms—hence the narrative of "historical injury" is used instead. Therefore, the extension of Islamophobia, which is a "culturalist" construction of violence, cannot be the end of the discussion; we must return to the social question and unequal and unjust modes of discrimination against Muslims (Gudavarthy 2021). Gudavarthy's view can be partially contested, though, since India was a British dominion and the Indian state post-independence carried over the colonial laws introduced under the British regime.

In the complexity of Indian secularism where the majority's bias is institutionalized through laws and state mechanisms, it becomes difficult to argue that India experienced post-secularization after the rise of the Hindu right. However, there is evident use of narratives and violence against Muslims. In this context, the place of the religious and personal becomes political and public, as in the case of the Muslim women in this study, who, using their religious agency, demand justice for their male family members.

Conclusion

Discussing four terrorism case studies, I have tried to understand and analyze the public and private spheres and the blurring between them in the lives of women whose male family members are incarcerated in India's war on terror. These women are not only at risk of bodily harm themselves but are also affected when their men are targeted. Their vulnerability and resistance together lead to the development of political agency under conditions of duress (Butler et al. 2016). Engaging in resistance by mobilizing their vulnerabilities in the public sphere, women like Nargis are building communities of support. Handling household finances and chores, dealing with police investigations, seeking legal aid for their male family members, and appearing in court and other public actions further indicates the collapse of the public-private divide in the lives of these women and a blurring of the public sphere in India.

Their resistance is demonstrated not only in their political protests but also through their day-to-day life, as they hold on to hope and remain optimistic about the release of their male family members and seeking justice. Their understanding of justice is derived from their sense of justice in religion, which they assert in the public sphere. This is the post-secular moment wherein religion and secularism interact, while maintaining the predominance of secularism under the UAPA. This moment occurs because these women, who are relegated to private space, come out to the public sphere as a response to the state targeting and incarcerating their male family members. With their "Muslimness"—that is, religious piety—they supposedly breach the "secularity" of the public sphere. In doing so, the state and religion interact in a more complex way over questions of Indian secularism and the rise of majoritarianism under the Hindu right. In discussing the women's vulnerabilities and resistance resulting from India's war on terror, I have tried to question Indian secularism and its public sphere, which is also patriarchal, as well as its post-secularization and the way the Indian state perpetuates a gendered form of Islamophobia.

NOTES

1. The National Investigation Agency is working as the central counterterrorism law enforcement agency.
2. Consent of the participants in this study was obtained before adding their real names in the chapter. Siddique Kappan was released from jail in February 2023 after spending two and a half years in jail without trial. He has been granted bail in the terror case by the Supreme Court of India.

3. Abdul Nasser Maudani served twelve years in prison and eight years on conditional bail. In 2014 the court had directed him to stay in Bengaluru till the trial was over. Currently the Supreme Court has relaxed the bail condition and permitted him to reside in his hometown in Kollam on the condition to present every two weeks at the designated police station.

4. SIMI is a banned organization that was formed in Aligarh in April 1977. It was outlawed in 2001 under the POTA.

5. The Delhi police's Special Cell, according to its Twitter page, has been constituted to prevent, detect, and investigate cases of terrorism, organized crime, and other serious crimes in Delhi.

6. Article 32 of the Indian Constitution gives individuals the right to go to the Supreme Court to seek justice when they feel that their rights have been unduly deprived.

7. Article 14 of the Constitution of India mentions that the state shall not deny to any person equality before the law or the equal protection of the laws within the territory of India.

8. Article 21 of the Constitution of India states that no person shall be deprived of his life or personal liberty except according to procedures established by law.

9. Yousuf is a prophet who is mentioned in the Bible and Quran. He was unjustly incarcerated and was later released when the accusations were proven false.

REFERENCES

Abu-Lughod, Lila. 1990. "The Romance of Resistance: Tracing Transformations of Power through Bedouin Women." *American Ethnologist* 17, no. 1: 41–55.

Appell, Annette Ruth, and Adrienne D. Davis. 2011. "Introduction: Mass Incarceration and Masculinity Through a Black Feminist Lens." *Washington University Journal of Law & Policy* 37, no. 1: 1–11.

Bhargava, Rajeev. 2013. "Reimagining Secularism: Respect, Domination and Principled Distance." *Economic and Political Weekly* 48, no. 50: 79–92.

Bose, Anuja. 2009. "Hindutva and the Politicization of Religious Identity in India." *Journal of Peace, Conflict and Development* 13 (February). https://www.bradford.ac.uk/library/library-resources/journal-of-peace-conflict-and-development/Issue-13-Article-8-formatted.pdf.

Butler, Judith, Zeynep Gambetti, and Leticia Sabsay. 2016. *Vulnerability in Resistance*. Duke University Press.

Calhoun, Craig, Mark Juergensmeyer, and Jonathan VanAntwerpen. 2011. *Rethinking Secularism*. Oxford University Press.

Gudavarthy, Ajay. 2021. *India after Modi: Populism and the Right*. Bloomsbury.

Habermas, Jürgen. 1964. "The Public Sphere: An Encyclopedia Article." Translated by Sara Lennox and Frank Lennox. *New German Critique* 3 (1974): 49–55.

Habermas, Jürgen. 2008. "Notes on Post-secular Society." *New Perspectives Quarterly* 25, no. 4: 17–29.

Harvell, Valeria G. 2010. "Afrocentric Humanism and African American Women's Humanizing Activism." *Journal of Black Studies* 40, no. 6: 1052–1074.

Hasan, Zoya, and Rita Menon. 2004. *Unequal Citizens: A Study of Muslim Women in India*. Oxford University Press.

Jamil, Ghazala. 2017. *Muslim Women Speak: Of Dreams and Shackles*. SAGE India.

Maktoob. 2020a. "Arrested Kerala Journalist Siddique Kappan's Wife Speaks to Maktoob. Hathras Case, UP Police" [Interview]. YouTube. October 13. https://www.youtube.com/watch?v=HJ5sBX-tP2I&t=191s.

Maktoob. 2020b. "Beyummah, A Mother Who Challenges UAPA" [Interview]. YouTube. September 8. https://www.youtube.com/watch?v=yqbBINUIehE.

Malik, Inshah. 2018. *Muslim Women, Agency and Resistance Politics: The Case of Kashmir*. Springer.

Mozumder, M.G.N. 2011. "Interrogating Post-Secularism: Jürgen Habermas, Charles Taylor, and Talal Asad." MA thesis, University of Pittsburgh.

National Crime Records Bureau. 2020. Ministry of Home Affairs, Government of India.

Sasi, K., director. 2014. *Fabricated!* [Documentary]. YouTube. https://www.youtube.com/watch?v=CoeVXOZnpKg&t=1098s.

Scott, Joan. W. 2017. *Sex and Secularism*. Princeton University Press.

Singh, Pritam. 2005. "Hindu Bias in India's 'Secular' Constitution: Probing Flaws in the Instruments of Governance." *Third World Quarterly* 26, no. 6: 909–926.

Wischermann, U., and I.K. Mueller. 2004. "Feminist Theories on the Separation of the Private and Public: Looking Back, Looking Forward." *Women in German Yearbook: Feminist Studies in German Literature & Culture* 20, no. 1: 184–197.

7

Quebec and Law 21, a Conceptual Ecosystem of Otherness

Between Omnipresence and Absence(s)

ZEINAB DIAB

> Secularism is a political discourse and not a transcendent set of principles, nor an accurate representation of history. Like all discourse, however, it has a purpose and effects that produce a particular view of the world—a view that shapes our reality while it passes to be that reality, even when it distorts our representation of reality.
>
> —*Scott (2018, 20)*

The question of visibility of religion has polarized Quebec for at least two decades, redrawing the political landscape in a convergence of parliamentary debate (Zubrzycki 2020). In an ethnocentric and nationalistic shift, secularism has become a tool to control the borders of the "nation," with Muslim women's hijabs becoming the marker of that symbolic border (Bilge 2010). Indeed, one finds "among the supporters of Quebec secularism many fervent militants of Quebec sovereignty, those tireless people of 1980 [first referendum] and 1995 [second referendum]" (Giroux 2020, 16). The "Act Respecting the Laicity of the State," commonly known as Law 21 in Quebec, is the consequence of a series of events that have marked the collective imagery. This imagery is imbued with expressions such as "reasonable accommodation," "ostentatious religious symbols," and "charter of values." They facilitated a stormy media narrative and political and electoral positions that rely on an Islamophobic context. According to Giroux (2020, 24), the provincial election in Quebec raised questions of nationalism, sovereignty, and identity through "an affective and political arrangement" that led to the adoption of Law 21.

Zine (2022, 22) writes that "while negative attitudes toward Muslim women who wear Islamic attire exist across Canada, Quebec has institutionalized gendered Islamophobia and codified anti-veiling into their provincial policies and practices." In this chapter,[1] I cover a body of work about Law 21 in Quebec and highlight critical gaps. First, I discuss several social events that have been significant in Quebec that cannot be dissociated from a holistic, comprehensive reflection on the adoption of this law. Second, I present a diagram of my literature review that has been developed from a conceptual ecosystem of Otherness. I maintain that regardless of the ideas put forward by the authors, Law 21 is almost systematically addressed to one or more categories of Otherness. In this sense, the law is designed to accommodate certain groups of people, thus shaping and specifying who is included or not. This could be qualified as "the fabrication of otherness reactivated by Law 21" (Larochelle 2020, 35). By suggesting that Law 21 serves to frame Quebec's identity and nationhood, and by presenting the writings on Law 21 in this specific framing of Otherness, I point out various "presences" constructing the narratives on Quebec's identity. I also highlight several significant absences that, by their omission, also structure this identity. Finally, I expose the omnipresence of the Arab Muslim woman in the collective imagery surrounding Law 21, an orientalist view in which the partisans of a "pure laine" Quebec find substance. My argument is simple: Since Quebec secularism was already a legal and social reality several decades before the adoption of Law 21 (Benhadjoudja 2017; Koussens et Amiraux 2014; Maclure 2020), this law now has a different function than establishing secularism—it serves as a political tool to define who is included in the "nation" and who should be excluded. Even if the law is said to be neutral, a detailed analysis of the court documents reveals that the Otherness most often referenced is that of Muslim women, and they are the most impacted by Law 21. Muslim women are the alterity par excellence who must be excluded from the Quebec "nation" and identity.

Islamophobic Context

It is important to remember January 29, 2017, when, fuelled by prevailing Islamophobia, a white nationalist Quebecer terrorist opened fire in a sacred space, a mosque, where forty people were gathered after prayers. He killed six men and seriously injured five others. According to Zine (2022, 18), this date "will go down in Canada's history as the day of the worst mass murder to take place in a house of worship." This Islamophobic-ethnonationalist terrorist act, committed by a man belonging to the white majority and resulting in Muslim victims, was nonetheless still not enough to shift the narrative of fear and hatred of Islam and Muslims in Quebec. Instead of implementing measures to counter violence and hate crimes against Muslim minorities, the government promoted its election campaign by further inciting contempt for Muslim communities. Thus, with a promise made during its provincial election campaign—legislating the wearing of religious signs and symbols—the Coalition Avenir Québec (CAQ) was elected on October 1, 2018. Law 21 was adopted with a derogation to the

Canadian Charter by Section 33 and a modification to the Quebec Charter; an approach aimed above all at cutting short any legal challenges. However, legal challenges nonetheless began the very day after its adoption. Organizations for the defence and protection of rights and freedoms have been very critical of this legislation, which violates the fundamental rights and freedoms of minority groups. In a judgment on April 20, 2021, the Superior Court of Québec validated the elements of Law 21. However, Justice Blanchard did not fail to underline the discriminatory nature of this law for Muslim women: "Of all the people targeted, women of the Muslim faith seem particularly vulnerable. Moreover, at the CSSM [Centre de services scolaires de Montréal], all the job application files, in this case eight, closed following the entry into force of Bill 21 concern Muslim women wearing the hijab" (Blanchard 2021, 172). The validation decision is currently being challenged: Law 21 has already been the subject of a second examination at the Court of Appeal of Quebec, in November 2022. The decision was rendered in February 2024, and contrary to the previous decision, it stipulated that English-speaking school boards must henceforth comply with Law 21 in the same way as French-speaking school boards. On the other hand, like Judge Blanchard, the three judges of the Court of Appeal also ruled that the law was not constitutional for elected officials. The matter is currently being brought to the Supreme Court of Canada by the English Montreal School Board (EMSB), the Fédération autonome de l'enseignement (FAE) and the National Council of Canadian Muslims (NCCM).

Two years after the January 29 attack against Muslim citizens, after a sad commemoration held on January 31, 2019, Premier François Legault repeated what he had mentioned on several platforms: "There is no Islamophobia in Québec" (Lecavalier 2019). The statement, the timing, and the context exposed the government's denial of Islamophobia as well as Legault's arrogance toward Muslim communities. As pointed out by Jamil (2021), "the refusal to know Islamophobia is an act of Islamophobia itself because it is a refusal of Muslim political claims." According to Eid, "of all the Canadian provinces, it is in Quebec that the aversion towards Muslim minorities is the most pronounced" (2020, 3), and Quebec is the province where the highest number of Islamophobic hate crimes have been reported.

Systemic denial of Islamophobia in the province goes hand in hand with denial of systemic racism. For example, incidents of racial profiling by police against Indigenous, Black, and Arab people, specifically arrests without cause, have risen by 400 percent over rates for white people (Kamel 2021). As a second example, on September 28, 2020, Joyce Echaquan, a thirty-seven-year-old Atikamekw Indigenous woman, died at Saint-Charles-Borromée hospital in Quebec. Before her death, she recorded a Facebook Live post in which a nurse and a beneficiary attendant can be heard making degrading remarks about her. Joyce Echaquan's death is considered by coroner Géhane Kamel as proof of the existence of systemic anti-Indigenous racism in Quebec's institutions because, according to her, "Mrs. Echaquan was indeed ostracized, and her death could have been avoided."

With the filing of the coroner's inquest report on Echaquan's death, there has been a lot of talk about systemic racism in Quebec, yet Premier Legault chooses to lock himself in denial, claiming a desire to protect "our values" and avoid a racism trial against Quebecers. This contempt for otherness is not limited to ethnic and religious racism; a bill targeting English-speaking minorities and allophones was also adopted by the National Assembly on May 2022. Bill 96, a reform of Law 101, aims to impose the use of French in basic services in a drastic manner, which many describe as dehumanizing. The parallels between Bill 96's targeting linguistic minorities and Law 21's targeting religious minorities are obvious, as journalist Toula Drimonis explains: "Just like it did with Bill 21, the CAQ chose to circumvent democracy because it was in the way. It's problematic to say the least, and while this routine brushing aside of dissent might appeal to some, Quebecers who value and respect the Quebec Charter of Rights and Freedoms should be concerned" (Drimonis 2021). It is therefore plausible to claim that racism in Quebec manifests itself concretely in institutions, whether through the police, health system, or law. Law 21 is indeed part of this set of coercive racist measures that target racialized, linguistic, religious, and otherwise marginalized people in society. All these social, political, and legal measures, including Law 21, effectively reinforce the white historical colonial structure (Romani 2020) and maintain domination over those considered outside of Quebec identity. As pointed out by Benhadjoudja (2022), not only is Law 21 Islamophobic, it is additionally a "racial secularism as settler colonial sovereignty in Quebec."

Adoption of Law 21

The National Assembly of Québec, with a CAQ majority, adopted Law 21 on June 16, 2019, by using Section 33 of the Canadian Charter of Rights and Freedoms to derogate from Sections 2 and 7 to 15, along with a modification to the provincial charter "in order to include that fundamental rights and freedoms must be exercised with respect for the secularism of the State" (*Loi sur la laïcité de l'État* 2019). As Romani explains, "The discriminatory nature of Law 21 is so established that it requires the government to have recourse to the derogatory provisions of the Québec and Canadian charters in order to escape—temporarily—from any prosecution based on discrimination that operates" (Romani 2020, 51). Thus, contrary to popular belief about this legislation, it does not only concern the ban on the wearing of religious symbols, but also the suspension of thirty-eight sections of fundamental rights and freedoms enshrined in the Quebec Charter, as well as the exemption from Sections 2 and 7 to 15 of the Canadian Charter. This breaks from the orientations promoted by Quebec's and Canada's charters concerning the principles of individual rights and freedoms (Lampron 2020), especially since Quebec was one of the first Canadian provinces to implement, in 1975, a charter for the respect of the rights of minorities. These current measures are therefore regressive.

It is mainly Section 6 of Law 21 that has motivated a series of legal challenges, the most recent of which have been those heard at the Superior Court of Québec. Section 6 mentions the prohibition of wearing religious symbols by state officials in Quebec (teachers, lawyers, peace officers, etc.). Additionally, Section 8 obligates the provision and reception of public services with an uncovered face, which refers to the niqab. Section 8 is very similar to Bill 94, introduced in 2010, when Quebec required "un visage découvert" or a "naked face" when providing or receiving public services. Natasha Bakht (2020) explains in her book *In Your Face* how the COVID-19 pandemic and the wearing of face masks, which has become widespread globally, exposed the fallacy of some of the main reasons for opposition to the niqab: security, communication, and identity.

Law 21, although presented as applying to all religions equally, disproportionately affects Muslim women teachers. As Judge Blanchard mentioned in his decision following the historic trial at the Superior Court, the law focused disproportionately on the question of the Islamic veil; very little emphasis was placed on other expressions of religiosity, such as the cross, the dastar, the kippah, or even the beard among Muslim and Sikh men (Blanchard 2021).

In December 2021, the reassignment of a teacher because of her hijab caused a stir. Parents (and kids) and politicians took the opportunity to express their disagreement with Law 21 when Fatemeh Anvari, a third-grade teacher at Chelsea Elementary School, was assigned to non-teaching duties because of her headscarf. This highly publicized event was certainly not the only one to occur that excluded, humiliated, and dehumanized Muslim women. My research has revealed several Muslim teachers who suffered a similar fate, if not even more severe. However, those women have remained in the shadows, for fear of reprisals if they assert themselves in the media; as Benhadjoudja (2018b) questions: "Can Muslim Women Speak?" Indeed, Muslim women who wear the hijab in the province of Quebec and speak out are forcefully called to order. The case of Dalila Awada is a poignant example. She entered an infernal spiral of hatred and legal proceedings (taking place over ten years) because she defended on many platforms the wearing of hijab during the Parti Québécois' "Charter of Values" campaign in 2013–2014. She states, "The debate (on secularism) is important to talk about, but it goes too far when you attack someone's integrity" (Nguyen 2014). When the federal government introduced Amira Elghawaby, the new special representative for combatting Islamophobia in Canada, a wave of hate was targeted at the visibly Muslim woman who wore a hijab. Columnists and political party leaders in Quebec immediately claimed that she had made racist remarks against Quebecers regarding Law 21. However, Law 21 is an institutionalization of gendered Islamophobia (Zine 2022) that, as mentioned, affects a disproportionate number of sections related to fundamental rights and freedoms in the two chapters operating in Quebec and directly impacts visibly Muslim women. Thus, it goes without saying that a representative whose job is to fight against Islamophobia will denounce and criticize Law 21. Indeed, this law perpetuates racism, sexism, and Islamophobia.

Furthermore, the space given for hearing the opinions and perceptions of hijabi women was severely restricted. Indeed, as Khaoula Zoghlami noted, during the parliamentary committee's discussion on Law 21, only one directly impacted female civil servant was given time to speak. Her testimony represented just 0.6 percent of the committee's total hearing time. According to Zoghlami, this highlights a paradox:

> While Muslim women's headscarves occupy public debates, the voices of women who wear these headscarves are, at best, excluded from discussions, at worst, completely inaudible [and] it is paradoxical that these self-appointed saviors who denounce the oppression of Muslim women and call for their liberation are not ready to listen to these Muslim women speak

about their experiences. Indeed, as long as they wear headscarves, these women will not be considered as full subjects and citizens of Québec...It is thus presupposed that the headscarf would not only hide women's bodies but would also harm their ability to think and act. (Zoghlami 2020, 202–203)

One of the basic principles of decolonial feminism is to listen to women and their demands, regardless of their origins; this was clearly not the case with the adoption of Law 21. The CAQ government and its allies assumed that Muslim women are without conscience or are conditioned in a form of "false conscience" and cannot speak for themselves. It is necessary to question whether "the demands at the heart of current feminism represent the deep concerns of minority, racialized women, or reflect more the experience of white women privileged by their colour" (Hamrouni and Maillé 2015, 11).

Islamophobia mixed with secularism discourse is betrayed in narratives about "Quebec's values" and veers into racism when used as a political instrument that aims to control the bodies of racialized Muslim women; the law is then reduced to a simple regulatory mechanism. For example, when Fatemeh Anvari was removed from her teaching position, even as crowds of parents and children loudly demonstrated for her return to class, we could read headlines such as "The Chelsea teacher shouldn't have been hired," and we heard Premier Legault say, "When you pass a law, you have to enforce it, so the school board should not have hired that person" (Sioui 2021). According to Muslim feminist critical race scholar Sherene Razack, "Racial thought, once integrated into laws and administrative measures, no longer seems to us violence inflicted on others, but a simple element of the law itself" (Razack 2011, 33). Quebec was already experiencing a shortage of qualified teachers when the law was passed, and the COVID-19 pandemic only worsened the problem. The lack of teachers became so serious during the pandemic that the government called on parents to "monitor" classes, even if those parents wore religious symbols. This situation has been described as a paradox by Muslim teachers wearing the hijab who have been hampered in their employability because of Law 21 (Lubeck 2022).

In this section, I have demonstrated how the adoption and implementation of Law 21 racializes Muslim women and perpetuates racism towards them. Not only are Muslim women deprived of a political voice concerning the adoption of this legislation, but they are also stigmatized, stripped of their fundamental rights, and increasingly restricted in their employment at a time when Quebec struggles with a lack of qualified female teachers in the public education system. The social context surrounding Law 21 discourse and practical measures taken to apply Quebec secularism exposes the law to be a racist mechanism that specifically targets veiled Muslim women.

A Law about Secularism or about Otherness?

This identity-ethnonationalist-racist-Islamophobic-gendered discourse mixed with the narrative of secularism hides several elements. But let's take a break and recall the very principles of secularism. To do this, I draw knowledge from the work of two leading experts on the subject, Jean Baubérot in France and Quebecer Francine Milot. Both recognize several types of secularism according to historical and local contexts; but, at the same time, they teach us that all kinds of secularism are articulated around four main principles: The principle of separation of religious institutions from the state, the principle of the state's neutrality, the principle of equal treatment of citizens, and the principle of freedom of belief and religion (Baubérot and Milot 2011). A serious question arises with those four principals: Is Law 21 a law on secularism?

It seemed to me, from the beginning of my research, that Law 21 emerged not because Quebec's state was not secular or that there was an urgent need to establish secularism, but rather—as Bilge (2010) and Benhadjouda (2017) emphasized many years ago in their research on secularism in Quebec—because discursive secularism has a particular function, that of establishing the contours of the Quebec's culture and its borders. According to Bilge (2010), an intersectional sociologist, there is a symbolic border between individuals belonging to the interior of a national community and others considered outsiders. A reactivation of this symbolic border would be triggered each time discourse on the hijab takes an ambient place in society. The hijab thus becomes a symbol of this boundary between "us" and "not-us." The hijab also becomes the archetype of all religious signs to be banned in order to preserve "Quebec's values," the "nation," and its "identity." The CAQ's objective has been, from its electoral win—and until today, within the framework of the two last provincial elections—to stir the ardour of the troops, to revive the fibre of Quebecer identity, and to stimulate pride in the latter (La Presse canadienne 2022). This Quebecer pride is precisely associated with a specific relationship to Otherness and is implanted in the collective imaginary with a feeling of superiority for belonging to the white francophone majority, "pure laine." Consequently, by reactivating the symbolic borders of the "nation" with a law that prohibits, above all, the wearing of the hijab, the concept of the "nation" becomes socially constructed as homogeneous and erases concrete diversity within Quebec society. In other words, Law 21 promotes and perpetuates racism and maintains whiteness by creating a Muslim Otherness focused on the hijab. According to Zine, with Law 21:

> Veiled Muslim women are rendered illiberal and "unimaginable" as citizens. Citizenship and national belonging become determined sartorially, as the nation is not only circumscribed by dominant cultural values and beliefs (that veiling is seen to undermine) but also is configured through the kinds of dress that signify belonging and allegiance to the same values. (2022, 20)

A Conceptual Ecosystem of Otherness:
Between Omnipresence and Absence(s)

A diagram emerged from my current research on Law 21 in Quebec and is presented as Figure 7.1. This diagram is framed as a conceptual ecosystem of Otherness and is structured around seven categories of Otherness: Muslim Otherness, international Otherness, French Otherness, Canadian Otherness, internal Otherness, "pures laines," and religious symbols. I developed this diagram based on a three-step literature review. First, I examined the fifteen expert reports submitted to Québec's Superior Court. Second, I analyzed the book *Modération ou extrémisme? Regards critiques sur la loi 21* (Celis et al. 2020), which synthesizes the writings of seventeen academics. Finally, when the decision written by Judge Blanchard became public, I counterposed it with my point of view. By approaching the writings surrounding Law 21 in terms of Otherness, it became possible to think beyond the pros and cons of this specific legislation to uncover three prominent absences and one omnipresence: Indigenous, Black, and American Otherness, while Muslim Otherness is transcendent in all the writings.

In this diagram, we can see that only one expert report actually attempts to understand what religious symbols are, but again, in an imperfect way. I placed it at the centre of this chart because the concept of secularism—associated with the erasure of visible religious symbols, and by extension the Islamic hijab—was presented in Law 21 as a central element of Quebec identity. Then, "pures laines" Otherness corresponds to the collective "we"—at this level of Otherness, there are authors who provide explanations of the political, historical, and social factors that led to the adoption of Law 21 and its representation as a protector of Quebec's identity and nation. The level of "internal Otherness" includes authors who have formulated analyses specifically related to Quebec's internal social, racial, religious, and linguistic dynamics. In this context of Otherness, internal differences within Quebec's territory are seen either as a driving force or as an obstacle

Figure 7.1. Law 21 in a Conceptual Ecosystem of Otherness

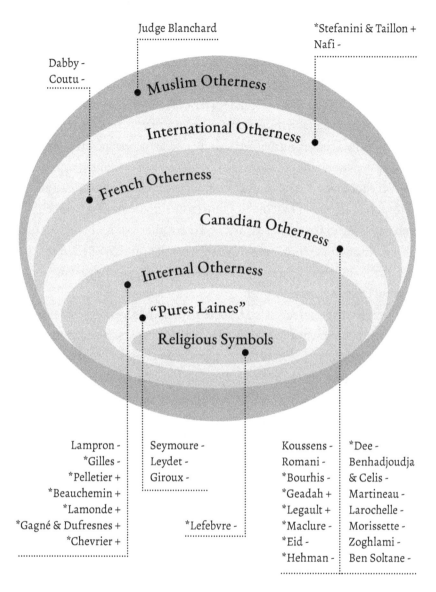

Judge Blanchard

*Stefanini & Taillon +
Nafi -

Dabby -
Coutu -

Muslim Otherness

International Otherness

French Otherness

Canadian Otherness

Internal Otherness

"Pures Laines"

Religious Symbols

Lampron -	Seymoure -	Koussens -	*Dee -
*Gilles -	Leydet -	Romani -	Benhadjoudja
*Pelletier +	Giroux -	*Bourhis -	& Celis -
*Beauchemin +		*Geadah +	Martineau -
*Lamonde +		*Legault +	Larochelle -
*Gagné & Dufresnes +	*Lefebvre -	*Maclure -	Morissette -
*Chevrier +		*Eid -	Zoghlami -
		*Hehman -	Ben Soltane -

✳ Author who acted as an expert in the
   Law 21 trial at the Superior Court of Québec.

‑ Author who was against Law 21.

✚ Author who was in favour of Law 21.

to the structuring of a national collective identity. As for Canadian Otherness, it encompasses Quebec's internal Otherness and is considered by authors, once again, to either facilitate or act as a barrier to the consolidation of Quebec's identity—especially in relation to Law 21 and its legal challenges. French Otherness includes Canadian Otherness in this schema, as the *"laïcité à la française"* is considered more prevalent and dominant than that of Canada. The level of international Otherness operates beyond all the reflections on and coercive measures imposed by Law 21 in structuring Quebec's white and francophone identity, raising questions about the severity of the law's provisions that contradict fundamental rights and freedoms enshrined in charters and international principles. Finally, there is Muslim Otherness, which encompasses all these intertwined forms of Otherness in this schema, as it is through the figure of the Muslim woman, and in relation to her, that Law 21 was conceived, ultimately forming an inverted mirror of what constitutes white Québécois identity. Muslim women in hijab are perceived as a threat to the Quebec nation, thus forming a radical Otherness (Karimi 2023). In this logic, they must be excluded from the nation to preserve Québécois identity and its values, which are positioned in opposition to the body of the hijab-practising Muslim woman. This logic of assigning radical Otherness operates similarly in France, where secularism, in its functioning, "assigns a radical otherness [that] deprives individuals [notably visibly Muslim women] of any form of legitimate identity and, beyond that, strips them of the fundamental sense of their presence in a territory" (Karimi 2023, 52). Even though Judge Blanchard was compelled to uphold the core of Law 21 due to its use of the notwithstanding clause in relation to the Canadian Charter, it is important to note that the tone of his decision was highly critical. He raised significant concerns and highlighted the injustices faced by Muslim women in Quebec. As Razack (2011) states, analysis of Law 21 and its political implications demonstrates that it primarily serves to exclude Muslim women and Islam from the legal framework in order to form and consolidate the white identity of certain groups. Even though the law is said to be neutral, a detailed analysis of legal documents and academic literature reveals that the Otherness most frequently invoked is that of Muslim women. Indeed, regardless of the arguments presented by the authors and experts who have written about Law 21, the legislation is regularly addressed in terms of Otherness, in a way that structures a Quebec identity whose imaginary boundaries are shaped by inclusive or exclusive positions, with the Muslim woman serving as the allegorical figure of the Other—the strange stranger (Ahmed 2004).

Law 21, in a framework of international Otherness, has been discussed especially regarding the little consideration given to the modification and derogation of charters of individual rights and freedoms while these charters are nevertheless governed by international law. Authors question the very essence of the urgency justifying the derogations included in Law 21, while its supporters see it only as a preventive technicality to avoid the courts. Coutu explains that in 1976, Canada, with the agreement of Quebec, ratified the International Covenant on Civil and Political Rights and agreed that a state party can derogate to that pact from its provisions only "in the event that an exceptional public emergency threatens the existence of the nation and is proclaimed by an official act," to the strict extent necessary and if "subject to such measures...do not result in discrimination solely on the basis of race, colour, sex, language, religion or social origin" (Coutu 2020, 235, 238). This international treaty does not, therefore, prohibit recourse to derogations, "but strictly conditions such recourse to the existence of precise circumstances of particular gravity, which do not, moreover, authorize the setting aside of certain fundamental rights, such as freedom of religion" (Coutu 2020, 238). However, to the argument of the will of Quebec's majority to adopt the "Act respecting the Laicity of the State," Coutu writes that it would rather be necessary to oppose a superior legitimacy, which stems from the international commitments of Canada and Quebec with respect to fundamental rights and freedoms. Nevertheless, three United Nations rapporteurs—holding mandates on issues relating to minorities, on contemporary forms of racism, on discrimination, race, xenophobia, and intolerance as well as on freedom of religion or belief—denounced Law 21 (Dabby 2020).

On French Otherness, Law 21 reaffirms an affiliation with French culture through a similar secularism, *"une laïcité fermée à la française."* The text of Law 21 in English introduces a new term, "laicity," an English translation of the word *laïcité*: "Until now, and in general in Canada, the term laïcité has been translated into English in legal texts as *secularism* rather than *laicity* and these terms are used in the Supreme Court of Canada as equivalent terms" (Dabby 2020, 243). It should also be noted that no explanation for this terminological choice is included in the law, and critics point out that this semantic shift through Law 21 is not consistent with pan-Canadian law. This is not an accident but a deliberate choice to distance from the term "secularism," generally accepted in the Anglo-Saxon world, and to appropriate the notion of secularism (*laïcité*) as understood in a French frame of reference (Lavoie 2018, 77). According to Lavoie (2018), ties to France have influenced the debates surrounding secularism in Quebec, even a *proximity* that is articulated in linguistic, cultural and legal terms, and mainly with an imprint of Catholicism. Just as in France, secularism appears in both legal and narrative forms to occupy significant space and justify claims of the dominant social group.

In their report submitted to the court, Stefanini and Taillon (2020) analyze European state law on regulating the freedom to express beliefs through the wearing of religious symbols and the provision and receipt of services with an uncovered face, situating Law 21 comparatively in this context. The two experts draw a panorama of different types of secularism in Europe and argue that "[b]y choosing secularism, Québec affirms not only its specificity, but also a certain affiliation with continental Europe. To the civil legal tradition (which dominates the whole of continental Europe), to the French language and culture (which Québec shares with Belgium, France, and Switzerland)" (Stefanini and Taillon 2020, 179). While the report extensively discusses European laws regarding the practice of face covering, which explicitly refs to the niqab, no passage mentions the global COVID-19 health crisis, which caused billions of people to wear protective face covering.

Regarding Canadian Otherness, the literature review as well as the conceptual diagram demonstrate that a large majority of expert reports in favour of Law 21 were submitted within this specific framework of Otherness, thus revealing a desire to reaffirm non-adherence to Canadian Anglo-Saxon culture. This seems to be not only because of the linguistic factor—Canada being anglophone and Quebec being francophone—but also because a specific relationship to religion is prevalent: Canada's religious heritage is Anglican while Quebec has Catholicism, even if it claims to be secular. Above all, there is also the historically conflicting relationship between English Canadians and French Canadians. The historical relationship of Quebecers with Canada serves the supporters of Law 21 to recall the oppressions they experienced under British colonial domination, which kept French Canadians in a subordinate social status and desiring distance and disaffiliation from Canada and, by extension, its multicultural policies. However, Gilles, reporting on behalf of the World Sikh Organization of Canada, used the same approach and framework to underline how "freedom of worship issues have historically resolved themselves by a compromise of tolerance...thus constituting a cultural and legal heritage." He illustrates how Law 21 breaks with Canada's history, specifically with the spirit of the "Acte de Québec" signed in 1774, which, according to Gilles, put an end to "the main discriminations relating to the Catholic population and [concretized] a sort of normative transformation" (Gilles 2020, 114, 4). There are therefore two parts to this story that seem to be instrumentalized according to the different positions surrounding Law 21. In this regard, Giroux argues that with the adoption of Law 21, nationalist secularism revealed its ambiguous relationship to colonialism: "The desire to be the colonizer instead of the colonizer dominates Québec thought," and she adds that secularism as it was done in Quebec in 2019 also "reveals a villainous, Islamophobic act, whose archive will be a stain in the history of Quebec" (Giroux 2020, 26, 24).

A wide range of authors focused their analyses on Quebec's inner Otherness. They questioned the consequences for the internal social cohesion of Quebec and on religious minorities, particularly Muslim women. For example, Eric Hehman (2020), a social psychologist, mentions how the social contexts in which laws are adopted can significantly affect the perception of the general population on the groups impacted by the adopted law. A government that passes a law sends a message that normalizes positive or negative behaviour. Similarly, Thomas Dee (2020) demonstrates how the presence of diverse teachers benefits both minority and majority students and has positive future societal impacts. Another expert, psychologist Richard Bourhis (2020), mentions how adoption of a law with the avowed aim of excluding all religious minorities bearing a religious sign from the Quebec school system—an effect that the Christian or nonbelieving Quebec majority does not have to suffer—has negative effects on the mental and physical health of the people concerned. Mental impacts include psychological distress, prejudice, stigmatization, discrimination, undermined self-esteem, feelings of frustration, and reduced motivation at work; as physical effects, he mentions weight gain, diabetes, high blood pressure, and heart disease. As Eid details, across Canada, Muslims are the most stigmatized and misunderstood group. Moreover, "some research conducted in Québec and the rest of Canada suggests that Muslim women who wear the hijab are particularly affected, in their personal lives, by Islamophobic stereotypes and prejudices...and veiled women suffer discrimination of an Islamophobic and/or Arabophobic nature in access to employment" (Eid 2020, 3).

Concerning articulation around the *pures laines*, authors have pointed out a persistent ambiguity in relation to religion, an ambivalence that is reactivated by the visibility of the religious Other, sparking the resurgence of a latent and persistent Catholicism, and this, despite a secularization and a secularism in place: *"Catho-laïcité"* (Celis et al. 2020, 18). This observation had already been elaborated by sociologist

Geneviève Zubrzycki (2020) who explains that Quebecers are Catholics in quarantine, their Catholicism revealing itself at the sight of the religious Other, and this, even if the social and individual apparatus has evacuated the religious since the Quiet Revolution of 1960. The secularism referred to in the text of Law 21 maintains the privileges of the dominant group, even if it defines itself as nonreligious; the Catholic religion is "invisible" and therefore compatible with this version of restrictive secularism, while it is incompatible for people from other religious groups where the external practice of religion is just as significant as internal belief. Thus, a critical reading of the religious neutrality referred to in Quebec's law on secularism reveals, in fact, a policy of colourblind denial that perpetuates white domination and inferiorizes Muslim women. This sartorial nationalism involves coercive unveiling to assert an assimilative code within a white settler-colonial context (Zine 2022, 20).

Finally, at the foundation of my conceptual schema are writings regarding the study of religious symbols. Even though such symbolism represents the very heart of the law, only one author (Lefebvre 2020) presented information on the wearing of religious symbols within several traditions. It turns out, however, that this expert report from the religious sciences viewpoint does not mention dastar wearing among Sikh women, even though Amrit Kaur, a teacher who wears it, was not only publicly against Law 21 but also had to move from Quebec because of the law (Maher 2019). Likewise, the wearing of kippah, tichel, or chiteil among Jewish women was not elaborated in this report, despite the very public objections of Caroline Gehr, a Jewish teacher (Savic 2019). There is also a marked absence in both literature and mainstream discourse regarding the Black Muslim experience. For example, some Black Muslim women wear a hijab tied in a bun with an uncovered neck, a type of hijab associated with Black identity (Khabeer 2016). This often goes undetected by Western observers, who, from an orientalist perspective, easily identify the veils of Muslim Middle Eastern women. All these absences in the literature demonstrate ignorance about the religion and culture of others and a fascination with the hijab of Muslim Arab women.

This framing of Law 21 also reveals two more prominent absences: American Otherness and Indigenous Otherness. In the first instance, given that Quebecers are geographically closer to Americans than they are to the French, this absence seems to be an exteriorization (rejection) of American belonging since it is an Anglo-Saxon culture and socially constructed as incompatible with Quebec's identity. Additionally, while some in Quebec repeated "we are not racist," and Premier Legault's reacted to the death of George Floyd by saying he was "shocked" by this incident, it merely indicates the perpetual denial of systemic racism in the province. Legault maintains that "racism is 'less present' in the province than in the neighbours to the south" (Carabin 2020). Another idea forwarded by Premier Legault can be framed as "We don't want America's secularism and freedom of religion," since such freedom occupies a central place in American debates, and American legal secularism mainly concerns the right to religious freedom. The secularism promoted by Law 21 does not protect the right to religion—indeed it infringes on the rights of religious minorities, a consequence that the majority group does not have to suffer. By dissociating itself from American belonging, the CAQ government dissociates itself from a racist narrative, even while it maintains a racial secularism (Benhadjoudja 2022).

Regarding Indigenous Otherness, it should be noted that the CAQ proposed its own definition of what constitutes a religion and a religious symbol, and Indigenous people denounced this bill from the start. They said it would steal their spirituality and identity (Niosi 2019). The CAQ government then declared that Law 21 would not apply to Indigenous people. What challenges us in this analysis, according to different levels of Otherness, is this failure to consider Indigenous spirituality in the very definition of what constitutes a religion. The legislator has inscribed its worldview and its own definition of religion and what constitutes a religious sign, a vision and definitions that derive from Catholicism, and especially in reaction to the hijabs of Muslim women. This observation thus exposes a lack of consideration for Indigenous realities and spirituality in this equation of Quebec identity and nationhood.

Conclusion

> It is through the right to exclude that a weakened state shows (at little cost) the strength it claims to possess and at the same time reassures those who suspect its destitution. (Razack 2011, 43)

In this chapter, I have discussed how with the adoption of Law 21 in Quebec, secularism became used as a political instrument for constructing the boundaries of identity for a "nation" in reaction to Canadian Anglo-Saxon culture and Muslim Otherness through its purported affiliation with French culture and by omitting considerations of American, Indigenous, and Black belonging. From a holistic perspective, I found that the social context and main ideas supported in the literature on Law 21 framed a conceptual ecosystem of Otherness. I suggested that this ecosystem represents Quebec's identity construction. Therefore, the presence of different forms of Otherness in the writings surrounding Law 21—but furthermore, one omnipresence and several critical absences—were significant to understanding the law's very purpose. As demonstrated in the case of veiled Muslim women, Law 21 marked the boundaries of the "nation," and by doing so, it reinforced the identity of "white and civilized" for the majority of Quebec (Larochelle 2020, 38). The legislators are constructing a "national sovereign identity" by marginalizing identities to control the symbolic border of the "nation" and distinguish who can or cannot be included in the nation. An orientalist perspective is clearly articulated in the discourse of Law 21 regarding the veiled Muslim woman. Even among experts who are invited to give their opinions about religious symbols, their overemphasis on the hijab of Middle Eastern women erases the Black Muslim experience. Similarly, discussion of head covering has been primarily associated with Muslim women and omits any discussion of Jewish and Sikh women who also cover their body and head in a similar way.

I also highlighted how the ongoing legacy of secularism and white settler colonialism in Quebec is observable within the framing of Law 21, as it ignores the histories and spiritual practices of Indigenous peoples, instead privileging a narrow understanding of a *catho-laïcité* nationalism. The law reinforces the idea of the Other and serves to further marginalize and exclude religious minority groups from full participation in Quebec society, constructing people whose religious identity is visible as incompatible in the "nation." Law 21 aims, above all, to reduce the visibility of Muslim women; it also reinforces the idea that Islam is incompatible with the West, and at the same time, systematically excluded from Western national symbolic borders (Benhadjoudja 2018a). I also explained how Law 21 allowed the CAQ government to mobilize a nationalist discourse by presenting a law on secularism as a solution for sovereign identity, a way to define the borders of the imagined "nation," and to delimit who is a Quebecer and who is not.

As Law 21 took shape in a social climate marked by Islamophobia and racism, the hijabs of Muslim teachers thus became a target for creating a legible boundary between the white *pures laines* us and the non-us. Moreover, Law 21 socially constructs the bodies of Muslim women, especially Arabs, as incompatible in the Quebec "nation" and legally allows their exclusion. This measure has had drastic consequences on their professional and social life as well as on their physical and mental health. It is therefore important to be concerned about the safety of these women since they are omnipresent in the social and legal discourse on Quebec secularism, which normalizes Islamophobic hatred and racism as a result of Law 21. However, because Quebec presents itself as a victim nation colonized by Canada (Benhadjoudja 2022), it becomes difficult to engage in any anti-racist and anticolonial conversations that could redress the harms to visibly Muslim women caused by Law 21.

NOTE

1.   All quotes in French have been carefully translated by the author.

REFERENCES

Ahmed, Sara. 2004. *The Cultural Politics of Emotion*. Routledge.

Bakht, Natasha. 2020. *In Your Face: Law, Justice, and Niqab-Wearing Women in Canada*. Delve Books.

Baubérot, Jean, and Micheline Milot. 2011. *Laïcités sans frontières*. Editions du Seuil.

Beauchemin, Jacques. 2020. "Rapport d'expertise pour le mouvement laïque québécois dans le dossier de contestation de la loi sur la laïcité de l'état." Rapport d'expertise, procès de la loi 21, Montréal.

Benhadjoudja, Leila. 2017. "Laïcité narrative et sécularonationalisme au québec à l'épreuve de la race, du genre et de la sexualité." *Studies in Religion/Sciences religieuses* 46, no. 2: 272–291. https://doi.org/10.1177/0008429817697281.

Benhadjoudja, Leila. 2018a. "Territoires de libération: Perspectives féministes musulmanes." *Tumultes* 50, no. 1: 111–130. https://doi.org/10.3917/tumu.050.0111.

Benhadjoudja, Leila. 2018b. "Les femmes musulmanes peuvent-elles parler?" *Anthropologie et sociétés* 42, no. 1: 113–133. https://doi.org/10.7202/1045126ar.

Benhadjoudja, Leila. 2022. "Racial Secularism as Settler Colonial Sovereignty in Quebec." *Islamophobia Studies Journal* 7, no. 2: 182–199.

Benhadjoudja, Leila, and Leila Celis. 2020. "Colonialité du pouvoir au temps de la loi 21—Pistes de réflexion." In *Modération ou extrémisme? Regards critiques sur la loi 21*, edited by Leila Celis et al. Presses de l'Université de Laval.

Ben Soltane, Sonia. 2020. "La loi 21 vue à travers le prisme 'des ségrations respectables.'" In *Modération ou extrémisme? Regards critiques sur la loi 21*, edited by Leila Celis et al. Presses de l'Université Laval.

Bilge, Sirma. 2010. "'...alors que nous, Québécois, nos femmes sont égales à nous et nous les aimons ainsi': La patrouille des frontières au nom de l'égalité de genre dans une 'nation' en quête de souveraineté." *Sociologie et sociétés* 42, no. 1: 197–226. https://doi.org/10.7202/043963ar.

Blanchard, Marc-André. 2021. "Jugement Cour supérieure du Québec [loi 21]." *SOQUIJ*. https://t.soquij.ca/Jd4m5.

Bourhis, Richard. 2020. *Fédération autonome de l'enseignement c. Procureure générale du Québec et al.* Rapport d'expertise, procès de la loi 21, Montréal.

Carabin, François. 2020. "Le racisme 'moins grave' au Québec qu'aux États-Unis, maintient Legault." *Journal Métro*, June 1. https://journalmetro.com/actualites/national/2456595/racisme-moins-grave-quebec-francois-legault/.

Celis, Leila, Dia Dabby, Dominique Leydet, Vincent Romani, eds. 2020. *Modération ou extrémisme? Regards critiques sur la loi 21*. Presses de l'Université Laval.

Chevrier, Marc. 2020. "Rapport d'expertise préparé pour le procureur général du Québec." Rapport d'expertise, procès de la loi 21, Montréal.

Coutu, Michel. 2020. "La passion des dérogations: exit l'État constitutionnel de droit?" In *Modération ou extrémisme? Regards critiques sur la loi 21*, edited by Leila Celis et al. Presses de l'Université Laval.

Dabby, Dia. 2020. "Le western de la laïcité. Regards juridiques sur la loi sur la laïcité de l'État." In *Modération ou extrémisme? Regards critiques sur la loi 21*, edited by Leila Celis et al. Presses de l'Université Laval.

Dee, Thomas. 2020. *English Montreal School Board et al. v. Attorney General of Quebec, Fédération autonome de l'enseignement v. Attorney General of Quebec et al.* Rapport d'expertise, procès de la loi 21, Montréal.

Drimonis, Toula. 2021. "Quebec and Bill 96: The Good, the Bad and the Ugly." *Cultmtl* (blog). May 18. https://cultmtl.com/2021/05/quebec-and-bill-96-the-good-the-bad-and-the-ugly-french-language/.

Dufresnes, Yannick, and Gilles Gagné. 2020. "Rapport d'expertise préparé pour le procureur général du Québec." Rapport d'expertise, procès de la loi 21, Montréal.

Eid, Paul. 2020. *Commission scolaire English-Montreal et al. c. Procureure générale du Québec, Lauzon, et al. c. Procureure générale du Québec, Fédération autonome de l'enseignement c. Procureure générale du Québec et al.* Rapport d'expertise, procès de la loi 21, Montréal.

Geadah, Yolande. 2020. "Rapport d'expertise du groupe pour les droits des femmes du Québec (PDF) concernant la contestation de la loi québécoise sur la laïcité de l'état." Rapport d'expertise, procès de la loi 21, Montréal.

Gilles, David. 2020. "Rapport pour la *World Sikh Organization of Canada Hak et al. c. Procureure générale du Québec*, CSQ 500-17-108353-197." Rapport d'expertise, procès de la loi 21, Montréal.

Giroux, Dalie. 2020. "La question nationale et de la laïcité au Québec: Psychopolitique d'une intrication." In *Modération ou extrémisme? Regards critiques sur la loi 21*, edited by Leila Celis et al. Presses de l'Université de Laval.

Hamrouni, Naïma, and Chantal Maillé, ed. 2015. *Le sujet du féminisme est-il blanc? Femmes racisées et recherche féministe.* Éditions du Remue-ménage.

Hehman, Eric. 2020. "Report re. Challenge to *An Act Respecting the Laicity of the State* (Bill 21)." Rapport d'expertise, procès de la loi 21, Montréal.

Jamil, Uzma. 2021. "Islamophobia and Whiteness in Canada." *Contending Modernities. Exploring How Religious and Secular Forces Interact in the Modern World* (blog). July 29. https://contendingmodernities.nd.edu/ theorizing-modernities/islamophobia-epistemic-ignorance/.

Kamel, Géhane. 2021. "Loi sur la recherche des causes et des circonstances des décès pour la protection de la vie humaine. Concernant le décès de Joyce Echaquan." Rapport d'enquête 2020-00275. https://www.coroner. gouv.qc.ca/fileadmin/Enquetes_publiques/2020-EP00275-9.pdf.

Karimi, Hanane. 2023. *Les femmes musulmanes ne sont-elles pas des femmes?* Hors d'atteinte.

Khabeer, Su'ad Abdul. 2016. *Muslim Cool: Race, Religion, and Hip Hop in the United States.* New York University Press.

Koussens, David, and Valérie Amiraux. 2014. "Du mauvais usage de la laïcité française dans le débat public québécois." In *Penser la laïcité québécoise. Fondements et défense d'une laïcité ouverte au Québec*, edited by Sébastien Lévesque. Presses de l'Université Laval.

Lamonde, Yvan. 2020. "Rapport d'expertise—Procureure générale du Québec." Rapport d'expertise, procès de la loi 21, Montréal.

Lampron, Louis-Philippe. 2020. "Les risques de la loi sur la laïcité—Bien au-delà de l'interdiction du port de signes religieux." Dans *Modération ou extrémisme? Regards critiques sur la loi 21*, edited by Leila Celis et al. Presses de l'Université Laval.

La Presse canadienne. 2022. "Congrès de la CAQ: La fierté plutôt que les grands enjeux de société." *Radio-Canada* (blog), May 19. https://ici.radio-canada.ca/nouvelle/1884854/congres-caq-grands-enjeux-propositions.

Larochelle, Catherine. 2020. "Petite histoire du nationalisme québécois et de ses racines orientalistes." In *Modération ou extrémisme? Regards critiques sur la loi 21*, edited by Leila Celis et al. Presses de l'Université Laval.

Lavoie, Bertrand. 2018. *La fonctionnaire et le hijab: Liberté de religion et laïcité dans les institutions publiques québécoises.* Presses de l'Université Laval.

Lecavalier, Charles. 2019. "'Il n'y a pas d'islamophobie au Québec,' dit François Legault." *Journal de Québec*, January 31.

Lefebvre, Solange. 2020. *Commission scolaire English-Montreal et al. c. Procureure générale du Québec et Fédération autonome de l'enseignement c. Procureure générale du Québec et al.* Rapport d'expertise, procès de la loi 21, Montréal.

Loi sur la laïcité de l'État. 2019. LQ. http://canlii.ca/t/6bnkx.

Lubeck, Andrea. 2022. "Des parents pour surveiller, mais pas de profs portant le hijab: Les Réseaux sociaux réagissent." *24 Heures*, January 14. https://www.24heures.ca/2022/01/14/parents-appeles-a-faire-de-la-surveillance-la-decision-decriee-sur-les-reseaux-sociaux.

Maclure, Jocelyn. 2020. *Commission scolaire English-Montreal et al. c. Procureure générale du Québec.* Rapport d'expertise, procès de la loi 21, Montréal.

Maher, Stephen. 2019. "'A Sadness You Can't Describe': The High Price of Quebec's Bill 21." *Maclean's*, August 12. https://www.macleans.ca/society/a-sadness-you-cant-describe-the-high-price-of-quebecs-bill-21/.

Martineau, Marie-Soleil. 2020. "La loi 21 et l'ethnisation genrée des inégalités sociales." In *Modération ou extrémisme? Regards critiques sur la loi 21*, edited by Leila Celis et al. Presses de l'Université Laval.

Nafi, Michael. 2020. "Une laicite christiano-centrique qui exclut au nom du principe de neutralite." In *Modération ou extrémisme? Regards critiques sur la loi 21*, edited by Leila Celis et al. Presses de l'Université Laval.

Nguyen, Michael. 2014. "Charte : Dalila Awada intente une poursuite pour diffamation de 120 000 $ contre des militants pro-laïcité." *Journal de Montréal*, May 5. https://www.journaldemontreal.com/2014/05/05/charte--dalila-awada-intente-une-poursuite-pour-diffamation-de-120-000--contre-des-militants-pro-laicite.

Niosi, Laurence. 2019. "Laïcité: Le gouvernement ne viserait pas les 'signes spirituels' autochtones." *Radio-Canada*, April 17. https://ici.radio-canada.ca/espaces-autochtones/1164620/laicite-autochtones-21-watso-caq-signes.

Pelletier, Benoît. 2020. *La Théorie du fédéralisme et son application au contexte multinational canadien*. Rapport d'expertise, procès de la loi 21, Montréal.

Razack, Sherene H. 2011. *La chasse aux musulmans: Évincer les musulmans de l'espace politique*. Translated by François Tétreau. Lux Editeur.

Romani, Vincent. 2020. "La loi 21 québécoise et l'indicible mot en r—Réfuter le racisme pour mieux dominer." In *Modération ou extrémisme? Regards critiques sur la loi 21*, edited by Leila Celis et al. Presses de l'Université Laval.

Savic, Lela. 2019. "Projet de loi 21: Un autre regard sur la laïcité." *Journal Metro*, May 28. https://journalmetro.com/actualites/montreal/2327483/projetdeloi21autreregard/.

Scott, Joan Wallach. 2018. *La religion de la laïcité*. Translated by Joëlle Marelli. Climats.

Sioui, Marie-Michèle. 2021. "La commission scolaire n'aurait pas dû embaucher l'enseignante voilée, selon Legault." *Le Devoir*, December 10. https://www.ledevoir.com/politique/quebec/653748/la-commission-scolaire-n-aurait-pas-du-embaucher-l-enseignante-voilee-selon-legault.

Stefanini, Marthe Fatin-Rouge, and Patrick Taillon. 2020. *Le droit d'exprimer des convictions par le port de signes religieux en Europe: Une diversité d'approches nationales qui coexistent dans un système commun de protection des droits. Rapport d'expertise: Droit comparé des États européens et de la Cour européenne des droits de l'homme*. Procès de la loi 21, Montréal.

Zine, Jasmin. 2022. *Under Siege: Islamophobia and the 9/11 Generation*. McGill-Queen's University Press.

Zoghlami, Khaoula. 2020. "Qui peut témoigner? Présences indésirables et paroles sous surveillance." In *Modération ou extrémisme? Regards critiques sur la loi 21*, edited by Leila Celis et al. Presses de l'Université Laval.

Zubrzycki, Geneviève. 2020. *Jean-Baptiste décapité: Nationalisme, religion et sécularisme au Québec*. 2nd edition. Boréal.

8

Good Islam, Bad Islam?

Secularism, Separatism, and Islamophobia in France

ROSHAN ARAH JAHANGEER

In a widely derided speech delivered on October 2, 2020, French president Emmanuel Macron (2020) claimed that "Islam is a religion that is currently experiencing a crisis all over the world."[1] Although his speech was meant to introduce a new bill to fight what he called "Islamist separatism" in France, his remarks angered Muslims globally and led to campaigns to boycott French products across the Middle East and South Asia (*Al Jazeera* 2020). "Islamist separatism," as defined in Macron's speech, is a type of religious radicalism that leads to separation from the rest of society, thus producing a counter-society within France that acts as a breeding ground for radicalism (Macron 2020). The bill, which underwent three name changes due to its controversial nature, eventually became law on August 24, 2021, under the title "Reinforcing Respect for Republican Principles"—although it is widely referred to as "the separatism law" (Légifrance 2021). Its stated aim is to reinforce secular republican values as a means to combat Islamist separatism in the French Republic. In practice, however, the separatism law grants the government nearly unlimited power to dissolve cultural, educational, religious, and civil rights associations and to limit foreign funding and home-schooling.[2] It also requires associations to sign a vaguely worded "republican contract" in order to access state subsidies, and includes measures to prohibit forced marriage and polygamy, virginity certificates, and inheritance laws that are based on the laws of a foreign country (Légifrance 2021). Furthermore, it extends the "neutrality principle," which forbids civil servants from wearing "religious symbols," to those who work for private or public companies involved in public service work, such as train drivers, healthcare workers and cleaners (CAGE 2022, 40).

Given its far-reaching nature, critics argue that the separatism law targets Muslim places of worship, associations, education, and families as part of France's efforts to remake Islam into a version that is compatible with French secularism (or *laïcité*). In this chapter, I argue that the separatism law accelerates France's surveillance and persecution of both Muslims and French Islam, which had already been initiated in the early 2000s with the establishment of a "new secularism" (Baroin 2003) that ushered in various anti-veiling laws. In the first section, I trace the emergence of the "new secularism," a concept that emerged in the lead-up to the enactment of the 2004 law that prohibits "religious symbols" (notably the hijab) in public schools (Légifrance 2004). I then examine the shift from secularism to separatism, a new framework adopted by Emmanuel Macron's government that goes even further in reshaping Islam and Muslim communities to better suit Republican exigencies. Finally, I discuss the closures or dissolutions of schools, mosques, and Muslim associations since the 2021 law, including, controversially, the high-profile NGO that advocates for Muslim civil and human rights, the Collective Against Islamophobia in France (*Collectif contre l'islamophobie en France*, CCIF).

France's "New Secularism" and Anti-veiling Laws

France's secularism dates back to 1905 with the law separating the Church from the state (Légifrance 1905). The law of 1905 granted accommodations to both Catholics and republicans by establishing religious freedom while also curbing the powers of the Catholic Church in matters of state governance and education. As historian John Tolan explains, "[The law of 1905] guaranteed freedom of conscience, the right to practice religion freely, and the policy that 'the republic neither recognizes, nor payrolls, nor subsidizes any cult,' with the explicit exception of chaplains in schools, hospices, the army and prisons" (Tolan 2017, 44). However, although the law of 1905 guaranteed state neutrality vis-à-vis religion, in practice, French secularism accommodated Catholicism by paying the salaries of chaplains in state institutions and the salaries of Catholic, Jewish, and Protestant clergy in departments that were still governed according to Napoleon's Concordat System.[3] In addition, the state continued to finance the upkeep of churches built before 1905 and later subsidized private religious schools—the majority of which were (and still are) Catholic schools (Ferrera, Lorcerie, and Geisser 2024).

However, by the mid-twentieth century, the arrival of a large Muslim population from the former French colonies ushered in the transformation of secularism in the metropole. The influx of male migrant labourers from North Africa during the post–World War I and World War II periods, and later during a stage of family reunification, produced a demographic shift that saw approximately 8–10 percent of the French population claiming Islam as their dominant faith. By the end of the 1970s and 1980s, there was greater visibility of female migrants from North Africa in France along with their children—those who were born and educated in France and who began attending public schools while wearing headscarves.

It was in the context of a "visible Islam," involving young girls wearing headscarves in public schools, that a transformation in secularism occurred. Scholars have named this transformation *"la nouvelle laïcité,"* or the "new secularism," which they consider to be a "falsified" or distorted overreach of what was intended in the original 1905 law (Baubérot 2012). During what was dubbed *l'affaire du foulard* (the headscarf affair) in 1989, three schoolgirls were expelled from a public high school for wearing headscarves, setting off a media and political firestorm centred on the assumed erosion of *laïcité* within the Republic's schools. Following this incident, the new secularism took on an increasingly limiting character vis-à-vis the Muslim minority within France, particularly with regard to "religious symbols." The incidents involving the headscarf—and the political responses to it—eventually led to the implementation of the law of March 15, 2004, banning the wearing of "religious symbols" in public schools (Légifrance 2004).

In the lead-up to the law of 2004, there had been renewed debate on *laïcité*, particularly in right-wing and centre-right parties. François Baroin, who was then vice-president of the National Assembly and spokesperson for right-wing political party Union pour un movement populaire (UMP),[4] penned a report entitled *Pour une nouvelle laïcité (For a new secularism)* (2003). His report explored the political uses that the right wing could make of the concept of secularism, which had previously been the purview of the left. It was within the context of the rise of the extreme right into mainstream French politics that Baroin was tasked to devise strategies so that the right-wing UMP could benefit from the social malaise that had provoked the electorate.[5]

According to the Baroin report, a key feature of the new secularism was that it should be a "cultural and identity-centred" secularism against an "Islam which is today the centre of preoccupations" (Baroin 2003). This new secularism was juxtaposed to 1905's historical secularism, which was centred on conflicts between the Catholic Church and the state—which was considered so commonplace as to be "irrelevant" for most French citizens. Baroin argued that redefining secularism—with Islam as its adversary instead of Catholicism—would help to restore the state's authority and also the right's authority to deal with issues of French identity and religious governance. Second, Baroin claimed that the new secularism required new political actors to take up the struggle against communitarianism and religious fundamentalism; these new actors should come from "immigrant" backgrounds (likely referring to those of Arab and Muslim descent) and serve as Republican elites, to show other immigrants (i.e., Arab/Muslims) that it was possible to integrate into French society by inculcating the secular values of the Republic. Finally, Baroin claimed that the headscarf worn by young girls in public schools was not actually a marker of religious belonging, but rather an attribute of fundamentalist Islam. He implied that young Muslim girls (and, by extension, women) were either fundamentalists themselves or influenced by them. Thus, Baroin advocated for state legislation against young girls' veiling in French public schools in the name of the "new secularism." His report contained several crucial elements for founding this new secularism. The new secularism entailed promoting (1) secularism as an essential part of French identity and taking Islam as its main adversary, not Catholicism; (2) "new actors from immigrant backgrounds" to support new secular values/policies and to serve as "model minorities" for other immigrants; and (3) anti-veiling legislation, based on the assumption that veiled Muslim girls/women promote a dangerous fundamentalism that threatens the values of the Republic (Baroin 2003).

Baroin's new secularism influenced subsequent commission reports that dealt with the question of secularism in public schools, including influential commissions led by Régis Debré (2004) and Bernard Stasi (2003), who cite Baroin's report as a "pillar" that orients their ideological perspectives and recommendations to ban "religious symbols" in public schools (Lorcerie 2008, 59). The new secularism also influenced the way that anti-veiling laws became accepted in France as a measure to "strengthen *laïcité*," through enforcing the "neutrality principle" even for non–civil servants, such as students and parents, who had previously been exempt from maintaining a "neutral" appearance. "In practice," Jim Wolfreys (2017, 94) writes, "*laïcité* has come to mean obliging Muslims, and Muslims alone, to make themselves invisible." This opinion is shared by legal scholar Rim-Sarah Alouane (2020), who argues that "[t]his modern and problematic definition of *laïcité* is weaponized to push for the adoption of increasingly restrictive legislation and policies regarding the wearing of religious symbols, which now constitutes an acceptable form of legal discrimination against French Muslims." As such, the new secularism set the stage for further laws controlling the lives and religious practices of Muslims in France.

For instance, in addition to the laws of 2004 and 2010 (Légifrance 2004, 2010) that, respectively, prohibit wearing religious symbols in public schools and covering the face in public space, further attempts have been made to ban female Muslim visibility in all areas of public life. In 2016, the mayors of forty French towns tried to ban the "burkini" on public beaches (Tayyen 2017). The burkini is a full-body swimsuit that covers a person's whole body except for the face, hands and feet, similar to a surfing rash guard. However, government officials described the burkini as "a beach version of the burqa" meant to "enclose, to hide women's bodies the better to control them" (Wolfreys 2017, 88). Although the government later overturned the bans, the burkini remains a recurring theme in politicians' discourses around Islam, and women wearing burkinis continue to be banned from swimming pools in some French cities (e.g., Grenoble) (Plummer 2022). Moreover, in August 2023, then–education minister Gabriel Attal announced that abayas and qamis (long, loose, dress-like robes and tunics worn by some Muslims) would no longer be allowed in public schools (Ministère de L'Éducation National 2023). Attal claimed that students wore these garments to defy the law on secularism and Macron went further in linking these garments to terrorism, saying in an interview that "we live in a society with a minority of people who, misusing a religion, challenge the Republic and secularism; and this has sometimes led to the worst: we can't pretend that the terrorist attack and Samuel Paty's assassination didn't happen in our country" (cited in Amnesty International 2023).[6] However, human rights groups such as Amnesty International (2023) have called the ban discriminatory, racist and sexist, as it continues to profile and police the bodies of Muslim girls in particular, exacerbating a process that had already been in place with the banning of long skirts, bandanas, hats, and hoodies, when worn by Muslim girls (Hajjat and Mohammed 2013). The ban also continues to conflate Muslim visibility with terrorism, violence, and aggression, painting anything that reflects Muslim practices in broad strokes. This discriminatory process has only accelerated with the legal turn from secularism to separatism.

From the "New Secularism" to Separatism

Following the attacks on the Bataclan in November 2015,[7] the French government activated an emergency law created in 1955 during France's war in Algeria, which plunged France into a state of emergency that lasted two years. During this time, the police amassed an unprecedented array of powers, including the power to raid homes, businesses, associations, and places of worship without warrants and to place individuals under house arrest even without sufficient evidence of wrongdoing (Rubin 2016). The 2015 measures were mostly focused on Muslim communities, with at least 407 people put under house arrest, often mistakenly, and at least 3,300 warrantless raids that only yielded five cases related to "potential terrorism offenses such as preparing to travel to the Middle East for training or gathering information for a potential attack" (Rubin 2016). Human rights groups decried these emergency measures as unfairly targeting Muslim communities—as scores of family homes were raided and property was destroyed by the police without explanation or recompense (Amnesty International 2016).

Although the state of emergency officially ended in July 2017, President Macron subsequently tabled a bill that permanently embedded many of the emergency measures into law. His counterterrorism law, known as the SILT law for strengthening "internal security and the fight against terrorism" (Légifrance 2017), gave police the power to search and seize property and to place individuals under house arrest without judicial authorization (Rubin and Peltier 2017); it also gave the government power to close places of worship "where terrorism, hatred or discrimination is promoted" (Boring 2021). Human rights organizations heavily criticized these measures as being ripe for civil rights abuses, particularly in the case of Muslim communities that already suffered disproportionately from racial profiling. Yet the government insisted on the need to implement these tougher measures to fight terrorism, which, according to former interior minister Gérard Collomb, constituted "a lasting response to a lasting threat" (Rubin and Peltier 2017).

Along with the counterterrorism bill of 2017, Macron also implemented what became known as the Systematic Obstruction policy (*politique d'entrave systematique*). What began as a secret plan, initially known as the "plan to fight radicalization" and later as the plan to fight against "Islamism and community withdrawal," was implemented in fifteen undisclosed areas across France in February 2018 (CAGE 2022, 26). The Systematic Obstruction policy gives the government unprecedented powers to monitor and shut down civic organizations, subject them to administrative controls, and seize their funding. The administrative controls involved prefects in every department who scrutinize any piece of legislation that may apply to a particular establishment in order to find an infraction that justifies closure; this may include regulations concerning hygiene, sports activities, minors, or fraud. While such controls may be interpreted as a positive intervention in potentially unsafe establishments, they are highly biased and designed to target Muslim organizations in particular.

In his speech to local prefects in 2019, former interior minister Christopher Castaner said,

> Our legislative and regulatory arsenal is ready. It is at your disposal and I ask you to use all its resources. As soon as there are doubts about a place or an association, I ask you not to hesitate to carry out inspections, checks. And if negligence is established, I ask you to choose administrative closures without hesitation. I mean [for example] drinking establishments that are becoming Islamist gathering places. I mean certain places of worship, certain schools and certain cultural and sports centres which are transformed into incubators of hatred.

Castaner's speech referenced the "legislative and regulatory arsenal" put in place in 2018 to fight "Islamism and community withdrawal," which was a precursor to the separatism law. He extolled the results already achieved in fifteen disadvantaged neighbourhoods across France in under two years, including 1,030 inspections of drinking establishments, cultural or sports establishments, schools, and places of worship. This led to the closure of 133 drinking establishments, thirteen places of worship, four schools, and nine cultural establishments, along with the seizure of over 17 million euros (Castaner 2019). While Castener and the government framed these closures as "successes" that should be extended and replicated across France, the reality is that the policy of Systemic Obstruction has led to further reduction of social, educational, religious, and cultural spaces in already disadvantaged neighbourhoods. To date, the policy—which was extended across all of France in 2019—has led to 24,877 Systematic Order controls being carried out, which has resulted in the closure or dissolution of 718 Muslim organizations, including schools, mosques, and businesses, and 46 million euros being seized by the government (*Élysée* 2022). Although by the government's account, the Muslim organizations that have been closed or dissolved were breeding grounds for "Islamist" activity, it is important to examine what is included under the government's definition of "Islamism."

Islamism was the subject of a senatorial commission established in 2019 that invited sixty-seven "experts" over eight months to testify on the threat of Islamist radicalism in France.[8] In a 2020 report entitled *Islamist Radicalisation: Facing and Fighting It Together* (Eustache-Brinio 2020), it defined Islamism as not only consisting of violent political movements or terrorist action, but also of nonviolent behaviours that resulted in withdrawal from society. The commission identifies, for example, individuals or groups that promote a "rigorous religiosity," which seeks to

> influence the daily life and relationships of French people of Muslim faith and foreign Muslims residing in France, to impose on them an orthopraxy, clothing, food, [and] ritual practices, but above all a standard of behaviour and relationships between men and women, in order to separate them from the rest of the French population. (Eustache-Brinio 2020, 1–2)

According to the commission's definition, Islamism does not necessarily advocate for or involve violent actions but rather an understanding of religion that prescribes certain behaviours or forms of "orthopraxy" or "correct conduct" that render Muslims different from others in a society.[9] They point out differences in clothing, food, and ritual practices that presumably set radical Islamists apart from everyone else. However, if one scratches the surface of this definition, what it says is that all those who dress differently (e.g., wearing a hijab, kippa, or turban), who have special dietary requirements (e.g., eating halal meat or abstaining from alcohol), or who perform specific "non-normative" ritual practices (e.g., praying, fasting) are essentially Islamists. The problem with this definition is that it characterizes mundane behaviours that are a common part of religious orthodoxy as Islamist. As French jurist Rayan Freschi concludes in his excoriating report on the persecution of Muslims in France, "It is patently clear that 'Islamism' in the hands of the French state effectively only describes Islamic orthodoxy" (CAGE 2022, 23).

Furthermore, this definition of Islamism has become the backbone of a framework that now includes the problematic concept of "separatism," as defined by the Macron government. Separatism as a concept has been used to denounce everything from communism to struggles against French colonialism, including in Algeria, Basque Country, Guyana, and Martinique (Khemilat 2021). It has also been used to suppress left-wing activists and organizations in France, painting them with the label "islamo-gauchisme" (or Islamo-leftism) by claiming that they support a radical Islamist agenda (Davis 2018). Under the Macron presidency, separatism has been combined with the previous definition of Islamism and applied to Muslims, who are accused of behaving as an "enemy within" (Khemilat 2021). In his previously referenced speech, Macron describes Islamist separatism as

> a conscious, theorized, politico-religious project, which materializes in repeated deviations from the values of the Republic, which often results in the constitution of a counter-society, which manifests as the de-schooling of children, the development of community-based sports and cultural practices which are the pretext for teaching principles which do not comply with the laws of the Republic. It is indoctrination and through it, the negation of our principles, gender equality and human dignity. (Macron 2020)

According to this definition, Muslims are accused of home-schooling their children and developing sports and cultural associations for nefarious purposes, which includes teaching children that men and women are not equal in society and that, presumably, they should not make friends with non-Muslim children (Macron 2020). However, what the government describes as "Islamist separatism" is an inadequate characterization of the intense social inequality and debilitating discrimination affecting those who live in disadvantaged neighbourhoods and who are castigated by elite politicians like Macron. For example, French scholar Fatima Khemilat affirms that Muslim families who home-school their children do not do so because they are "Islamist separatists" who wish to inculcate hatred for French values into their children, but rather who wish "to find an alternative to the endemic educational failures in working-class neighbourhoods of France, as shown by the repeated conclusions of the National Council for the Evaluation of the School System (Khemilat 2021, para. 15).[10] I would also argue that home-schooling is a way to mitigate the harmful impacts of the aforementioned anti-veiling laws that target the clothing practices of young Muslim girls in particular and which have led to their expulsion from public schools and a denial of their right to education (Jahangeer 2022; Amnesty International 2023).

Moreover, the behaviour Macron decries as "separatist" is likely the result of racism and discrimination that Muslims have experienced in public spaces, which has been exacerbated by high levels of discrimination and unemployment experienced by those living in socioeconomically disadvantaged neighbourhoods. For instance, in 2005 the unemployment rate for French university graduates from North African backgrounds was 26.5 percent, compared with a national rate of 5 percent (Wolfreys 2017, 137). Evidence also demonstrated that regardless of their qualifications, the children of immigrants (frequently referred to as "third-, fourth- or fifth-generation immigrants" due to their supposed "refusal" to integrate) were more likely to end up in unskilled or part-time work and on temporary contracts, in addition to living in run-down estates (Wolfreys 2017, 131). As Khemilat writes, behaviour stigmatized as "separatist" should be understood not as a sign of religious radicalization but as a strategy aimed at reducing the social inequalities suffered by people who experience this "Muslim condition," which should not be understood as religiosity but rather as "a common social, economic or even spatial experience of a minority" (Khemilat 2021, para. 17).

The separatism law passed in 2021 entrenches the idea of "Islamist separatism," even though the law itself was renamed as the law "to reinforce republican principles" to avoid the appearance of targeting Muslim communities in particular (Nossiter 2021). Nonetheless, the separatism law, which further entrenches the Systematic Obstruction policy, targets France's Muslims. It perpetuates the distinction between "good" Islam (silent, politically passive, invisible) and "bad" Islam (visible, politically engaged, assertive) by using state power to quash Muslim dissent as well as any behaviours it does not agree with. The law itself contains 101 provisions, the most significant of which are summarized as follows:

- It dramatically expands governmental powers to dissolve an organisation, by enabling them to bypass the court process.
- Places of worship can be shut down temporarily to stop the work of "hate preachers."
- Cultural associations will be subject to tighter fiscal and administrative control.
- Organisations seeking public funds will have to sign a "Republican Contract" and abide by its conditions.
- The strengthening of *laïcité*, requiring political, philosophical and religious neutrality for any civil servant—including banning the wearing of religious symbols. This legal requirement has now been extended to non–civil servants, employees of public or private bodies involved in a public service mission like train drivers, health care workers, cleaners and much more.
- Referents on *laïcité* will ensure that *laïcité* and republican values are observed in the public sector. They will draft annual

reports where they will highlight the transgressions they witnessed.

- The law targets Islamic private education and homeschooling by introducing new executive tools facilitating the suspension or closure of Islamic private schools, and greater monitoring of homeschooling. (CAGE 2022, 40–41)

Read together, the separatism law further restricts any possibility of an autonomous Muslim civil society in France, as it brings to bear the state's surveillance and regulatory apparatus down on Muslims that do not fit its ideal definition of Islam—a definition that is devoid of any meaning outside of the one that the French state decides on. As Freschi writes, "The government seeks to coerce Muslims into accepting its ideological framework—in other words, to choke off Muslim dissent and Islamically orthodox behaviours" (CAGE 2022, 23). This ideological framework consists of "reinforcing republican principles," which in practice forces Muslim organizations and individuals to conform to whatever definition of secularism is most expedient at the time. As Wolfreys (2017, 90) argues, "*Laïcité* is often presented as a given, a fixed and immutable aspect of the 'republican tradition,' but its meaning at any time has been dependent on political battles and therefore subject to change, modification, compromise and distortion." Furthermore, Freschi writes that under the separatism law, "[The legal system] has been weaponised in order to severely restrain Muslims' ability to freely practice their religion and express their dissent. Hence, the boundaries of their freedom of religion, of opinion and of association are here clearly tightened" (CAGE 2022, 41). This tightening is particularly concerning, as it makes it abundantly clear that the separatism law and its entrenchment of the Systematic Obstruction policy are responsible for an unprecedented level of social control and persecution of both Muslims and French Islam.

The Chilling Effects of the Separatism Law

In addition to the forms of surveillance and persecution that I noted earlier, one of the immediate casualties of the separatism law was the prominent human rights association, the CCIF. The CCIF was one of the most well-known civil society organizations in charge of defending the rights of Muslims in France. Its main purpose was to collect data on Islamophobic incidents in France, which it published in yearly reports, and to legally defend those who filed complaints against Islamophobic acts. It was a highly respected organization whose work was trusted by both national and international organizations and NGOs, such as the National Consultative Commission on Human Rights, the French Ombudsman, Amnesty International, and the Organization for Security and Co-operation in Europe (Bechrouri 2023).

However, following the brutal murder of Samuel Paty, a public school teacher who had been publicly accused by a student's father of showing derogatory cartoons of the Prophet Muhammad in his class-room, the CCIF was pulled into the controversy. In a social media post that went viral, the student's father had shared the name of the teacher and the school where he worked; this is where the eventual killer learned both the name and location of the teacher and later went to murder him (*France 24* 2020). However, prior to the incident, the father had also contacted the CCIF to make a complaint about the teacher's lesson and had urged his social media followers to do the same. Although the CCIF had recorded the father's complaint and had advised him to take down his social media post, it took no further action as it was still in the pro-cess of confirming the facts of the case. Nonetheless, the minister of the interior, Gérald Darmanin, accused the CCIF of having played a role in Paty's murder due to having communicated with the father to record his complaint, a charge that was eventually used to push for an order to officially dissolve the association (Polloni 2020).[11]

Ibrahim Bechrouri, a French scholar who had worked as a spokesperson for the CCIF between 2016 and 2018, wrote about the sequence of events that led to the CCIF's dissolution. Bechrouri (2023, 210) argues that the CCIF had been in the process of advocating against the Macron government's new separatism law and that it had been targeted in order to shut down its efforts and to send a message to all other Muslim organizations that opposed the government's actions: "Successfully targeting the CCIF, an organization known for its strength and use of the law by Muslim activists, was a way of sending a message to Muslim organizations in France. From now on, they will have to tread lightly, accept government action unquestioningly or risk disappearing." Other human rights organizations, such as Human Rights Watch, also opposed the CCIF's dissolution and warned of the "chilling effect" that it would have on the freedom of expression and association in France (Bechrouri 2023, 210). More concerning still is the conflation between calling out Islamophobia—especially state-organized or systemic Islamophobia—and legitimizing terrorism. In the official order to dissolve the CCIF, Macron, Prime Minister Jean Castex, and Darmanin argued that

> under the guise of denouncing acts of discrimination committed against Muslims, the Collective Against Islamophobia in France defends and promotes a particularly broad notion of "Islamophobia," not hesitating to include as "Islamophobic acts" administrative police measures, or even judicial decisions, taken as part of the fight against terrorism...in doing so, the Collective Against Islamophobia in France must be considered as participating in the legitimization of such acts. (Légifrance 2020)[12]

Their argument—that naming the government's anti-terrorism efforts "Islamophobic" (including the Systematic Obstruction policy discussed above) in turn legitimizes terrorism—is not only flawed but actually suppresses freedom of speech as well as the role of civil society in acting as a watchdog against state abuse. It also seeks to restrict definitions of Islamophobia to only non-state actors and depoliticized "hate acts," thus removing Muslim associations' agency in representing members of their communities that have been targeted by the abuse of state power. As Khemilat (2023, 194) argues, "such measures make it almost impossible to challenge the government's security policies, or openly Islamophobic speeches made by public officials, without being suspected of 'separatism,' inciting hatred, or advocating terrorism."[13]

Since the CCIF's dissolution in 2020, other prominent Muslim associations have been dissolved, including BarakaCity, a humanitarian NGO, and the Coordination contre le Racisme et l'Islamophobie, an anti-discrimination organization that also worked to combat Islamophobia (Syrah 2021). Moreover, a number of Muslim-owned business have be targeted for closure or suspension of government subsidies, including bookstores, restaurants, mosques (Syrah 2021) and schools, as well as one of the only private Muslim schools to receive funding from the government: the Averroès lycée in Lille (Ferrara, Lorcerie, and Geisser 2024).[14] In addition to these closures or suspensions, Bechrouri and others have also noted that the separatism law has been used in insidious ways to restrict the freedom of assembly rights not only of Muslim organizations, but also of left-wing, and occasionally even right-wing, organizations that the government finds objectionable, such as Collectif Palestine Vaincra and Action Palestine (Khemilat 2023), GALE (an anti-fascist group), Nantes révoltées (a left-wing organization), as well as the French chapter of Amnesty International (Bechrouri 2023). These examples demonstrate that separatism has accelerated and also effectively replaced secularism as a tool of governance that not only restricts the visibility of Muslims in France, but also their ability to autonomously organize in order to meet the needs of their community. Separatism, in practice, dangerously narrows Muslims' freedom of association, expression, and their right to non-discrimination under democracy.

Conclusion

While the "new secularism" of 2003 set the stage for further laws restricting the rights of Muslims in France, including the separatism law, both are part and parcel of a long French history of trying to remake Islam into a shadow of itself—recognizable only to French republicans. Although the "new secularism" was initially the project of a right-wing political party, it is today adopted as an essential component of republican principles by all parties across the political spectrum. A central part of the secular and now also separatist project is to make Islam invisible by criminalizing nonviolent Islamic orthodoxy, as seen through anti-veiling laws and attempts to ban burkinis in public places. It is clear that anti-veiling laws remain a central component of both secular and separatist projects; for instance, in the debates around the separatism law, some senators initially wanted to ban minors from wearing religious symbols (e.g., hijabs) in public spaces. In addition, Marine Le Pen, leader of the extreme right-wing RN party who lost to Emmanuel Macron in the 2022 French presidential elections, proposed banning the hijab in public space and issuing fines to those who wore it (AFP 2022). Although the RN was narrowly defeated by a hastily assembled "Republican Front" coalition (Henley 2024) during France's 2024 snap parliamentary elections, the difficulty of governing such a split parliament presents an opportunity for the RN's resurgence in the 2027 presidential elections. Regardless of the extreme right's continuing threat to French democracy, Macron's government remains responsible for adopting similar tactics and policies. His government's separatism law has produced the erasure of an autonomous and vibrant Muslim civil society, as we have seen with the forced dissolution of the CCIF in 2020, which threatens the rights of France's largest religious majority. French political journalist Edwy Plenel writes that the French model of integration is based on the unequal, hierarchical relationships established during the colonial era. He argues that France still adheres to "the neo-colonial demand to assimilate that seeks to compel one section of our compatriots (of Islamic culture, Arab origin, black skin, etc.) to erase themselves and dissolve, in short, to whiten themselves. The requirement, in other words, to disappear in order to be accepted" (cited in Wolfreys 2017, 99–100). It is a type of neocolonial control of Islamic practices and institutions that denies the development of an autonomous Muslim civil society. It seems that for Muslims in France, now as in the past, the price of citizenship is self-erasure.

NOTES

1. I would like to thank Dr. Kirsten Wesselhoeftt, Dr. Shirin Shahrokni, and Thomas Kureeman for reading and commenting on earlier drafts of this chapter.
2. The section of the 2021 law that limits home-schooling is especially concerning given that it makes public schooling obligatory, barring exception, in a context where Muslim students are banned from wearing "religious symbols" in state-funded public schools. Furthermore, the French state's increasing surveillance and control of private Muslim schools has led to high-profile closures of once-lauded lycées such as the Averroès school in Lille (see Ferrara, Lorcerie, and Geisser 2024).
3. "On July 15, 1801, Bonaparte established a concordat with Pope Pius VII, recognizing Catholicism as the majority religion in France but granting free practice of religion to Lutherans, Calvinists, and Jews. The clergy of the four recognized cults were employees of the French government" (Tolan 2017, 42–43).
4. The UMP changed its name to *Les Républicains* in 2015, under Nicolas Sarkozy.
5. The National Front (FN) was an extreme far-right party in France founded in 1972 that was led by Jean-Marie Le Pen from 1972 to 2011. The FN came in second place during the first round of the 2002 presidential elections, provoking panic among France's political class. Le Pen's daughter, Marine Le Pen, took over leadership in 2011 and later changed the name of the party to le Rassemblement Nationale (National Rally, RN).
6. Samuel Paty was murdered by a young French man of Chechnyan background on October 16, 2020, barely two weeks after Macron's October 2, 2020, speech on Islamist separatism. Paty was said to have shown cartoons of the Prophet Muhammad in his class.

7. The Bataclan attacks killed 130 people and wounded at least 350 people. It was preceded by an attack on satirical newspaper *Charlie Hebdo* headquarters in January 2015 that killed eleven journalists. Despite the state of emergency, another attack occurred on July 14, 2016 (Bastille Day), in Nice, which killed eighty-six people. While ISIS claimed responsibility for the Bataclan attacks (Castillo 2015), no evidence indicated that it had been involved in the Bastille Day attacks (Jones, Chrisafis, and Davies 2016).

8. The senatorial Commission of Inquiry into Islamist Radicalization and the Means of Combating It was formed at the request of political party Les Républicains (Sénat 2019)

9. "Orthopraxy" originates from the Greek word *orthopraxia*, meaning "right practice."

10. "PISA 2015 confirms the high level of social inequalities within French schools. Indeed, France is one of the OECD countries for which the correlation of performance with socio-economic background is the strongest (20% in France, against 13% on average in the OECD)" (Centre national d'étude des systèmes scolaires n.d.).

11. Although the order to officially dissolve the organization was issued by the government on December 2, 2020 (Légifrance 2020), the CCIF had already anticipated that it would be ordered to disband. In order to save its data, archives, funding, and membership lists, the CCIF chose to dissolve itself (Bechrouri 2023). In doing so, it was able to transfer all of its materials to Belgium, where it now operates under the name Collectif Contre l'Islamophobie en Europe (Collective Against Islamophobia in Europe, CCIE).

12. My translation of the original French text.

13. My translation of the original French text.

14. The Averroès school in Lille was one of only three private Muslim schools to receive funding from the government; this is compared to 7,500 mostly Catholic schools to receive government funding, and over a hundred Jewish private schools. The decision to revoke state funding from the Averroès school, which has ranked among the top private schools in the country, has been accused of being "politically motivated" and subject to double standards, especially when compared with another Catholic school that had also been subject to state inspection (Ferrara, Lorcerie, and Geisser 2024).

REFERENCES

AFP. 2022. "Le Pen Vow Headscarf Bans in Tight French Election Battle."
    France 24, July 4. https://www.france24.com/en/live-news/20220407-le-
    pen-vows-headscarf-fines-in-tight-french-election-battle.

Al Jazeera. 2020. "'Boycott French Products' Launched over Macron's Islam
    Comments." October 25. https://www.aljazeera.com/news/2020/10/25/
    social-meboycott-french-products-online-against-macrons-islam.

Alouane, Rim-Sarah. 2020. "The Weaponization of Laïcité." *Berkeley Center for
    Religion, Peace & World Affairs*. October 7. https://berkleycenter.
    georgetown.edu/posts/the-weaponization-of-laicite.

Amnesty International. 2016. "France: Upturned Lives: The Disproportionate
    Impact of France's State of Emergency." February 4. https://www.
    amnesty.org/en/documents/eur21/3364/2016/en/.

Amnesty International. 2023. "France: Authorities Must Repeal Discriminatory
    Ban on the Wearing of Abaya in Public Schools." October 3. https://
    www.amnesty.org/en/documents/eur21/7280/2023/en/.

Baroin, François. 2003. "Rapport de François Baroin 'Pour une nouvelle
    laïcité.'" *Réseau Voltaire*. June. http://www.voltairenet.org/rubrique506.
    html?lang=fr.

Baubérot, Jean. 2012. *La laïcité falsifiée*. La découverte.

Bechrouri, Ibrahim. 2023. "'L'esprit de défense': Separatism, Counterinsurgency,
    and the Dissolution of the Collective Against Islamophobia in France."
    Modern & Contemporary France 31, no. 2: 199–218.

Boring, Nicolas. 2021. "France: President Signs New Antiterrorism Law." *Library
    of Congress*. https://www.loc.gov/item/global-legal-monitor/2021-08-23/
    france-president-signs-new-antiterrorism-law/.

CAGE. 2022. *"We Are Beginning to Spread Terror": The State-Sponsored Persecution
    of Muslims in France*. March 2. https://www.cage.ngo/articles/
    we-are-beginning-to-spread-terror-the-state-sponsored-persecution-
    of-muslims-in-france.

Castaner, Christophe. 2019. "Discours d'ouverture de M. Christophe Castaner
    lors du séminaire des préfets consacré à la lutte contre l'islamisme et
    le repli communautaire." *Ministère de l'Intérieur.* November 28. https://
    www.interieur.gouv.fr/fr/Archives/Archives-ministres-de-l-Interieur/
    Archives-Christophe-Castaner/Actualites/Discours-d-ouverture-de-
    M.-Christophe-Castaner-lors-du-seminaire-des-prefets-consacre-a-la-
    lutte-contre-l-islamisme-et-le-repli-communautai.

Castillo, Mariano. 2015. "Paris Suicide Bomber Identified: ISIS Claims Responsibility for 129 Dead." *CNN*, November 16. https://www.cnn.com/2015/11/14/world/paris-attacks/index.html.

Centre national d'étude des systèmes scolaires. n.d. *Inégalités sociales et migratoires à l'école.* http://www.cnesco.fr/fr/inegalites-sociales/.

Davis, Muriam Haleh. 2018. "Racial Capitalism and the Campaign Against 'Islamo-Gauchisme' in France." *Jadaliyya.* https://www.jadaliyya.com/Details/37858.

Debré, Jean-Louis. 2004. *La laïcité à l'école: un principe républicain à réaffirmer—Rapport de la mission d'information de l'assemblée nationale, vol. I.* Paris: Odile Jacob.

Élysée. 2022. "Compte rendu du Conseil des ministres du mercredi 12 janvier 2022." January 12. https://www.elysee.fr/emmanuel-macron/2022/01/12/compte-rendu-du-conseil-des-ministres-du-mercredi-12-janvier-2022.

Eustache-Brinio, Jacqueline. 2020. "Radicalisation islamiste: Faire face et lutter ensemble." *Sénat*, July 7. http://www.senat.fr/rap/r19-595-1/r19-595-1-syn.pdf.

Ferrera, Carol, Lorcerie, Françoise, and Geisser, Vincent. 2024. "France's Biggest Muslim School Went from Accolades to Defunding—Showing a Key Paradox in How the Country Treats Islam." *The Conversation*, January 26. https://theconversation.com/frances-biggest-muslim-school-went-from-accolades-to-defunding-showing-a-key-paradox-in-how-the-country-treats-islam-220725.

France 24. 2020. "Police Say French Teacher's Killer Sent Texts to Parent Angry over Mohammad Cartoons." *France 24*, October 20. https://www.france24.com/en/france/20201020-french-teacher-s-killer-sent-message-to-parent-angry-over-prophet-mohammad-cartoons.

Hajjat, Abdellali, and Marwan Mohammed. 2013. *Islamophobie: Comment les élites françaises fabriquent le "problème musulman."* Paris: La Découverte.

Henley, Jon. 2024. "French Elections: What is the Republican Front—and Will It Head Off National Rally?" *The Guardian*, July 4. https://www.theguardian.com/world/article/2024/jul/04/french-elections-what-is-the-republican-front-and-will-it-head-off-national-rally.

Jahangeer, Roshan Arah. 2022. "Secularism, Feminism, and Islamophobia: A Study of Anti-Veiling Laws in France and Quebec." Doctoral dissertation, York University. https://yorkspace.library.yorku.ca/items/a9fd3c25-946c-4486-8dd5-5d9d13da4a34.

Jones, Sam, Angelique Chrisafis, and Caroline Davies. 2016. "Nice Truck Attack: Islamic State Claims Responsibility." *The Guardian*, July 16. https://amp.theguardian.com/world/2016/jul/16/ islamic-state-claims-responsibility-for-nice-truck-attack.

Khemilat, Fatima. 2021. "France's New 'Separatism' Law Stigmatises Minorities and Could Backfire Badly." *The Conversation*, August 15. https:// theconversation.com/frances-new-separatism-law-stigmatis- es-minorities-and-could-backfire-badly-162705.

Khemilat, Fatima. 2023. "La loi contre le 'séparatisme': mort et résurrection d'une 'justice d'exception.'" *Modern and Contemporary France* 31, no. 2: 183–198.

Légifrance. 1905. "Loi du 9 décembre 1905 concernant la séparation des Églises et de l'État." December 9. https://www.legifrance.gouv.fr/affichTexte. do?cidTexte=JORFTEXT000000508749.

Légifrance. 2004. "LOI n° 2004-228 du 15 mars 2004 encadrant, en application du principe de laïcité, le port de signes ou de tenues manifestant une appartenance religieuse dans les écoles, collèges et lycées publics." March 15. https://www.legifrance.gouv.fr/eli/loi/2004/3/15/ MENX0400001L/jo/texte.

Légifrance. 2010. "LOI n° 2010-1192 du 11 octobre 2010 interdisant la dissimula- tion du visage dans l'espace public." Octobre 11. https://www.legifrance. gouv.fr/eli/loi/2010/10/11/2010-1192/jo/texte.

Légifrance. 2017. "LOI n° 2017-1510 du 30 octobre 2017 renforçant la sécurité intérieure et la lutte contre le terrorisme (1)." October 30. https://www. legifrance.gouv.fr/jorf/id/JORFTEXT000035932811/.

Légifrance. 2020. "Décret du 2 décembre 2020 portant dissolution d'un groupement de fait." December 3. https://www.legifrance.gouv.fr/jorf/ id/JORFTEXT000042602019.

Légifrance. 2021. "LOI n° 2021-1109 du 24 août 2021 confortant le respect des principes de la République." August 21. https://www.legifrance.gouv.fr/ jorf/id/JORFTEXT000043964778.

Lorcerie, Françoise. 2008. "La 'loi sur le voile': Une entreprise politique." *Droit et société*, 53–74.

Macron, Emmanuel. 2020. "Fight against Separatism—the Republic in Action: Speech by Emmanuel Macron, President of the Republic, on the Fight against Separatism." *Élysée*, October 2. https://www.elysee.fr/en/ emmanuel-macron/2020/10/02/fight-against-separatism-the-republic-in-action-speech-by-emmanuel-macron-president-of-the-republic-on-the-fight-against-separatism.

Ministère de L'Éducation National. 2023. "Principe de la laïcité à l'école." *Le bulletin officiel de l'éducation nationale, de la jeunesse et des sports.* August 31. https://www.education.gouv.fr/bo/2023/Hebdo32/MENG2323654N.

Nossiter, Adam. 2021. "Macron's Rightward Tilt, Seen in New Laws, Sows Wider Alarm in France." *New York Times*, February 16. https://www.nytimes.com/2020/11/25/world/europe/france-macron-muslims-police-laws.html?searchResultPosition=18.

Plummer, Robert. 2022. "French Burkini Ban Upheld as Grenoble Loses Legal Challenge." *BBC World*, June 21. https://www.bbc.com/news/world-europe-61883529.

Polloni, Camille. 2020. "Contre le CCIF et BarakaCity, Gérald Darmanin manie la menace de dissolution." *MédiaPart*, October 19. https://www.mediapart.fr/journal/france/191020/contre-le-ccif-et-barakacity-gerald-darmanin-manie-la-menace-de-dissolution.

Rubin, Alissa J. 2016. "Muslims in France say Emergency Powers Go Too Far." *New York Times*, February 17. https://www.nytimes.com/2016/02/18/world/europe/frances-emergency-powers-spur-charges-of-overreach-from-muslims.html.

Rubin, Alissa J., and Elian Peltier. 2017. "French Parliament Advances a Sweeping Counterterrorism Bill." *New York Times*, October 3. https://www.nytimes.com/2017/10/03/world/europe/france-terrorism-law.html?searchResultPosition=1.

Sénat. 2019. *Commission d'enquête sur la radicalisation islamiste et les moyens de la combattre.* November 14. http://www.senat.fr/commission/enquete/radicalisation_islamiste.html.

Stasi, Bernard. 2003. "Commission de réflexion sur l'application du principe de laïcité dans la république: Rapport au président de la république." *La Documentation française*, December 11. http://www.ladocumentationfrancaise.fr/var/storage/rapports-publics/034000725.pdf.

Syrah, Lou. 2021. "Lutte contre le 'séparatisme': Un an de chasse aux sorcières." *Médiapart*, October 28. https://www.mediapart.fr/journal/france/281021/lutte-contre-le-separatisme-un-de-chasse-aux-sorcieres.

Tayyen, Sana. 2017. "From Orientalist Sexual Object to Burkini Terrorist Threat: Muslim Women throgh Evolving Lens." *Islamophobia Studies Journal* 4, no. 1: 101–114.

Tolan, John. 2017. "A French Paradox?: Islam and Laïcité." *Georgetown Journal of International Affairs* 18, no. 2: 41–50.

Wolfreys, Jim. 2017. *Republic of Islamophobia: The Rise of Respectable Racism in France.* Oxford University Press.

III

Combatting
Compounded
Islamophobia

9

Compounded Islamophobia

The Impact of Anti-Black Racism and Gender-based Discrimination on Muslim Mental Health in Canada

FATIMAH JACKSON-BEST

In December 2020, news outlets reported two separate occurrences of physical attacks committed against Black Muslim women and girls in Alberta, Canada (Snowdon 2020; Junker 2021). On June 6, 2021, the Afzal-Salmans, a Southeast Asian Muslim family, were murdered while taking an evening walk in London, Ontario. Just four years before these instances, a gunman entered the Islamic Cultural Centre of Quebec City and murdered six Muslim men. While shocking, these are not isolated examples of Muslims in Canada being killed or experiencing violence. The country is often lauded for its diversity and multiculturalism, but statistics show a steep increase in targeted, hate-motivated murders of Muslims in Canada (Badaloo 2022). Data from Statistics Canada (2023) indicates that Muslims experienced the second highest rate of police-reported hate crimes committed between the years 2018 and 2021. Additionally, data collected from Muslim and non-Muslim Canadians over the last fifteen years have shown societal indications of rising Islamophobia. The Canadian Islamophobia Industry Research Project, led by Jasmine Zine at Wilfred Laurier University, reported on several polls, including a 2007 Environics survey that indicated 66 percent of Muslim respondents were concerned about discrimination, and 30 percent were "very concerned." In 2016, a Leger poll in Quebec showed that francophone Canadians' views of Islam had gradually declined since 2012, and 48 percent of those surveyed in the province had a negative view of Islam (Wilfred Laurier University n.d.). This sentiment closely mirrored views across the rest of the country. According to a 2017 Angus Reid survey, 43 percent of Canadians "had unfavourable views of Islam as compared to other faiths" (Wilfred Laurier University n.d.). Cumulatively, these examples and data affirm Furqan et al.'s (2022, E747) statement that "Islamophobia occurs at the individual, societal and structural levels, and manifests in many ways." One impact of Islamophobia is on the mental health of Muslim people, which includes the marginalization and trauma Islamophobic incidents cause and extends to the mental healthcare they try to access and may receive. Notably, the family of the Edmonton mother and daughter who experienced violent anti-Black and gendered Islamophobia in 2020 discussed the pair being retraumatized after the attack as they navigated support services that were ill-equipped to deal with the complex needs of victims of hate crimes (Junker 2021). The inability of mental health services to meet the needs of Black communities has been reported in Canadian, American, and European research, with institutional and practitioner racism being among the main barriers that Black people encounter when attempting to access care (Fante-Coleman and Jackson-Best 2020; Booker, Jackson-Best, and Fante-Coleman 2023; Rivenbark and Ichou 2020).

This chapter focuses on the impact of Islamophobia on the mental health of Muslims and explores how mental healthcare–seeking and the therapeutic relationship can be impacted by Islamophobia. Because Islamophobia is often gendered and racialized, the chapter also explores how anti-Black Islamophobia (Mugabo 2016; Jackson-Best 2019) and gendered Islamophobia affect Black Muslim women who exist at the intersection of race, religion, and gender. Fundamentally, the chapter wrestles with secular understandings of religion, race, gender, and mental health, which all rest on assumptions of humanity—a notion that has historically excluded Black people and effectively leaves them out of the secular project (Mugabo 2016).

The chapter concludes with recommendations for mental health providers regarding care provision for Muslim clients. Guidance for Muslim clients is also given, specifically to foster capacity for self-advocacy that engages both the self and community in the process of finding and receiving mental healthcare.

Secularism, Symbolism, and Canadian Legislation

In early 2021, the federal government declared that January 29 would be recognized as the National Day of Remembrance of the Québec City Mosque Attack and Action against Islamophobia. Just over a month after the murder of the Afzal-Salman family, there was a national summit on Islamophobia, which brought together Muslim community members, leaders, and activists to discuss Islamophobia in Canada. While these initiatives hold some significance, they are also critiqued for lacking the structural approach needed to stop Islamophobia. Commemorations and summits also lack the political teeth to strike down systemic Islamophobic legislation, such as those laws enacted in Quebec under the guise of fostering religious neutrality (Mugabo 2016; Commission des Droits de la Personne et des Droits de la Jeunesse n.d.). This includes Bill 62, which bans Muslim women from wearing the niqab (a veil that leaves a gap for the eyes) or the burqa (a veil that fully covers the head and body) while doing certain activities, as well as Bill 21 (discussed by Diab in Chapter 7), which bans some civil servants who are in positions of authority from wearing religious symbols while at work and has disproportionately impacted Muslim women who wear the hijab (International Civil Liberties Monitoring Group, Islamic Social Services Association, and Noor Cultural Centre 2020). Bills such as these, which are promoted as religiously neutral, circumvent responsibility of the state for the ways in which groups like Black people are disproportionately affected by them. As Diab has shown, these types of laws do not operate on neutral ground concerning religious differences. Rather, they define religion and categorize people, demarcating who is or is not an acceptable citizen or human.

Mugabo also writes that "[s]ecularism solidifies religion as a category that allows non-Black people of color to be categorized as human" (2016, 168). This secular solidification of non-white as non-human is perpetuated by the processes of colonization and enslavement of Black people, who are effectively excluded from the category of human altogether. Mugabo further states that "secularism is constitutive of anti-Blackness" (169). According to this logic, secularism has never been a route toward the acknowledgement of Black humanity, and it mainly serves those who have structural privilege due to colour, class, ability, and gender. Mugabo illustrates this through recounting her own experience as a Black Muslim woman operating in activist spaces that were organizing against Quebec's Charter of Values in 2013, and how she faced anti-Blackness due to some white members' beliefs that the Charter affected Muslims and Muslim women but not Black communities. The lack of acknowledgment that people can be Black *and* Muslim *and* woman, and thus triply affected by the Charter, led to her disillusionment and eventual permanent exit from white feminist–led and Quebec nationalist organizing spaces. The alienation Mugabo describes is palpable and mirrors the experiences of many Black Muslims in comparable spaces and within the broader Canadian society.

Compounded Islamophobia:
Anti-Black Racism and Gendered Islamophobia

> None of it compares to those first few weeks back
> at home, awake at three in the morning clutching a
> kitchen knife under my pillow in the sweltering heat
> because I couldn't bring myself to close the window for
> fear you had somehow escaped and were waiting for
> the right moment..."Emotionally, I have been strug-
> gling because nothing in my life has had the same
> effect on me as this has." (Blunt 2023)

This quote from the 2023 court testimony of an eighteen-year-old Black Muslim woman who was stabbed at her restaurant job in Winnipeg, Canada, describes the physiological effects of the violent incident and the mental health toll it has taken on her as she deals with the persistent trauma. The young woman made a point to state that she has met challenging times before the incident due to her race, gender, and religion but this experience was the most difficult one she has faced thus far. While the perpetrator claimed that the stabbing was random and not hate-motivated, critics and activists have highlighted his targeting of a Black, visibly Muslim woman wearing a hijab as opposed to the other people who were also in the restaurant at the time and did not share her characteristics.

Canadian research on Islamophobia and mental health high-lights the association between this phenomenon and poorer mental health outcomes, particularly among Muslims who experience the compounded effects of Islamophobia and other forms of inequal-ity, such as gender-based discrimination and anti-Black racism (Furqan et al. 2022). Social work scholar Akua Benjamin defines anti-Black racism as the "policies and practices which are rooted in Canadian institutions such as education, health care, and justice that mirror and reinforce beliefs, attitudes, prejudice, stereotyping and/ or discrimination towards people of Black-African descent" (Black Health Alliance n.d.). Anti-Black racism is as old as Canada itself, as evidenced by the country's engagement in the enslavement of African people for over 300 years. It persists contemporarily through systemic forms of violence, which are deployed through policing and the justice system, income inequality, inequities in mental health treatment, and unequal burdens of disease and illness, such as those experienced during the COVID-19 pandemic, where Black people in, for example, Ontario, Canada, were at an increased risk of contracting the virus and dying from it (Dryden and Nnorom 2021). It is not a stretch to assert that anti-Black racism produces deleterious conditions for people of African descent. When compounded with Islamophobia, it is inevitable that Black Muslims will experience more violence and negative mental health outcomes.

Additionally, Canadian research shows that visibly Muslim women are disproportionately targeted for racialized and gendered Islamophobic violence (Furqan et al. 2022). A 2020 report found that Muslim women are overrepresented in hate-motivated violence and that Islamophobia functions according to stereotypes about this group, who are "essentialized as subjugated victims and dangerous cultural vectors" (International Civil Liberties Monitoring Group, Islamic Social Services Association, and Noor Cultural Centre 2020). In neoliberal, secular societies like Canada, women who wear markers of their Islamic faith, such as the hijab, niqab, or burqa, become easy targets for Islamophobic violence because of their heightened visibility in the public sphere. When we consider some of the tangible examples of Islamophobia in Canada, such as the 2020 assaults on Black Muslim women living in Alberta, it is important to recognize the confluence of factors that made these women targets: specifically, their Muslim identity, race, and gender. Intersectionality (Crenshaw 1989, 1991) is a helpful paradigm through which we can better understand these factors and the phenomenon of compounded Islamophobia. At its core, intersectionality is about power, and the "multiple, simultaneous and dynamic interchanges among categories of social difference as it interlinks with power and privilege, and systemic oppression and its operation at the micro, mesa, and macro levels" (Loutfy et al. 2015, 2). Through this definition, we understand that Islamophobia can function (and become strengthened) because of the existence of gender-based discrimination and anti-Black racism, which already work to devalue people who are not white and male.[1] For Black Muslim women and Black Muslims, Islamophobia cannot be separated from centuries of racialized violence and the dehumanization of people of African descent via colonialism and enslavement. Nor can it be isolated from gender-based discrimination of women. Islamophobia becomes merely another capillary in matrices of domination within secular states like Canada. Recounting her tenuous experience in spaces organizing against the Charter of Quebec Values, Mugabo (2016) recalls a quote from a February 2015 interview that featured Samah Jabbari, the then spokeswoman of the Canadian Muslim Forum. Jabbari made arguments against the Charter, and towards the end of the interview stated, "We [non- Black Muslims] won't accept to be the slaves, nor the negroes of Quebec." (Mugabo 2016, 166). This quote encapsulates how the Muslim subject is characterized as brown or Arab, but never Black—even by other Muslims. It also exposes how hierarchy-making functions in Muslim communities, putting Black people at the bottom due to their perceived inferiority and enslavability, and placing brown and Arab Muslims who have not experienced similar systems of domination above them.

Addressing gender-based discrimination and anti-Black Islamophobia, which is the distinct kind of racism experienced by Black Muslims from both non-Muslims and non-Black Muslims (Mugabo 2016; Jackson-Best 2019), is critical to the work of eradicating Islamophobia. However, combatting anti-Black Islamophobia is complicated by the wide-scale erasure of Black Muslims' experiences from dominant discourse about Islamophobia, which typically centres on non-Black Muslim women. While non-Black Muslim women undoubtedly experience gendered Islamophobia, it is important to acknowledge that one of the functions of anti-Black racism is to strip humanity from Black people and remove opportunities to express pain, hurt, and even religiosity (Mugabo 2016). This process of dehumanization renders it difficult for people of African descent to be considered as victims of inequality while, at the same time, the idealized Muslim is characterized as being Middle Eastern or Southeast Asian by Muslim communities and non-Muslims. The result is that Black Muslims must fight to have their humanity and experiences acknowledged, even as they disproportionately experience Islamophobic violence in secularized societies like Canada, with its history of colonization and enslavement of Black people. To counter this, we must remember that when oppression exists in any form, there cannot be full liberation for anyone. Also, we must centre communities that have been historically marginalized in our advocacy and activism.

Islamophobia and Mental Health

> I went through moments of depression. I went through moments of really heightened anxiety. And I noticed that it really, really had an impact on just my overall wellbeing...I finally got connected with people that I could relate to in that could support me. I then started to talk about it. (Khan 2021, 54)

This quote from a study participant of a master's thesis project on the mental health impacts of Islamophobia experienced by Muslim women in Canadian post-secondary settings sheds light on some of the mental health struggles they navigated. The work highlights interpersonal experiences of Islamophobia and connects these to larger processes of structural violence and the complex power dynamics that enable Islamophobia to occur, and which create ongoing traumatic landscapes in which Muslims relive the experience, whether personally, structurally, or vicariously, and must find the internal fortitude to deal with it.

American research on the prevalence of mental illness in Muslim communities indicates there is a strong relationship between experiences of discrimination and mental health challenges (Phillips and Lauterbach 2017; Shattell and Brown 2017). Canadian research on the effects of Islamophobia on mental health corroborates these findings and highlights how prolonged stress on affected individuals can make them susceptible to other illnesses and disorders (Badaloo 2022). Cumulatively, the North American research on Islamophobia and mental health indicates that it is a threat to the physical and mental well-being of those subjected to it, and over time it can damage an individual's mental health and potentially exacerbate other mental and physical health challenges. The negative mental health effects of Islamophobia may begin as early as childhood, which is evidenced by an exploratory study conducted with school-aged Muslim children in Ontario, Canada. The authors reported that this group routinely encountered hateful comments within their wider (non-Muslim) communities and experienced safety issues at school, particularly after the 2017 Quebec City mosque shooting (Elkassem et al. 2018). Children reported regularly experiencing oppression, fear, and hypervigilance because of their Muslim identity and as a result of their religious markers (Elkassem et al. 2018; Furqan et al. 2022). For example, hijab-wearing Muslim girls expressed feeling targeted due to their head covering, with several stating "I get a lot of points and stares for my hijab during games…they were pointing at me and laughing, pointing at my hijab," and "wearing the hijab can be hard. People might bully you and make fun of you. Like what are you wearing? What is that piece of garbage on your head?" (Elkassem et al. 2018, 12). This xenophobia may be exacerbated by mental health service providers who lack adequate understandings of the hijab, which can lead to further marginalization of Muslim youth seeking mental healthcare (Fante-Coleman et al. 2023). While anti-hijab sentiment may be dismissed as being benign or even a rite of passage for Muslim girls and women in the West, its proliferation is dangerous due to the ways members of this group are often constructed as representatives of the Islamic faith. Hijab-wearing Muslim girls and women also become easy targets for laws like Quebec's Bill 21 that use secularism and liberal Christianity as benchmarks for religious normalcy while simultaneously removing the right to religious expression from these very groups. Muslim girls and women are often left to carry the burden of these secular initiatives, and they can internalize interpersonal and structural Islamophobia, which may have negative impacts on their mental health (Khan 2021).

Mental Healthcare Institutions and the Therapeutic Relationship

Mental healthcare in Canada can be characterized by two key periods: the asylum era and the deinstitutionalization movement. Canada's first asylums mirrored most early healthcare services in that they were largely run by religious bodies, typically representatives of the Christian Church (Chaimowitz et al. 2014; Appleton 1967). The isolation and treatment of disease was the most common approach in asylums, and patients were constructed as passive receptacles of treatment modalities. The deinstitutionalization movement began in the 1960s as mental healthcare policy and practice underwent significant changes, which included the decentralization of mental health services and provision of community-based programs and care (Davis 2006; Simmons 1990). By then, mental healthcare had become implicated in the movement for patients' rights, taking cues from ongoing struggles for civil rights in the United States, the women's rights movement, and calls for minority rights (Davis 2006). Despite these changes, community-based mental healthcare models have been critiqued for their narrow treatment approaches that focus on managing symptoms while excluding factors that influence patients' worldviews, such as their identity and religion, and the persistent characterization of the patient as a passive receiver rather than an active agent in their own care (Davis 2006). Furthermore, modern psychiatry in Canada has been challenged to balance being cognizant of a patient's religious and/or spiritual needs and delivering care in a secular fashion, so as not impose healthcare providers' views (or lack thereof) onto people in their care (Chaimowitz et al. 2014).

Research on Islamophobia and mental healthcare–seeking highlights systemic and institutional issues that abound in spaces where mental health treatment is provided (Latif, Rodrigues, and Galley 2020; Jiswari and Arnold 2018; Furqan et al. 2022). The impacts are most salient in the therapeutic relationship between Muslim clients and non-Muslim healthcare providers and in the ways Muslim clients access mental health services and programs. This can be attributed to mental healthcare models that are largely based on one-size-fits-all conventions, in which the idealized patient is typically white, male, heterosexual, and free of disabilities. It can also be assumed that the ideal patient is not a Muslim. This highlights one of the major systemic and institutional issues that Muslim service-seekers face within mental healthcare settings, even before Islamophobia becomes part of therapeutic interactions. In practice, a one-size-fits-all model means that although each patient comes to a mental healthcare environment with their own unique racial, religious, and cultural understandings, which organizations like the Canadian Psychiatry Association and the Canadian Association of Social Workers acknowledge they have a fundamental right to (Chaimowitz et al. 2014; Canadian Association of Social Work 2022), mental health systems and models are not built to address and incorporate this diversity into how clients are regarded, treated, or diagnosed. Instead, mental health models generally view the mind and the body as separate, disregard the multiple manifestations of trauma, including vicarious and intergenerational trauma, and exalt the Western biomedical model that focuses on illness as opposed to holistic wellness (Dwornik 2021). This can lead to clients feeling that their identities are overlooked and not meaningfully considered or included in their care. It can also contribute to difficulty in finding the right kind of mental health supports, leaving clients feeling disconnected from their care, which can lead to them dropping out of services and worsened mental health. This was the case for some Black Muslim youth in Ontario who cited a lack of consideration for their intersecting identities and the proliferation of anti-Black racism and Islamophobia in the mental healthcare services they had accessed (Fante-Coleman et al. 2023).

There may also be practitioner-based anti-Muslim discrimination experienced by Muslim clients when seeking mental health supports. Participants in a study by Latif and colleagues (2020) discussed the lack of connection they experienced with mental health providers who did not share their culture and lacked understanding about their religion, and whose secular views of identity prevented nuanced conceptualizations about their lived realities as Muslim women in Canada. Given Islamophobia's insidiousness and how it is adopted in secularist discourse, professionals who provide mental healthcare may knowingly or unknowingly internalize and then project anti-Muslim ideas and sentiments onto their clients. Practitioner-based Islamophobia may be caused (in part) by unconscious secularist ideals about Islam, but it has the same outcomes as intentional secularist beliefs among mental healthcare providers, in that Islam is viewed in binary terms as either a problem that needs to be minimized or a potential solution if it fits into narrowly prescribed parameters of acceptability by those in positions of power (see Hurd, Chapter 1 in this collection). Furthermore, groups that experience overlapping forms of marginalization, such as Black Muslims, may face intensified barriers because of practitioner-related secularism and discriminatory beliefs about race and religion. For example, a counsellor may subscribe to stereotypes about the supposed inherent criminality and perceived dangerousness of Black people, which leads to increased interactions with the justice system and emergency services, placing them on a negative pathway into the mental health system (Fante-Coleman and Jackson-Best 2020). Such stereotypes pathologize Black people and pigeonhole community members into assumptions that are rooted in anti-Black racism and Islamophobia. These then prevent Black clients from developing therapeutic relationships with mental health providers who could help to improve their mental health. Further to this point, when service providers have Islamophobic beliefs or discriminatory ideas about Muslim women and their role in Islam, rigid roles may be ascribed to the women that limit the care they are offered or affect the help they are willing to receive. An example of this is found in a study of Canadian Muslim women's mental health released by the Canadian Mental Health Association, which indicated that "cultural stereotyping or a 'picture'-based understanding of Muslim women clients led to a perceived inability to connect women's particular mental health stressors with positive solutions" (Latif, Rodrigues, and Galley 2020, 8). Conversely, the research project also found that feeling as though their service provider had a connection to or an understanding of their religious and cultural background was a success factor for Muslim women engaged in therapeutic mental health settings.

The role of service providers as representatives of mental health institutions cannot be understated, and their potential to be cultivators of positive therapeutic relationships for Muslim clients is significant. For many Muslims in Canada, finding a Muslim therapist is difficult. It is even more challenging for those who are seeking free or low-cost care. Muslims without financial resources or insurance are limited in their ability to find a therapist who shares and/or understands their sociocultural and religious background. Many Muslim patients end up working with a provider who has little or no knowledge of who they are, what they believe, or how these attributes could positively inform mental health treatment. This is not to say that therapists who are not Muslim cannot provide high-quality, culturally responsive, and safe care to Muslim clients. However, in some therapeutic interactions Muslim patients may be tasked with explaining religious conventions or encounter mental health practitioners who are unable or unwilling to implement the services and supports that meet their unique needs. Even worse, some care providers may also have Islamophobic attitudes or beliefs that they project onto Muslim clients. All these factors can exacerbate conditions like stress, anxiety, and depression and increase the deleterious conditions for people seeking help.

Conclusion

Islamophobia's existence on individual, societal, and institutional levels (Furqan et al. 2022) necessitates approaches to mental healthcare provision that acknowledge the negative impacts it can have on Muslim clients' lives and on the therapeutic relationship itself. Gendered Islamophobia and anti-Black Islamophobia are interconnected forms of discrimination tied to secularism that put Muslims who are Black and/or identify as women at increased risk for Islamophobic abuse and violence. Mental health services should be aware of and respond to the heightened risk faced by Muslims and especially Black Muslim women, who experience compounded Islamophobia due to race, religion, and gender. Additionally, in mental healthcare environments, it is critical for providers to be aware of their attitudes to religion in general and Muslims in particular and actively to work against reproducing all forms of discrimination that may impact Muslim clients, particularly those who are Black, Black women, women, as well as those from communities of colour.

Policy Recommendations

The information presented speaks to the urgency of this issue and the need for transformational change to prevent and take steps to eradicate Islamophobia. There are opportunities for mental health service providers to effect positive change, framed in what follows as recommendations. Importantly, these recommendations cannot take the place of institutional and structural change, which are imperative for transforming mental healthcare systems. Guidance is also included for Muslim clients, to help them develop strategies for increasing individual and collective ability to self-advocate in mental healthcare settings. Like the recommendations, this guidance cannot be a sustainable alternative to transformational change among mental healthcare providers and the institutions they work within and represent. Instead, the recommendations and guidance must be understood as strategies that can assist clients and providers to receive and deliver the best care possible.

Recommendations for Mental Health Providers

1. Be self-reflective about prejudicial and discriminatory views of Black Muslims, Muslims, Muslim women, Black communities, etc. Commit to engaging in continuous training and education to address Islamophobia, your lack of information or knowledge about Muslims, and internalized myths and stereotypes about Muslims and Islam.

2. Adapt modalities of mental healthcare whenever possible to meet Muslim clients' needs. Furqan et al. (2022) state that a trauma-informed approach can be useful in understanding the multiple manifestations of Islamophobia in Muslim communities. Trauma-informed approaches can be incorporated into a range of treatment protocols and modalities of care, such as cognitive behavioural therapy, psychotherapy, or behavioural therapy.

3. Increase awareness about how institutional and organizational policies, practices, and frameworks are influenced by secularism and reinforce Islamophobia. It is essential to be cognizant of the ways Islamophobia manifests in institutions, but it cannot end at awareness. Service providers must also take

proactive steps towards undoing Islamophobia in professional settings and organizational and practice-based change.

4. Avoid the reproduction of discriminatory dynamics in healthcare interactions with Muslims. This is particularly true for mental health providers' engagements with all Muslim clients, but it also extends to Muslim colleagues. Contributing to a safe and inclusive work environment is important for everyone.

5. Adopt alternative models of care that are Muslim-centred. This may be achieved through designing and deploying high-quality mental health programming created by and for Muslim communities that members can access. Black communities in Canada have recognized barriers to care and sought to address them through designing programs and frameworks for mental healthcare that centre Black experiences and needs and provide alternatives to Western models. There has been an uptick in Muslim-led mental health organizations and programming, and more are needed. This includes free and low-cost options for community members who face financial barriers.

Guidance for Muslim Clients

1. Know the system as well as possible. This can be challenging, given that mental health systems are confusing for most, but approaching them systematically is useful. When entering an agency or institution for mental health support, do not be afraid to ask about your healthcare provider. Are they Muslim? Are Muslim practitioners available? If paired with a non-Muslim provider, continue asking questions: Have they ever had a Muslim client? What do they know about Islam? Gather other information that will provide insights into who you will be engaging with. Having some context about the organization itself is also helpful. Understanding whether it is a community-based agency, a hospital, or a program that offers

a limited number of sessions with a practitioner can also help empower people through building knowledge and confidence. It can also inform what kinds of follow-up or supplementary mental health supports may be needed or pursued.

2. Seek support of trusted family and/or friends throughout your care. Some community members may have acute mental health needs and are unable to collect information about the mental health provider or facility they are accessing. This necessitates greater involvement and support from trusted family and friends. Stigma is a significant barrier to care within community and family networks. However, these networks can also be facilitators of mental healthcare (Fante-Coleman and Jackson-Best 2020). Providing transportation to appointments or support via follow-up and checking in are just two supportive provisions.

3. Advocate against community-based mental illness stigma. Muslim communities, like many others, have deeply held beliefs about mental illness. Start at the individual level by working to undo the ways we connect mental health to spirituality. It is also important to divest from stigmatizing behaviours, words, and actions that are used to characterize mental illness and those who are experiencing mental health challenges.

NOTE

1. Muslim men are also included in gendered Islamophobia. The report by the International Civil Liberties Monitoring Group, Islamic Social Services Association, and Noor Cultural Centre (2020, 1) states that they are characterized as "violent terrorists and patriarchs." However, given that Muslim women more often experience violent and physical Islamophobia, the analysis in the report and other research focuses on this group.

REFERENCES

Appleton, Violet E. 1967. "Psychiatry in Canada a Century Ago."
  Canadian Psychiatric Association Journal 12, no. 4: 345–361.
  doi:10.1177/070674376701200040.

Badaloo, Anna-Liza. 2022. "Two Decades of Islamophobia: The Invisible Toll
  on the Health of Muslims in Canada." *The Monitor*, January 1. https://
  monitormag.ca/articles/two-decades-of-islamophobia-the-invisible-
  toll-on-the-health-of-muslims-in-canada/.

Black Health Alliance. n.d. "Anti-Black Racism." https://blackhealthalliance.ca/
  home/antiblack-racism/.

Blunt, Marney. 2023. "Man Sentenced to Six Years in Prison for Random
  Stabbing at Winnipeg Olive Garden." *Global News*, September 7. https://
  globalnews.ca/news/9946223/man-sentenced-to-six-years-in-prison-
  for-random-stabbing-at-winnipeg-olive-garden/.

Booker, Melissa, Fatimah Jackson-Best, and Tiyondah Fante-Coleman. 2023.
  "Anti-Black Racism and Building Organizational Partnerships:
  Implications for Recovery-oriented Practice in Mental Health."
  Journal of Recovery in Mental Health 6, no. 2: 4–32.

Canadian Association of Social Work. 2022. "CASW Social Policy Principles."
  https://www.casw-acts.ca/en/governance/casw-social-policy-principles.

Chaimowitz, Gary, Doug Urness, Biju Mathew, Julia Dornik, and Alison
  Freeland. 2014. "Freedom of and from Religion." *Canadian Journal of
  Psychiatry* 59, no. 12: 1–3.

Commission des droits de la personne et des droits de la jeunesse. n.d. "Religious
  Neutrality of the State." https://www.cdpdj.qc.ca/en/our-positions/
  issues/religious-neutrality-state.

Crenshaw, Kimberlé. 1989. "Demarginalizing the Intersection of Race and Sex:
  A Black Feminist Critique of Antidiscrimination Doctrine, Feminist
  Theory and Antiracist Politics." *University of Chicago Legal Forum* 1, no. 8:
  139–167.

Crenshaw, Kimberlé. 1991. "Mapping the Margins: Intersectionality, Identity
  Politics, and Violence against Women of Color." *Stanford Law Review* 43,
  no. 6: 1241–1299. https://doi.org/10.2307/1229039.

Davis, Simon. 2006. *Community Mental Health in Canada*. University of British
  Columbia Press.

Dryden, OmiSoore, and Onye Nnorom. 2021. "Time to Dismantle Systemic
  Anti-Black Racism in Medicine in Canada." *CMAJ: Canadian Medical*

Association Journal 193, no. 2: E55–E57. https://doi.org/10.1503/
cmaj.201579.

Dwornik, Ania. 2021. "The Interface of Mad Studies and Indigenous Ways of
Knowing: Innovation, Co-Creation, and Decolonization." *Critical Social
Work* 22, no. 2: 25–39.

Elkassem, Siham, Rick Csiernik, Andrew Mantulak, Gina Kayssi, Yasmine
Hussain, Kathryn Lambert, Pamela Bailey, and Asad Choudhary. 2018.
"Growing Up Muslim: The Impact of Islamophobia on Children in a
Canadian Community." *Journal of Muslim Mental Health* 12, no. 1: 3–18.
http://dx.doi.org/10.3998/jmmh.10381607.0012.101.

Fante-Coleman, Tiyondah, Melissa Booker, Ameerah Craigg, Deneece Plummer,
and Fatimah Jackson-Best. 2022. *Factors That Impact How Black Youth
Access the Mental Healthcare System in Ontario. Toronto: Pathways to
Care Project.* Black Health Alliance. https://www.pathwaystocare.ca/
research/ptc-focus-group-report-eng.

Fante-Coleman, Tiyondah, and Fatimah Jackson-Best. 2020. "Barriers and
Facilitators to Accessing Mental Healthcare in Canada for Black Youth:
A Scoping Review." *Adolescent Research Review* 5: 115–136. https://doi.
org/10.1007/s40894-020-00133-2.

Furqan, Zainab, Arfeen Malick, Juveria Zaheer, and Javeed Sukhera. 2022.
"Understanding and Addressing Islamophobia through Trauma-
Informed Care." *Canadian Medical Association Journal* 194, no. 21:
E746–E747. https://doi.org/10.1503/cmaj.211298.

International Civil Liberties Monitoring Group, Islamic Social Services
Association, and Noor Cultural Centre. 2020. "Islamophobia in
Canada: Submission to the UN Special Rapporteur on Freedom
of Religion or Belief." https://www.ohchr.org/sites/default/files/
Documents/Issues/Religion/Islamophobia-AntiMuslim/Civil%20
Society%20or%20Individuals/Noor-ICLMG-ISSA.pdf.

Jackson-Best, Fatimah. 2019. *Black Muslims in Canada: A Systematic Review of
Published and Unpublished Literature.* Tessellate Institute and The Black
Muslim Initiative.

Jiswari, Athir N., and Carrie Arnold. 2018. "Cultural Humility and Mental
Health Care in Canadian Muslim Communities." *Canadian Journal of
Counselling and Psychotherapy* 52, no. 1, 43–64. https://cjc-rcc.ucalgary.ca/
article/view/61133.

Junker, Anna. 2021. "Attack was 'Horrific and Brutal': Family of Black Women Targeted at Southgate Centre in December Speak Out." *Edmonton Journal*, January 7. https://edmontonjournal.com/news/crime/family-of-somali-women-attacked-at-southgate-centre-in-december-speak-out.

Khan, Zainab. 2021. "The Impact of Islamophobia on the Mental Health of Muslim Post-Secondary Students." Master's thesis, York University. https://yorkspace.library.yorku.ca/server/api/core/bitstreams/06b0c377-94e4-4e2a-85a9-c16779984cd9/content.

Latif, Ruby, Sara Rodrigues, and Andrew Galley. 2020. *Muslim Women's Mental Health: A Community-Based Research Project.* Canadian Mental Health Association.

Loutfy, Mona, Wangari Tharao, Carmen Logie, Muna A. Aden, Lori A. Chambers, Wei Wu, Marym Abdelmaseh, Liviana Calzavara. 2015. "Systematic Review of Stigma Reducing Interventions for African/Black Diasporic Women." *Journal of the International AIDS Society* 18, no. 1: 1–7. https://doi.org/10.7448/IAS.18.1.19835.

Mugabo, Delice Igicari. 2016. "On Rocks and Hard Places: A Reflection on Antiblackness in Organizing Against Islamophobia." *Critical Ethnic Studies* 2, no. 2: 159–183. https://doi.org/10.5749/jcritethnstud.2.2.0159.

Phillips, David, and Dean Lauterbach. (2017). American Muslim Immigrant Mental Health: The Role of Racism and Mental Health Stigma. *Journal of Muslim Mental Health* 11, no. 1: 39–56. https://doi.org/10.3998/jmmh.10381607.0011.103.

Rivenbark, Joshua G., and Mathieu Ichou. 2020. "Discrimination in Healthcare as a Barrier to Care: Experiences of Socially Disadvantaged Populations in France from a Nationally Representative Survey." *BMC Public Health* 20, no. 31: 1–10. http://dx.doi.org/10.1186/s12889-019-8124-z.

Shattell, Mona, and Paula J. Brown. 2017. "Racism, White Privilege, and Diversity in Mental Health." *Journal of Psychosocial Nursing and Mental Health Services* 55, no. 7: 2–3. https://doi.org/10.3928/02793695-20170619-01.

Simmons, Harvey G. *Unbalanced: Mental Health Policy in Ontario, 1930–1989.* Toronto: Wall & Thompson, 1990

Snowdon, Wallis. 2020. "Woman in Hijab Assaulted in 2nd 'Hate-Motivated' Attack in Edmonton this Month." *CBC News*, December 16. https://www.cbc.ca/news/canada/edmonton/southgate-lrt-assault-hijab-hate-motivated-1.5843642.

Statistics Canada. 2023. "Police-Reported Hate Crime, 2021." https://www150. statcan.gc.ca/n1/daily-quotidien/230322/dq230322a-eng.htm.

Wilfred Laurier University. n.d. "The Canadian Islamophobia Industry Research Project." https://www.wlu.ca/academics/faculties/faculty-of-arts/ faculty-profiles/jasmin-zine/canadian-islamophobia-industry- research-project/index.html.

10

Combatting Islamophobia in Canada

Interventions and Gaps

KHALED AL-QAZZAZ *and*
NAKITA VALERIO

Over the last few years in Canada, and
especially during the COVID-19 pandemic, there has been a marked
increase in Islamophobic incidents and hate crimes, as well as significant systemic abuses against Muslims at the governmental and societal
levels. At the time of writing this chapter, more Muslims had been
killed in targeted, hate-motivated attacks in Canada than in any other
G7 nation. Among the most horrific tragedies the country has seen are
the murders of six Muslim men by Islamophobic shooter Alexandre
Bissonnette at the Islamic Cultural Centre of Quebec City on January 29,
2017; the stabbing of Mohamed-Aslim Zafis by neo-Nazi Guilherme
von Neutegem on September 12, 2020; and the truck killing of the
Afzaal family by white supremacist Nathaniel Veltman in London,
Ontario, on June 6, 2021. These have been coupled with a major rise in
person-to-person assaults and harassment incidents throughout the

pandemic, especially against Black Muslim women in the province of Alberta (Yourex-West 2021). At the same time, high-level political rhetoric has demonized Muslims for political gain—notably during the 2015 election, with the introduction of the "barbaric cultural practices" hotline and the niqab ban by the outgoing Conservative government—but has ebbed and flowed since then. When it comes to contending with Islamophobia, ongoing systemic abuses remain largely unaddressed, including discrimination by the Canadian Border Services Agency, the targeted profiling of Muslim charities by the Canada Revenue Agency, and more (Emon and Hasan 2021; NCCM 2020). Additionally, the foreign policy of the Liberal government during the Israeli war on Gaza in 2023–2024 has left many Muslims in Canada at a loss for how to proceed with a governing class rendering itself supportive atrocities and indignities against Palestinians (and, by extension, Muslims).

Muslim thinkers, activists, advocates, organizations, and grassroots movements have done their best to advocate for addressing systemic Islamophobia and clamping down on hate groups to curb violence against Muslims; however, the lack of a comprehensive analysis of such approaches may be a factor in the absence of a totalizing national approach across organizations and regions. While it is easy to speculate on some of the reasons for this—including limited resources as a result of these systemic barriers, similarly staggered development in Muslim community organizations (especially across regional boundaries), a lack of communication, and sometimes hastiness on the part of both government and advocates, or even territorialism—it suffices to say that the approaches taken now are not always rooted in research-based strategies for policy implementation. While they do not always need to be, we hope that this chapter's analysis can benefit Muslim communities in advocating against Islamophobia in the future. This chapter aims to inform by investigating existing interventions, to develop a bigger picture of them, and to offer strategies for a collaborative and novel Canadian approach that is responsive to this context while building on its past lessons.

Although there is a significant amount of necessary scholarly literature on theoretical topics in Islamophobia, as well as on manifestations of its various phenomena (both structural and interpersonal) in Canada, there remains a practical gap for Canadian organizations, institutions, and activists seeking to learn from past approaches to disrupting Islamophobia both here and abroad, in other secular or post-secular Western contexts. Following this, our chapter seeks to examine the following critical questions: What approaches have been taken here, in Canada? What areas have been covered by these approaches? What gaps or challenges remain? And most importantly, what do these findings tell us about how we *ought to* approach the disruption of Islamophobia here? This chapter offers preliminary responses to these questions and touches on recent approaches to offer beneficial examples for the way forward.

Methods

Research for this chapter was undertaken using a multi-method approach, including examining existing secondary literature on the topic, analyzing media reports and Muslim organizational information found online, and pulling information from large-scale national studies conducted by the Institute for Religious and Socio-Political Studies (I-RSS) about Muslims and Muslim organizations in Canada. This chapter offers only a general overview of anti-Islamophobia approaches and themes that organizations and advocates have utilized in Canada; more work is needed to develop a full composite picture of those approaches by region. The work done here offers a blueprint and key recommendations for future work. Literature on the topic, media reports, and online data were pulled using key terms related to the topic and further dividing those terms by region, including Ontario, the Maritimes, the Prairies, the West Coast, and the North. Zeinab Diab in this book (Chapter 7) offers an excellent look at the development of institutionalized and systemic Islamophobia in Quebec specifically and future research building on it might include then examining the unique trajectory of responses or anti-Islamophobia actions taken in Quebec while replicating such work in other regions.

Approaches

Approaches taken to combat Islamophobia in Canada follow several key methods, trends, and themes, and they can be further divided by scope (approaches being national, regional, or local). One key finding in compiling these approaches is that, despite some national organizations aiming to unify their voices around advocacy efforts, the general approach of Muslim communities remains fragmented and quite disparate. Muslim organizations and advocates often operate in isolation, duplicating some efforts or focusing on reactionary endeavours at the expense of a longer-term, strategic, collaboration. While some key exceptions exist and will be expanded on below, more remains to be done to remedy this issue.

Political Advocacy, Legal Recourse, and Policy Change

One of the more visible areas where Muslim activists and organizations have worked to combat Islamophobia is in political advocacy and policy change. These efforts are conducted in two primary streams of action: through mandate-specific organizations or through the efforts of general Islamic institutions that include advocacy as *part* of their overall efforts. In Canada, several national organizations focus primarily on Islamophobia, including the National Council of Canadian Muslims (NCCM), the Canadian Muslim Public Affairs Council, the Muslim Advisory Council of Canada, and Justice for All Canada. Each of these groups conducts programming and political advocacy efforts, primarily at the federal level, for domestic Islamophobia issues, including both overt hate and violence as well as broader systemic issues. NCCM often leads the charge for supporting hate-crime victims and has a reporting mechanism on its website to collect data informing its hate-crimes map. They also seek policy change, countering Islamophobic laws like Bill 21 in Quebec and regularly presenting briefs to elected officials and in Parliament. NCCM was instrumental in planning a national summit on Islamophobia for the Government of Canada in July 2021.

Many national organizations that cater to Muslim communities generally (in religious rites, education, and social services) also engage in anti-Islamophobia political advocacy on behalf of their communities. Organizations like the Muslim Association of Canada (MAC), the Islamic Circle of North America, the Canadian Council of Imams, and others release statements or policy briefs on issues of Islamophobia and also conduct significant advocacy efforts with elected officials and governmental bodies/agencies.

A more recent development in this series of approaches is actual legal actions taken against different levels and agencies of government or private enterprises about systemic violations of Muslim rights. These include an appeal against Quebec's Bill 21 filed in 2021 by the Canadian Civil Liberties Association and NCCM, as well as a Charter challenge by MAC filed against the Canada Revenue Agency in 2021 related to invasive audits conducted by the agency from 2016 to 2022. Other legal actions that relate to combatting anti-Palestinian racism impacting Muslim students include a University of British Columbia student group coordinator suing Hillel BC and their former contractor for defamation after they placed pro-Hamas stickers bearing the student group logo around the UBC campus during the Israeli assault on Gaza in November 2023. NCCM specifically advocated for UBC to conduct an independent investigation into the incident and its continued aftermath.

Relatedly, given the concept of *ummah* (a structure of Muslim nationhood that crosses political borders) within Islamic worldviews, it should come as no surprise that some national Muslim organizations, including those listed above, also advocate against Islamophobia and oppression of Muslims globally, seeing little distinction between the rights and needs of Muslims abroad and those in Canada. These groups seek to leverage Canada's place on the world stage to instigate change for Muslims facing conflict, occupation, genocide, and state discrimination, as well as provide humanitarian assistance and safe havens where possible. Advocacy for the right to speak out about those issues domestically, without repercussions, is also a focus for groups like Justice for All. At the time of writing this chapter, amid the Israeli war on Gaza (2023–2024), Muslim professional organizations and lobby groups have also flexed what influence they hold by withholding political funding for politicians and organizing awareness campaigns. Further, anti-Islamophobia political advocacy is also being done by Muslim academics and activists outside of formalized institutions and structures, through channels like governmental consultation or through media activism.

Security

Immediate responses to vandalism, graffiti, building damage, and overt violence have been met with increased security measures by Muslim houses of worship and community centres. In the wake of the Quebec City mosque shooting, for example, mosques across the country began inviting law enforcement officials to attend larger congregational prayers, which continues in many major cities to this day, although the practice has fallen out of favour in jurisdictions where law enforcement has cracked down heavily on Palestinian protesters. In solidarity, activists in such cases call for Muslim organizations to refrain from inviting police and politicians into congregational spaces and where it still happens, it tends to be publicly condemned. Additionally, under the federal government's Security Infrastructure Program, developed in 2007, private, non-profit organizations linked to a community at risk of hate-motivated crime can make security improvements to their community gathering spaces and the program will pay 50 percent of the costs (Public Safety Canada 2023). These projects might include the installation of additional lighting, alarm systems, fences, or surveillance cameras. It is unclear, however, how many Muslim organizations have accessed these funds across the country.

Finally, some grassroots volunteer groups like the Salam Project were founded in 2017, after the Quebec City mosque shooting, and ramped up in 2019 after the Christchurch, New Zealand, massacre. The Salam Project is run by volunteer experts who team up with Muslim law enforcement officials to provide training on safety and security for mosques and Muslim community organizations. They operate primarily in the Greater Toronto Area and Ontario, but they have also delivered training in New Brunswick, Manitoba, and British Columbia. Other regions with higher-density Muslim populations like Alberta and Quebec stand to be influenced by the project's future reach.

Education

Education initiatives around Islamophobia have taken several approaches and tend to cater to specific audiences, such as educators, corporate or union groups, as well as the general public. Most education initiatives fit into three streams based on the approach: building awareness about Islam and Muslims (especially in response to misconceptions); teaching about Islamophobia in either a diversity, equity, and inclusion or anti-racism framework; or training educators or institution leadership teams on how to teach about Islamophobia themselves. These initiatives could include public lectures, workshops and seminars, online video series, and educational resources such as activities and lesson plans.

Public education about Islam and Muslim heritage in general tends to focus on depicting Muslim history in Canada or globally, as well as illustrating basic beliefs and practices of the religion to better understand not only Muslim ways of being but also what their rights in public spaces are. Documentary series such as *A New Life in a New Land* (2010) by Milo Productions are aimed at educators and are meant for use in the classroom, making them curriculum resources to support the needs of Muslim students. Some of the practical advice therein is aimed at helping non-Muslim educators navigate Muslim needs during holidays, in parent-teacher relationships, and issues related to immigration/refugee status. Groups like Islamic History Month Canada, the Aga Khan Museum, and NCCM have also published guidebooks or curated resource lists for educators on Islamic religious practices and other topics. Some of these resources outline the legal framework for the protection of religious freedoms and focus on developing accommodations for Muslim worship. The former Alberta Muslim Public Affairs Council, now NCCM Alberta, took a different approach, focusing on historical Islamic polities like Al-Andalus as a model for acceptance and pluralism in the classroom and Canada through the creation of curricular resources like *Building Acceptance* (2016). The Tessellate Institute has opted to focus on stories of Muslim youth and identity in their video-based curriculum package for upper grades.

Teaching about Islamophobia directly (whatever the theoretical framework attached to it) has far more educational resources and approaches attached to it in this context. Toolkits and reports like *Rivers of Hope* (by the organization of the same name; 2018) or *Islamophobia at Work* (by the Canadian Labour Congress; 2019) and their accompanying live workshops or webinars represent efforts to educate the general public on Islamophobia. A webinar entitled *Challenging Islamophobia in the Youth Sector* (2020), created by Youth REX and NCCM, depicts how youth-sector stakeholders can work together to challenge Islamophobia and support Muslim youth in Ontario. It includes a discussion of what Islamophobia is, the experiences of Muslim youth, and how to be a meaningful ally. NCCM has also produced *A Teachable Moment About Islamophobia*, a variety of training programs and workshops aimed at educators, parents, and parent councils. It explores how Islamophobia may impact schools and classrooms and includes an overview of what Islamophobia is, common myths, and how Muslim children are impacted by negative public discourse.

Most recently, in the wake of the murder of the Afzaal family on June 6, 2021, and in preparation for the first anniversary, Muslim youth who were friends with slain fifteen-year-old Yumnah Afzaal developed the Youth Coalition Combating Islamophobia based in London, Ontario, where the attacks happened. One priority of this ambitious group, amid planning commemorative vigils annually, has been the development of curricular resources for all grade levels that include activities for understanding implicit bias, Islamophobia personally and systemically, and a review of what occurred on June 6 from a trauma-informed perspective.

Building safe and inclusive classrooms and workspaces is another subject for which there are numerous resources, some general and a few focused on dealing with Islamophobia more specifically. In this vein, NCCM has created a training program called *Inclusive Schools*, and the Canadian Council for Muslim Women has created a toolkit entitled *My Canada: Finding Common Ground* (2010). The latter resource was launched to provide Muslim youth with a platform to engage in dialogue about the issues they face and identify solutions, as well as to prevent alienation of Muslim youth. The toolkit includes a video of diverse Muslim youth and a manual outlining practical recommendations for conducting workshops and facilitating dialogue with Muslim youth. It covers topics like leadership, media relations, civic engagement, creative expression, and community resources.

It is important to note that, until recently, each of these streams tended to be isolated from one another, with different organizations creating their own resources or delivery tools and relatively little communication between them. This changed in the fall of 2021 when, with the financial support of Ontario's Ministry of Education, MAC—after compiling a bibliography with the support of I-RSS of existing anti-Islamophobia resources in Canada (Hill 2021)— developed a more comprehensive and holistic educational tool that combines not only the three streams but also the existing mediums. The result was the creation of an online portal called Islam Awareness, which includes extensive videos, lesson plans, infographics and posters, and other resources in the three main streams outlined above: introducing Islam to educators; dismantling Islamophobia in schools (from an anti-racism lens); and building safe, Islamophobia-free classrooms. Of note is the fact that the introduction to Islam goes beyond a cursory look at the more superficial aspects of the religion and instead dives deeply into understanding an Islamic worldview, ethical framework, and even philosophical foundations. The rich way the religion is portrayed goes beyond some approaches that tend to be reactive or focus only on addressing public misconceptions and stereotypes about Islam and Muslims.

A final area where Muslim organizations have operated (in a very limited manner) in education is advocacy for the inclusion of Islam, Islamic heritage, religious literacy—and information about Islamophobia specifically—in official provincial curriculums. Groups like the Edmonton Council of Muslim Communities (ECMC) have tried for years to attain such inclusions in places like Alberta; however, the degree of success of these efforts remains to be seen.

Integration

In attempts to improve conditions for Muslims in Canada and centre the importance of Muslim issues in governmental policy circles, Muslim communities and some organizations have focused on increasing the sociopolitical and economic integration of Muslims. This includes normalizing and professionalizing specific Islamic practices and processes such as halal food certification and halal financing in mainstream society. It has also meant pushing for Muslims to occupy key positions, from elected officials at all levels of government to key advocacy positions in governmental agencies and prominent nongovernmental organizations. In the federal elections of 2019 and 2021, for example, twelve Muslims were elected to office, representing various political parties. Additionally, establishing key academic positions for Muslim scholars, such as the ECMC Chair for Islamic Studies at the University of Alberta or the Institute of Islamic Studies at the University of Toronto, has been instrumental in bringing Muslim voices and Islamic leadership into that domain.

Where Muslim communities have not fared as well (through no fault of their own) is in economic integration. Although there is a common perception that Muslim communities are generally middle or upper-middle class due to their propensity for higher education (compared to the Canadian national average of 33.3 percent, 54 percent of working-age Muslim men and women held degrees in 2021, up from 49.9 percent in 2015 [Statistics Canada 2021; Hamdani 2015]), this reality has not translated into employability for large parts of Muslim communities. In fact, 16.7 percent of Canadian Muslims were unemployed in 2021 compared to the national average of 10.3 percent (Statistics Canada 2021). This rate is up from 13.9 percent in 2015 (compared to the national average of 7.8 percent at the same time), being exceeded in unemployment only by Indigenous, First Nation, Métis, and Inuit peoples (Hamdani 2015, 24). Foreign-trained professionals from Muslim-majority countries also disproportionately face underemployment, with the latest available statistics showing a range of 67 percent to a whopping 91 percent not working in their field (see Hamdani 2015 and Zietsma 2010). Further, the average annual net income of Canadian Muslims in 2021 was $36,120 (only increasing $5,457 in six years) versus $44,920 (up from $40,650 in 2015) nationally, with lower pension incomes than the average population (possibly due to higher self-employment or employment in non-pensionable jobs) (Statistics Canada 2021; Hamdani 2015, 28). Despite experiencing comparatively high unemployment, Muslims still only claimed 1.7 percent of income from social security in 2021 (versus 1.2 percent of all Canadians), a number down from 2.2 percent in 2015 (Statistics Canada 2021; Hamdani 2015, 29). Despite these economic realities, housing issues, and food insecurity for many Muslims, anti-Islamophobia efforts in Canada have not focused on these issues as being directly related to their cause, despite overwhelming evidence that systemic barriers and discrimination are the likely culprits in producing many of these glaring inequities.

Intra-community Support

A fair share of the academic literature on Islamophobia in Canada is rightfully focused on the detrimental effects of Islamophobia on Muslim youth and families as well as on the socioeconomic impact of systemic discrimination and how this alters Muslim families, communities, and organizational foci. That being the case, Muslim community activists and organizations have understandably directed their attention to the mitigation of Islamophobia's negative effects instead of combatting the phenomena directly. Part of this approach might be rooted in what we have elsewhere called a *stranger* syndrome, where Islamophobia in Canada is framed in the minds of Muslims as part of a continuum of hatred from the time of the prophets until the present moment that will never be abated or expunged entirely (Al-Qazzaz and Valerio 2020). This results in a shift from trying to *eliminate* Islamophobia to trying to *manage* the impact it has on Muslims. As such, community support groups and efforts around Muslim mental health have arisen at the grassroots and institutional levels, as have key Muslim identity projects that aim to fortify Muslim youth, especially as they continue to experience religious identity crises.

While it is beyond the scope of this chapter to attempt a complete picture of all interventions that fit into this category, it is important to highlight a few key examples. In 2021, with financial support from the Government of Canada through the Canadian Heritage Society, Nisa Helpline launched their Anti-Racism Action Program-funded Changemakers Youth Initiative. This program focuses on empowering young, racialized Muslim women in leadership and development, community education, and digital media literacy, to help this particular demographic navigate the ongoing stressors and challenges of living in an Islamophobic context with compounded oppressions. The workshops and toolkits are directed inward at Muslim communities' most marginalized members, in the hopes of offering opportunities, awareness, and support for their plight.

A relatively novel approach has been taken by Sisters' Dialogue (SD), an Albertan non-profit organization founded in 2021 in response to a string of violent public attacks against Black Muslim women over a period of six months (and for those occurring since). The grassroots-turned-non-profit group has founded a Safewalk program in collaboration with the Edmonton Federation of Community Leagues to offer walking partners for visible Muslimahs in public and on public transportation, in the hope of preventing further incidents. SD also funds free and accessible psychotherapy sessions for Muslim women who have been targeted in hate crimes or experienced public Islamophobic aggression; they also periodically hold community art therapy sessions, playback theatre sessions for victims, Muslimah sharing circles and care packages, public panels on critical topics related to Islamophobia, political advocacy efforts rooted in community listening, and the support of Muslimah religious identity projects like the Nusaibah Collective, which will be expanded on below.

Generally speaking, community care and mental health support are just beginning to be prioritized in Muslim communities in Canada, and there remains significant work to be done. While some crisis management and social service organizations like Nisa Homes, Nisa Helpline, Naseeha Helpline, and others continue to operate out of necessity, it is only recently that organizations like Canadian Muslim Counselling and i-Impact (formerly Mercy Mission Canada) have begun to develop longer-term solutions and movements in communities. Such solutions might include virtual counselling services, in the case of the former organization, or other innovative developments like Taskeen Wellness, launched in 2021 by the latter. Taskeen aims to "provide culturally responsive education, mentorship, and support to interested community residents (parents, youth, and others) who wish to be trained as *Wellness Advocates*" (Mercy Mission Canada n.d.).

Muslim Identity Projects

Another area of intervention that focuses on inward community support to mitigate the ongoing effects of Islamophobia is the development of Muslim identity-building projects. These have been created in response to a significant amount of literature indicating a crisis of identity and even faith among Muslim youth, especially as they navigate spaces of belonging and exclusion (Al-Qazzaz and Valerio 2020). As far as is apparent, such initiatives are not yet widespread, but early successes are promising for an impactful future.

One upcoming project that marries intra-community support with identity-building endeavours is another comprehensive online portal in development at the time of writing. Similar to the aforementioned Islam Awareness project undertaken by MAC, this portal is meant to support Muslim youth mental health in the public education system. In partnership with the Ministry of Education in Ontario, MAC aims to provide a roadmap for healthy Muslim character development and wellness, an understanding of mental health support within a holistic Islamic framework, and awareness and systems navigation assistance for educators and parents of Muslim youth experiencing mental health issues.

Another such program, MAC iRISE, developed in 2019 and implemented in nine Islamic schools across the country, is a holistic character education pedagogy where students embody Islamic values and acquire relevant life skills to meet twenty-first-century challenges, while still being grounded in the concept of *Rabbaniyah* (God-centred consciousness and focus). Unlike short-term or extracurricular character programs, MAC iRise is integrated throughout the school experience both inside and outside the classroom by teachers and school staff and has seen considerable growth and success.

Based on the foundational concept that increased religiosity and a strong religious identity, and especially related praxis, can serve as tools for fostering resilience for Muslims experiencing Islamophobia (see Narayanan 2011; Ridzuan 2020; Skalisky et al. 2020; Saputro et al. 2021; Rahman et al. 2020; Al Eid et al. 2020), another identity-based program called the Nusaibah Collective has been piloted for the past three years in Alberta. As a community-based, grassroots project aimed at creating authentic, Islam-forward, Hereafter-focused, and traditional knowledge-rooted connections between Muslimahs of all backgrounds in Canada, the collective focuses on "reigniting a passion for the Qur'an and its consistent recitation under the guidance of a qualified scholar; gathering together (virtually)...making our belief transparent through the actions of our tongues and limbs; and building a loving community" (thenusaibahcollective.ca 2024, "Home"). As part of participation in the collective, members have given their feedback throughout their experience indicating that the intervention is significantly transformative for participants, particularly given the ever-present spectre of Islamophobia combined with various constraints within Muslim communities (thenusaibahcollective.ca 2024, "About"). Other such programs are available through mosques and Islamic institutions across the country.

Some identity-building projects within Muslim communities rightfully cater to the intersecting identities embodied by many Muslims and aim to mitigate the effects of multiple stressors caused by compounded oppressions. As researcher Fatima Chakroun (2022) pointed out in her national study on Muslim organizations in Canada for I-RSS, these groups typically spring up in response to a perceived lack of space or awareness about the unique challenges Muslims with intersecting identities face. One such example is the Black Muslim Initiative, launched in Toronto in 2018 to address issues at the intersection of Islamophobia and anti-Black racism, focusing on education, advocacy, and resource development for Black Muslims while also conducting and supporting independent research.

Research

Another arena where Muslims and Muslim organizations are combatting Islamophobia is in academia and research. According to a recent literature review examining scholarship on Muslims in Canada (Valerio

2022), though progress has been made in certain areas and disciplines, some research and publications continue to discuss still-dominant narratives about Muslims. There is an overrepresentation of topics like radicalization and securitization in public discourse and academic literature in which Islamic worldviews are sometimes subtextually and other times overtly understood and portrayed on false continuums from secular (acceptable) to "extremist" (practising, unacceptable) (Valerio 2022). This issue has been tackled in Muslim communities in two ways: within public universities and through the development of independent research institutes and/or projects.

In public universities, two developing examples at the University of Toronto are noteworthy: the Muslims in Canada Archive (MiCA) (Institute of Islamic Studies 2022)and the Muslims in Canada Data Initiative (MiCDI). MiCA aims to "acquire, organize, preserve, and make accessible records of and about Canadian Muslim individuals and organizations that possess enduring value for the preservation of the history and documentary heritage of Muslims in Canada" (Institute of Islamic Studies n.d., 2022)—a heritage that is currently limited due to lack of attention on the archiving process. Similarly, garnering sufficient statistical data on Muslims in Canada remains another area where communities and researchers alike struggle. As Valerio notes in her literature review, MiCDI "launched as of early 2021 intending to build upon coming census data from 2021, as well as supporting a future Environics survey that will be developed in the wake of that data...Once that study has been conducted, the intention is to have post-doctoral research fellows produce a series of reports on the findings of the study and its accompanying processed datasets" (Valerio 2022). These additions will be critical for centring Muslim-driven research in academic circles and public discourse.

Outside of public universities, independent research institutes have been established and conduct rigorous academic research on Muslims in Canada, with the aim of both contributing to scholarly literature and informing Muslim community organizations and governmental agencies and officials of their findings. The Tessellate Institute (TTI) was founded as a non-profit organization in 2007; it later obtained charitable status and tweaked its mission to focus on exploring and documenting the lived experiences of Muslims in Canada to provide educational projects and programs that highlight Canada's Muslim heritage. In 2012, this mission was further refined to, in their own words, "be an intellectual platform through which Muslim and non-Muslim voices can combat Islamophobia, highlight positive Muslim contributions to Canadian society, and enhance the public debate on issues related to being Muslim in contemporary Canada" (Tessellate Institute n.d.).

I-RSS was founded in 2018 and "produces original and relevant research, filling the gaps in North American academic policy circles... developing original research publications and hosting forums which facilitate discussion around [their] research...[and emphasizing] the practical application of research findings, producing policy analyses and providing recommendations on issues concerning Muslims to Islamic organizations while inform[ing] all levels of government for better engagement with North American Muslims." Similarly, I-RSS "affirms that changing a culture of misunderstanding and misinformation requires intentional, collaborative effort to develop research-based knowledge and anti-oppressive frameworks for critical analysis about Islam and Muslims" (I-RSS 2021, "About Us").

Additionally, in 2021, the Canadian Association for the Study of Islam and Muslims (CASIM) was established to "foster scholarship on Islam and Muslims" through online talks, conferences, and the promotion of literature written by Canadian authors (CASIM 2024, "About CASIM"). Other independent research initiatives also exist and tend to be conducted by existing non-profit organizations to inform their policy development and programming. Studies have been conducted by the Black Muslim Initiative, the Muslim Advisory Council of Canada, NCCM, Islamic Relief Canada, Coalition of Muslim Women—Kitchener-Waterloo, and others.

Relationship/Bridge Building

Borrowing much from anti-racism activism, solidarity and relationship building are still significant tools wielded by Muslims and community organizations. These groups can more aptly be termed as soft educational partners, meaning that the intention behind them is often tradition sharing and community building while they combat Islamophobia in a secondary sense. Though these efforts at unity can be important, a disproportionate emphasis on them in Muslim communities should be balanced, as it lends too much credence to the idea that if people just "get to know Muslims," Islamophobia might disappear. These notions are usually couched in an understanding of Islamophobia as a fear or hatred based on ignorance, obscuring the central role of power in the equation as well as the industry of Islamophobia itself. Solidarity or relationship-building efforts, while important for fighting Islamophobia in popular discursive environments, do little to address the entities and movements that curate those environments and even less to address major systemic issues.

Many such endeavours centre on interfaith work, with members of other religious groups joining together in support of Muslim causes and against Islamophobia. Sometimes these are longer-term relationships; other times, and more often, these relationships can be timely and built from major crises or events, such as vigils after Islamophobic attacks or in media responses to incidents of global hatred against Muslims. Other times, gatherings are less overt in their messaging and might instead be a show of solidarity at Ramadan iftars and Eid prayers or other major Muslim events. Some of the more promising work on relationship building that takes a novel and decolonizing approach is in the area of Muslim-Indigenous relations – a burgeoning space of friendship and resilience that is centred on deep connection and understanding, an ethic of respectful incommensurability, and refusing superficiality (see Hossain 2024).

Deradicalization of Anti-Muslim Groups

Less work has been done by Muslim activists and organizations to deradicalize white supremacists and members of patriot and anti-immigrant neo-Nazi groups. Groups like NCCM successfully advocated for certain groups like the Soldiers of Odin and paramilitary groups like the III%ers to be outlawed, which happened in 2021 (Department of Justice 2021); however, other unified and more concerted efforts have not been attempted. While it is understandable that the targeted group of these hateful communities should not have to be responsible for helping their members leave and seek social rehabilitation, the possibility of lending Muslim community support, resources, and attention to organizations engaged in such work potentially remains. One key example that shows promise is the Alberta-based Organization for the Prevention of Violence and its Evolve Program, which provides personalized, accessible, and free counselling and mentorship for individuals struggling with indoctrination in violent extremist movements of all varieties. The organization also publishes original research and timely reports on the status of violent extremists, with a specific focus on white supremacists and far-right groups in Canada. It is worth noting that within this area of approaches, deradicalization of anti-Palestinian groups has not been included in these efforts.

Gaps in Approaches

Developing this preliminary composite picture of existing approaches to combatting Islamophobia in Canada aids in identifying where some efforts are duplicated or overrepresented (draining resources and attention) while also illuminating gaps. Some of the key gaps are as follows.

Shared Data Collection

While some groups have compiled and collected hate crime and incident data from independent reporting mechanisms, there is no national system for data collection and sharing, one that would include an expanded understanding of Islamophobia beyond that category alone.

Systemic Islamophobia Assessments

Some data collection focuses on overt interpersonal violence as the primary manifestation of Islamophobia in Canada. However, to date, there is a dearth of information and assessment tools for measuring systemic Islamophobia in other areas such as health and economic equity, barriers to community thriving, and so forth. The creation of assessment tools and training to measure embedded Islamophobia in institutions would be beneficial. It should be noted that a very valuable report by Jasmin Zine from 2022 entitled "The Canadian Islamophobia Industry: Islamophobia's Ecosystem in the Great White North" has helped shed light on the Islamophobia industry, here understood as the "grouping or network that is comprised of far-right media outlets and Islamophobia influencers, white nationalist groups, far-right groups, soft-power fringe right groups, Muslim dissidents, think tanks and their designated security experts, and the donors who fund... campaigns...that involve the demonization and vilification of Islam and Muslims, and often work in concert to foment controversies and spread Islamophobic narratives and conspiracy theories" (quoted in report of Standing Committee on Human Rights 2023, 31).

Addressing Compounded Discrimination

Efforts have been made by academics and some community orga-nizations to understand and address how Islamophobia intersects with other aspects of identity to create compounded experiences of discrimination and disenfranchisement; however, more work remains to be done especially to bring this into popular discursive environments in a more consistent manner.

Understanding the Impact of Islamophobia on Muslim Bodies, Families, and Communities

While the literature on the psychological impact of Islamophobia in Canada is developing, there is less sociological work done on the detrimental effects of Islamophobia on health outcomes, family health and wellness, and overall community success markers.

Focus on Deradicalization

As mentioned previously, there is more that could be done by Muslim community organizations and leadership to support the important work of deradicalizing members of anti-Muslim hate groups. Additionally, support for governmental policies and legislation designed to disband Islamophobic movements is crucial.

Long-term, Strategic, Comprehensive Vision

The pictures painted above make clear that although some collaborative efforts undoubtedly occur in Muslim communities across the country, only a very small percentage of existing Muslim organizations in Canada focus on Islamophobia, and even then, efforts tend to be highly localized, insular, and sometimes reactionary in responding to overt violence. While the reasons for this fracturing are well understood, a broader understanding of the various impacts of Islamophobia as well as pushing beyond territorial boundaries for more collaborative efforts and resource sharing would improve both responses and advocacy efforts on the issue.

Research-based Approaches

With limited resources, it comes as no surprise that few community and institutional responses to Islamophobia are based on research, especially given issues in data collection. Continuous consultation is needed with Muslim communities to develop a comprehensive, unbiased national academic research agenda about Islam and Muslims. A national coalition of Muslim academics who could inform such an agenda would be beneficial.

Emphasis on Purely Religious Discrimination

The current frameworks for understanding Islamophobia have often fallen under the umbrella of anti-racism efforts, and while racialization (and its subsequent dehumanization) is an important part of the Islamophobia equation, it further obscures the discriminatory realities faced by many Muslims on religio-praxis grounds alone. Anti-Islamic rhetoric shows us what Namira Islam (2018) calls *soft Islamophobia* in liberal or left-leaning anti-Islamophobia spaces, where there is prevalent "discomfort with and erasure of Islam as a faith in favour of 'cultural' Muslims." This point is crucial because it not only encompasses the reality that Islamophobia affects every single aspect of a Muslim's life— since Islam can be understood as an entire way of life—but it also points to a need within anti-Islamophobia organizing to go beyond survival. It is not enough to eliminate all of the hate groups or even all of the systemic inequities that Muslims face. It is not enough to stop interpersonal hatred, violence, and microaggressions. Islamophobia will still exist and persist until the day that the rights of Muslims to practice their religious way of life to the fullest possible extent are upheld, enshrined, and celebrated in shared pluralistic spaces, reflecting the deep equity of Muslims globally with other peoples and the ability to live side by side even incommensurably.

Collaboration Efforts

A long-term, established platform comprised of multiple, diverse key stakeholders to develop a national vision to promote coherent advocacy and share experiences is necessary. Similarly, the formation of multi-stakeholder alliances within Muslim communities and across others to combat Islamophobia, hate, and violence from extreme groups is critical.

Capacity Building and Resource Distribution

To avoid unnecessary duplication of efforts and resources as well as the depletion of momentum from burnout, there needs to be a central focus on capacity building for advocacy within Muslim communities. It should be multi-representational, legal- and research-based, yet still connected to grassroots priorities and experiences.

Conclusion

From this preliminary, big-picture study of anti-Islamophobia interventions in Muslim communities across Canada, it is clear that organizational and activist foci have been incredible, though sometimes fragmented and disparate, resulting in endeavours that may have replicated existing efforts or some approaches being overrepresented ways while neglecting others. However, improvements can be made in both inward supportive and outward advocacy efforts. Particular attention should be paid to adopting a nuanced and comprehensive definition of Islamophobia to ensure no critical areas of intervention are overlooked (especially in terms of systemic interventions) and to develop a long-term, collaborative, strategic vision—one nationally rooted in research and data sharing that expands the markers for assessing the impact of Islamophobia. Future research should focus on additional development of this large-scale, composite picture of approaches to combatting Islamophobia as well as comparative analyses with the work of Muslim organizations and communities in other Western, secular contexts.

REFERENCES

Al Eid, Nawal A., et al. 2020. "Religiosity, Psychological Resilience, and Mental Health Among Breast Cancer Patients in Kingdom of Saudi Arabia." *Breast Cancer: Basic and Clinical Research*, January.

Al-Qazzaz, Khaled, and Nakita Valerio. 2020. *Policy Paper: Lessons from Examining Canadian Muslim Youth Challenges and Pathways to Resilience*. Institute for Religious and Socio-Political Studies.

Annalakshmi, Narayanan. 2011. "Islamic Worldview, Religious Personality, and Resilience Among Muslim Adolescent Students in India." *Europe's Journal of Psychology* 7, no. 4: 716–738.

Canadian Association for the Study of Islam and Muslims (CASIM). 2024. "About CASIM" https://casim.ca/about-casim/.

Canadian Council for Muslim Women. 2010. *My Canada: Finding Common Ground* Toolkit. https://youthrex.com/toolkit/my-canada-finding-common-ground/.

Canadian Labour Congress. 2019. *Islamophobia at Work: Challenges and Opportunities*. https://documents.clcctc.ca/human-rights-and-equality/Islamophobia/IslamophobiaAtWork-Report-2019-03-20-EN.pdf.

Chakroun, Fatima. 2022. "Muslim Organizations in Canada: A Composite Picture of Service and Diversity." *Religious and Socio-Political Studies Journal* 1, no. 1. https://rssjournal.ca/index.php/rss/article/view/muslimorgsincanada-fchakroun-rssj.

Dayrit, Flordeliza, and Michael Milo. 2010. *A New Life in a New Land*. https://www.anewlife.ca/about.

Department of Justice. 2021. "Government of Canada takes action to protect Canadians Against Hate Speech and Hate Crimes." June 23. Government of Canada. https://www.canada.ca/en/public-safety-canada/news/2021/02/government-of-canada-lists-13-new-groups-as-terrorist-entities-and-completes-review-of-seven-others.html.

Emon, Anver, and Nadia Hasan. 2021. *Under Layered Suspicion: A Review of CRA Audits of Muslim-Led Charities*. NCCM and University of Toronto. www.layeredsuspicion.ca.

Hamdani, Daood. 2015. "Canadian Muslims: A Statistical Review." *Canadian Dawn Foundation*. March 29. www.cdndawnfoundation.ca.

Hill, Elizabeth. 2021. "Annotated Bibliography: Islam and Anti-Islamophobia Resources for Educators." Institute for Religious and Socio-Political Studies and Muslim Association of Canada. https://islamawareness. ca/wp-content/uploads/2021/12/Annotated-Bibliography-Islam-and-Islamophobia-Resources-for-Educators-IRSSMAC-2021.pdf.

Hossain, Memona. 2024. "'Standing with Each Other': Indigenous-Muslim Relation-Making on Turtle Island." *Religious and Socio-Political Studies Journal* 2, no. 1: 4–32.

Institute of Islamic Studies. 2022. "Muslims in Canada Archives (MiCA) Included in Federal Budget 2022." April 7. https://islamicstudies.artsci. utoronto.ca/research-labs/muslims-in-canada-archives-mica/.

Institute of Islamic Studies. n.d. "Muslims in Canada Archives (MiCA)." https:// islamicstudies.artsci.utoronto.ca/projects/mica/.

Institute for Religious and Socio-Political Studies (I-RSS). 2021. "About Us." https://i-rss.org/about-us/.

Islam, Namira. 2018. "Soft Islamophobia." *Religions* 9, no. 9: 280. https://doi. org/10.3390/rel9090280.

Mercy Mission Canada. n.d. "Taskeen Wellness." https://mercymission.ca/ taskeen-wellness/.

Muslim Association of Canada. 2021. Islam Awareness Online Courses and Resource Portal. https://islamawareness.ca/.

National Council of Canadian Muslims (NCCM). 2020. "Policy Paper: CBSA Oversight Bill." https://www.nccm.ca/wp-content/uploads/2020/10/ CBSA-Policy-Paper-9.pdf.

National Council of Canadian Muslims (NCCM). 2024. "Training and Workshops." https://www.nccm.ca/connect/training/ Accessed July 25, 2024.

Nusaibah Collective. 2024. "Home" and "About." https://thenusaibahcollective.ca.

Public Safety Canada. 2023. "Communities at Risk: Security Infrastructure Program: FAQs." Government of Canada. https://www.publicsafety. gc.ca/cnt/cntrng-crm/crm-prvntn/fndng-prgrms/scrt-nfrstrctr-prgrm/ bt-prgrm-en.aspx.

Rahman, Ab, et al. 2020. "Critical Review of Reciting Al Qur'an in Restoring Resilience and Mental Health Among Quarantined Covid 19 Patients." *Journal of Critical Reviews* 7, no. 5: 1126–1135.

Ridzuan, Abdul Rahim. 2020. "Resilience and Patience (Sabr) in Islamic View When Observing the Movement Control (Order MCO) during the Covid 19 Pandemic." *International Journal of Psychosocial Rehabilitation* 24, no. 1: 5485–5497.

Rivers of Hope. 2018. *Rivers of Hope: A Toolkit on Islamophobic Violence by and for Muslim Women.* https://www.riversofhope.ca/toolkits.

Saputro, I., H.F. Nashori, and I. Sulistyarini. 2021. "Promoting Resilience among Family Caregiver of Cancer through Islamic Religious Coping." *Indigenous: Jurnal Ilmiah Psikologi* 6, no. 2: 55–66.

Skalisky, J., S. Wanner, B. Howe, and K. Mauseth. 2020. "Religious Coping, Resilience and Involuntary Displacement: A Mixed-methods Analysis of the Experience of Syrian and Palestinian Refugees in Jordan." *Psychology of Religion and Spirituality* 14, no. 4: 539–547.

Standing Committee on Human Rights. 2023. "Combatting Hate: Islamophobia and its Impact on Muslims in Canada." November. Canadian Senate. https://sencanada.ca/content/sen/committee/441/RIDR/reports/Islamophobia_FINAL_e.pdf.

Statistics Canada. 2024. "Special Interest Profile, 2021 Census of Population: Religion." https://www12.statcan.gc.ca/census-recensement/2021/dp-pd/sip/details/page.cfm?Dguid=2021A000011124&PoiId=8&AgeId=3&Lang=E&FocusId=1&TId=0#sipTable.

Tessellate Institute. n.d. "What is TTI?" https://tessellateinstitute.ca/what-is-tti/.

Valerio, Nakita. 2022. "Trends and Issues for Muslims in Canada: A Literature Review." *Institute for Religious and Socio-Political Studies.*

Yourex-West, Heather. 2021. "Why are Alberta's Black, Muslim Women Being Attacked?" *Global News*, March 26. https://globalnews.ca/news/7721850/hate-crime-alberta-attacks-black-muslim-women/.

YouthREX. 2020. "Challenging Islamophobia in the Ontario Youth Sector"—Webinar and Resources. https://youthrex.com/webinar/challenging-islamophobia-in-the-ontario-youth-sector/.

Zietsma, Danielle. 2010. "Immigrants Working in Regulated Occupations." *Perspectives.* Statistics Canada Catalogue no. 75-001-X. February.

Zine, Jasmin. 2022. "The Canadian Islamophobia Industry: Islamophobia's Ecosystem in the Great White North." *Islamophobia Studies Journal* 7, no. 2: 232–249.

Contributors

Khaled Al-Qazzaz is an educator, philanthropist, and human rights activist. He is the founding executive director of the Institute for Religious and Socio-Political Studies (I-RSS) in Canada. He is also a member of the International Justice Circle of Human Rights Watch and is the director of Education and Communications for the Muslim Association of Canada. Khaled established a K–12 international school in Egypt in 2005 and executed the portfolios for foreign relations, human rights, and women's rights for the first democratically elected government of Egypt, until the military coup in 2013. Khaled co-founded and led the QED Foundation, serving vulnerable migrants and refugees. In the same year, Khaled established the Zajel Institute to empower members of the Arab diaspora and exile communities. He holds a master of applied sciences in mechanical and industrial engineering from the University of Toronto and pursued a doctor of education in educational administration at Walden University.

Jinan Bastaki is an associate professor of legal studies. She holds an LLB from the London School of Economics, an LLM from the University of California (Berkeley), and a PhD from the University of London (SOAS). Bastaki focuses on forced displacement, human rights, refugee law, and citizenship. To this end, she also examines how Islamophobia impacts the rights, belonging, and access of Muslims. In 2018, her paper on nationality-based detention of migrants won the International Committee of the Red Cross and the International Institute of Humanitarian Law's (IIHL) best essay prize. Her work has appeared in the *Journal of Refugee Studies, Citizenship Studies, Refugee Survey Quarterly*, and others. Prior to her current appointment, Bastaki was associate professor of international law and vice-dean of research and graduate affairs at UAEU, a visiting scholar at the University of Oxford's Center for Socio-Legal Studies, and an instructor for the IIHL.

Dustin J. Byrd is a professor of philosophy and religion at the University of Olivet. He specializes in the critical theory of the Frankfurt School, psychoanalytical political theory, and contemporary Islamic and Russian thought. He is the founder and editor-in-chief of Ekpyrosis Press and also the founder and co-director of the Institute for Critical Social Theory. He also serves as the editor-in-chief of the journal *Critical Perspectives* (formerly *Islamic Perspective*). His recent publications include *The Dark Charisma of Donald Trump: Political Psychology and the MAGA Movement* (Ekpyrosis Press, 2023), *Syed Hussein and Critical Social Theory: Decolonizing the Captive Mind* (Brill, 2023), and *The Frankfurt School and the Dialectics of Religion: Translating Critical Faith into Critical Theory* (Ekpyrosis Press, 2020). www.dustinjbyrd.org.

Zeinab Diab is a PhD candidate at the Institut d'études religieuses (IÉR) at the Université de Montréal in Quebec, Canada. Her research focuses on the "Act Respecting the Laicity of the State" (Law 21) adopted in Quebec in June 2019, its political implications and human effects on visibly Muslim women and their communities, and the survival and resistance strategies developed by these actors. Her work lies at the intersection of religious studies and critical Muslim studies, capturing Islamophobia, secularism, Otherness, fundamental rights, freedoms, and nationalist and feminist political discourses. Zeinab regularly speaks in the media and various academic and community spaces as a part of her community-engaged participatory action research. She is one of the advisors to the National Council of Canadian Muslims (NCCM) and engaged in a large-scale Law 21 research project, entitled "What is it like to be a Muslim Woman in Québec?"

Alain Gabon is an associate professor of French studies in the Department of Foreign Languages & Literatures—Classics at Virginia Wesleyan University. He has written and lectured extensively in the US, Europe, and beyond on contemporary French culture, postcolonialism, literature, and film as well as on Islam and Muslims in France, Europe, and the world. His works have been published in academic journals and books, for think tanks like the UK Cordoba Foundation, and in mainstream and specialized media such as *Saphirnews*, *Milestones: Commentaries on the Islamic World*, and *Les Cahiers de l'Islam*. He is a regular contributor to the *Middle East Eye*, the Bridge Initiative at Georgetown University, and the *9/11 Legacies*.

Elizabeth Shakman Hurd is professor of religious studies and political science at Northwestern University, where she focuses on the politics of religion in US foreign and immigration policy, the politics of secularism and religious freedom, American borders, and the US in the Middle East. Her books include *Heaven Has a Wall: Religion, Borders, and* *the Global United States* (University of Chicago Press, 2025), *The Politics of Secularism in International Relations* (Princeton University Press, 2008), *Beyond Religious Freedom: The New Global Politics of Religion* (Princeton University Press, 2015), and four co-edited volumes on secularism, religion, and politics in international affairs, including, most recently, *At Home and Abroad: The Politics of American Religion* (Columbia, 2021). Hurd co-directs the Northwestern Global Religion & Politics Research Group, is a core faculty member in the MENA Studies program, and co-curates the Teaching Law and Religion Case Archive, an open-access resource for teaching about law and religion globally.

Fatimah Jackson-Best is an assistant professor in the Department of Health Research Methods, Evidence, and Impact and the Department of Medicine at McMaster University. In 2018–2019 she collaborated with the Black Muslim Initiative and Tessellate Institute to publish the first known systematic review of works focused on Black Muslims in Canada. She has conducted workshops on anti-Black Islamophobia, Islamophobia, and gendered Islamophobia at McMaster University and the University of Toronto. To improve access to mental health and addiction services for Black children, youth, and their families in Ontario, Fatimah led a project with the Black Health Alliance called Pathways to Care from 2018 to 2023. Her research explores the impact of Islamophobia on the mental health of Black Muslims and Muslim women in Canada. Her work has been published in *Canadian Psychology, Child and Adolescent Social Work Journal, Journal of Recovery in Mental Health*, and *Adolescent Research Review*.

Roshan Arah Jahangeer is a Mauritian-Canadian, Muslim feminist scholar and settler living in Tkaronto (Toronto), Canada. She completed a PhD in political science from York University and works as contract faculty in York's School of Gender, Sexuality, and Women's Studies. She was the inaugural postdoctoral fellow in Islamophobia in Health Professions Education at the Temerty Faculty of Medicine,

University of Toronto. Her research explores the transnational circula-
tion of anti-veiling laws between France and Quebec and their impacts
on Muslim women in the contexts of secularism, feminism, and
Islamophobia. Her work has been published in the *Canadian Journal of
Women and the Law, Canadian Medical Education Journal, the Conversation,*
and the *Montreal Gazette*. She has worked with community organizations such as the Canadian Council for Muslim Women and Institut F,
and she was previously a research director and board member at the
Tessellate Institute.

Areesha Khan is a young scholar with an interdisciplinary economics
and development studies background. This book chapter is part of her
master's dissertation, which she wrote amid the implementation of and
nationwide protests sparked by India's Citizenship Amendment Act and
the National Register of Citizens, which were said to be anti-Muslim.
She is driven by her mother's and her own lived experience and looks at
the real lives of Muslim women worldwide against the discourse built
around their identity. She is interested in exploring how the economy
is embedded in society and vice versa, along with questions of caste,
gender, and religion in South Asia.

Sharmin Sadequee is a cultural anthropologist researching Islam and
Muslim communities in North America with particular attention to
religion, race, law, and secularism. She spent over fifteen years record-
ing the experiences of settler-immigrant and natural-born American
Muslims within the US legal and political system and how they push
back by engaging in various rights movements. Her ethnographic
manuscript is tentatively titled *Governing Muslims: Terror Trials, Islam,
and Secular Crisis in the United States*. Her other postdoctoral research
examines ethnonationalism, Islam, and environmental sustainability
through the lens of a regenerative mosque and Islamic cemetery in
the United States. She has received support from the Social Science
Research Council, the American Council of Learned Societies, and

Shenandoah University's Center for Islam in the Contemporary World. Her work has been published in *Surveillance & Society, Anthropology Now, The Immanent Frame*, and *The Maydan*.

Saul J. Takahashi is a professor of human rights and peace studies at Osaka Jogakuin University. His main research interests include global Islamophobia and human rights in Palestine. Saul worked with refugees at Amnesty International, then served in the Office of the UN High Commissioner for Human Rights from 2009 to 2014, travelling throughout the West Bank and Gaza and documenting human rights violations. Saul holds an LLM in international human rights law from the University of Essex and also serves as a senior non-resident fellow at the Hashim Sani Centre for Palestine Studies, University Malaya, and as an expert on the global network and on the question of Palestine. Saul is the author of *Human Rights and Drug Control: The False Dichotomy* (Hart Publishing, 2018), and *The Palestinian People Continue to Suffer: Why the UN Can't Solve the Problem* (in Japanese, Gendai Jinbun-sha, 2015). His page on Researchmap is https://researchmap.jp/saul_takahashi.

Nakita Valerio is a Vanier scholar, based on Treaty 6 territory in Canada, completing doctoral religious studies at the University of Alberta. Nakita specializes in Muslim women's Qur'anic literacy and leadership in Morocco. Her other areas of research include Muslim-Jewish Moroccan history, memorizers of the Qur'an, and traditional Islamic knowledge networks in North America, along with numerous studies of Muslims in Canada in her prior capacity as research director for the Institute for Religious and Socio-Political Studies (I-RSS). She remains editor-in-chief of the University of Alberta's *RSS Journal*. Nakita founded the Nusaibah Collective and serves as an advisor to University of Alberta's Chester Ronning Centre for the Study of Religion and Public Life, as sponsor for the Fatima Al-Fihri Graduate Award in Islamic studies, and as an alumni faculty of arts representative in numerous capacities at the University of Alberta. She is also the secretary of the Canadian Association for the Study of Islam and Muslims (CASIM). Finally, she co-founded a primary school in rural Morocco, where she lived for several years.

Jasmin Zine is a professor of sociology, religion, and culture at Wilfrid Laurier University. Her recent book, *Under Siege: Islamophobia and the 9/11 Generation* (McGill-Queens University Press, 2022) explores the experiences of the millennial generation of Canadian Muslim youth who came of age during the global War on Terror and times of heightened anti-Muslim racism. *Under Siege* was named on the *Hill Times* list of best books of 2022. She is author of a major report on the Canadian Islamophobia industry (2022) that examines the networks of hate and bigotry that purvey and monetize Islamophobia. She has consulted on combatting Islamophobia for UNESCO and prominent European organizations. She is a sought-after media commentator and has given numerous invited talks and keynotes across Canada, the US, and around the world. Dr. Zine is co-founder and vice-president of the International Islamophobia Studies Research Association (IISRA).